WINNING THRU TRIAL

7 Winning Ways to Become Mighty

Charles P. Malone

AC Power Media, LLC

Copyright © 2023 by Charles P. Malone. All Rights Reserved.

No portion of this book may be reproduced, stored in a retrieval system, or transmitted in any way, by any means or form, electronic, mechanical, photocopy, recording, or otherwise, without the prior written permission from the publisher or author, except as permitted by U.S.A. copyright law.

Published in the United States of America by AC POWER MEDIA, LLC, Mailing Address: 4174 E. Palo Verde St., Gilbert, AZ 85296

Cover stock Image purchased from Dreamstime LLC, Address: 1616 Westgate Circle, Brentwood, TN 37027 – Invoice no. 8491658   05/19/2012 @ 10:05am

Back Cover Design © 2023 by Steele Graphics

Special discounts available on quantity purchases by schools, corporations, educators, and others. Contact the publisher for details.

U.S. trade bookstores and wholesalers, please contact AC Power Media, LLC @ (480) 329-7489 or FAX: (480) 336-9065 or by email to: cmijustwriteit@gmail.com and please copy cmalone44@gmail.com   *Email for Info and orders: cmijustwriteit@gmail.com

ISBN: 979-8-9874555-2-4This book is a work of non-fiction based primarily upon the author's personal experiences in life and from his personal opinions gained from experiencing both success and failure. There is no intention by the author or publisher to provide medical or legal advice that might be considered implied warranties of merchantability or fitness. Although the author may share experiences from his own life and share information and resources, the reader is cautioned to do their own due diligence on anything of material concern.

Neither the author nor the publisher shall be liable for any loss or profit or any other personal or commercial damages, including but not limited to special, incidental, consequential, or other damages, perceived or otherwise.

ORDER BOOKS BY CHARLES P. MALONE ON AMAZON.COM

INFO ABOUT NEW BOOKS AND PUBLISHED ARTICLES WRITTEN BY CHARLES P. MALONE AT: www.facebook.com/ijustwriteit

WINNING THRU TRIAL

Contents

PREFACE	1
1. The Sweetness of Trial	7
The Sweetness of Trial (2nd Half)	45
2. When Trial Strikes	80
3. Attitude Begets Behavior	126
4. Choice Defines Character	174
5. Seek the Best Gifts - Look for the Miracle.	238
6. Without Battle, There is No Win!	284
7. BE MIGHTY! (The story of Mighty Jake)	313
8. CONCLUSION	366
About the Author	375

PREFACE

TRIAL – Miscellaneous definitions include:
A test of performance.

2. A test of a person's endurance or forbearance.

3. A test to assess suitability or performance.

4. A test of faith, patience, or stamina through subjection to suffering or temptation (Merriam-Webster).

Did you notice a common denominator amongst the general definitions of the word "Trial" mentioned above? During your last trial, did you think of it as a "Test?" Me either. It felt more like punishment!

I remember disobeying my mother when my horse (I wasn't supposed to be riding after a rain) did a summersault with me clinging onto the saddle and crashing into the wet earth beneath, with the horse on top of me. Of course, I was only ten years old and probably too young to know anything about trial. Still, I bet my parents thought the month I spent in St. Joseph's Children's Hospital in Phoenix, AZ., undergoing four surgeries to save my right arm, was a trial.

But trial became real for this ten-year-old boy with a plaster-of-Paris body cast starting at the tips of his fingers on his right hand and encasing his boyish frame down to his waist, just "below" where his pants would usually button – except now they didn't. If that was a test of my ability to withstand all the pranks, remarks, laughing, and finger-pointing from classmates while I tried to live a normal life during the six-month healing process, I am confident I did not pass.

Think back to a time when trial entered your life. Were you prepared for it? Did you see "opportunity" in your trial? How did you react to your trial when it first hit? Was God your first call? Do you believe there is purpose in trial? The premise I have taken as the author of this book, "Winning Thru Trial," is that trial has purpose–to provide experience. But it will be up to each of us to choose what we will make of the experience gained, in our life's journey of "becoming."

While writing my first book, "The Sweetness of Trial," my goal was to provide a faith-based experience for the reader, to acquire a feeling which would neutralize the bitterness often felt when something/someone is lost or taken from us. It is a feeling I felt personally as I knelt by the side of my wife in prayer, pleading to God to heal our daughter from breast cancer, to help me recover from two years without substantial income, to save me from the depths of depression, to help cure my bitterness over losing still another business after many long years of sacrifice–and more. Yet, in those often desperate and humbling times of pleading came the soft and gentle embrace of a still, small voice, "Be still, and know that I am God."

There are likely few other times when we are privileged to "taste" the sweetness of Heavenly Father's love purer than during trial. I started writing "Winning Thru Trial" before "Sweetness" was even finished because I felt the promptings early that my experiences with failure were to be shared, not hidden under a bushel, as awkward as it might be to admit failure instead of taking a stage somewhere claiming to have scaled Mt. Everest, blindfolded. But I have learned through time in the ring of life that it isn't about how many times you get knocked down that defines you as a failure because, in my mind, the "only" way you fail in anything after being knocked to the floor, is when you stay down.

I wanted to write a book as my testimony to the world that what defines you as a "winner" is getting back into the ring to go another round, no matter how many times you are knocked down, because each time you meet Goliath in whatever form he takes you gain experience. Like compound interest, experience today will help form perspective, insight, and wisdom to fight tomorrow again.

In this world of "agency," God created the ring of life with unlimited rounds, the last round known only to Him who created us. It is our opportunity to see life with unlimited potential to become all that we can while in the ring.

When my father passed away, I gravitated to my mother when I needed a "listening ear and reassuring approval or direction." It wasn't that I was looking to her to solve my life's problems, particularly… but I wanted the assurance that someone who had been through life and had their share of trials had survived to this point and could offer some confirmation that I, too, would live to fight another day.

When my mother passed away, and I finally moved through the grieving process, I felt an emptiness of not having someone to "confirm" my feelings when facing difficult situations. Perhaps you know the same empty feeling?

One day, I will take my place on the threshold of eternity, leaving this life for that of another, leaving behind for a time those I call family, friends, and acquaintances. It is my fondest hope that the contents of this book will offer to you, the reader, a written testimony filled with inspiring stories of becoming, a strategy for preparing yourself for the next trial, some humor (in light of the book title) to bring a smile, and assurances from biblical scripture and real-time life-experiences that what you are going through (trial) has a purpose in molding you into a Christ-like son or daughter of God.

My purpose in writing this book is to offer you, the reader, a brighter hope of overcoming adversity and, in the process, provide some guidance based upon true principles of success toward achieving greatness – "this" type of greatness...

There is an account in the Old Testament of a man whom God loved and trusted so much that He allowed Satan, the master deceiver, to test the man's integrity and loyalty through incomprehensible trial(s). You know him and his story as Job.

Job lost "everything" dear and precious to him, yet he never blamed God; his faith "became unshakable" through his trials. In the end, Job "proved himself" and became one of the most remarkable men of all the people of the East, "receiving twice as much as he had before" (See Job 42).

You see, trial isn't punishment as the world would see it, but God's way of opening doors to our gifts and talents that otherwise would not have surfaced. Without Goliath (trial), there would have been no King David, no "win" in the ring of life.

How does one "win" thru trial, anyway? Aren't we just supposed to "endure" our trials? And why would someone – "anyone" - want to read a book about trial? But if you knew a battle was coming at some point in your life, wouldn't you want to be "prepared" with a battle plan?

You will find "Winning Thru Trial" to be a book of instruction on how to not only prepare yourself to endure the next trial... but also to grow in personal development. You will come to appreciate and embrace a "new" definition of "winning" as it applies to overcoming trial while in the storms of life, to be more in line with how Heavenly Father intended this "test" to be graded–to continue "becoming" all God intended for us to be; to get back up when we fall... and to "fail forward" to win!

"Winning Thru Trial" teaches the reader how to "prepare" for the next trial by conditioning the mind and heart through the "Five P's:" Proper Preparation Prevents Poor Performance!

You will learn to "look for the 'Opportunity' in trial," but not the world's definition of opportunity.

What would a book about trial be without a chapter on "choice?" Within Chapter Six, you will learn the value of attaining the mindset of "Failing Forward."

"Be Mighty" is the clarion call we have ascribed to our grandson Jacob Priestley (Facebook "Adventures with Mighty Jake"), who has inspired thousands with his story of autism and terminal mitochondria disease. We, his family and friends worldwide, have taken up his call to Be Mighty, as the concluding chapter in this book teaches. I think you will be inspired to join us.

The premise behind this book is that trial will happen to everyone, in one form or another–and it will hurt! But so what? Failing hurts! Losing hurts! Why not accept that life is "designed" to hurt to remove earthly "impurities" so that what remains is part of your "becoming?" (aka Winning.)

"Winning Thru Trial" will take you by the heart and teach you how to see trial differently. The stories herein will inspire you to believe that if "they" can get through their trial to "become,"... so can you. The "Winning Ways" taught within the pages of this book are priceless gems to prepare you when in the ring of life, to see trial as an ally in "becoming" greater (aka more like Jesus Christ) than you would have become "without" it–to help you recognize the changes which have occurred within you as you emerge on the other side of trial–when sunshine has once again cleared the clouds of doubt and worry, and replaced with the sweetness of "the steadfast love of the Lord," [which] never ceases; His mercies never [coming] to an end... (Lamentations 3:22)

Without trial, without opposition, there is no victory! There is no "win!" But your journey toward "Winning" starts now! The road to "becoming" awaits!

Chapter One

The Sweetness of Trial
Where It All Began...

As I knelt by the side of my bed at the conclusion of the Sabbath, knowing that Monday would bring another week of endless job searching, I recognized a sweetness that is not present during times of plenty; tears that form today are absent when ritual overtakes sincerity and purpose.

Much has been written about the 'good' that comes from trial. I have read much of it. In addition to reading about it, I have experienced firsthand the change from being served with trial so that we may prove ourselves. A loving Heavenly Father promised only to "tee it up"... but left it up to us to hit it straight and true and experience the benefits of "reacting positively" to negative inertia.

Yet, my trials seem to last long into the night of nights... far-reaching and deep. My pain is not dulled knowing others have similar trials, some even worse, having escalated into a loss of business, home, family, and friends. This is my Gethsemane, my personal walk through the valley of darkness... my cross to bear.

Could I retrace my steps during times of plenty, I would remember how

I reacted to trial then. These were different trials, one affecting the health of a loved one ... or a wayward child stumbling without light, trials that hurt and caused me to react ... and read, pray, and grow. But it was trial, nonetheless, that found me kneeling by my bedside ... or tearing up while driving and having to pull over into a vacant lot, and not just praying a prayer ... but crying a prayer, a pleading prayer, for guidance and light.

At first, early on as a young convert of 18 years of age, I prayed to be released from my trials ... for God to solve my problems; to interfere, make things better. But as I aged and gained experience in trial, I realized there was a sweetness found during times of famine that was not experienced in times of plenty.

"Learn of me and listen to my words; walk in the meekness of my Spirit, and you shall have peace in me" (Doctrine & Covenants 19:23).

Over the years, I have tried to define the "sweetness" that comes from trial. I know that for me, it did not come easily or soon. When the trial first hits, it seems to come as a thief during the night, unexpected and swift. We are often confused and lost, unable to find a bearing to give us hope. But if we are able to stand firm in the faith ... however impossible it may seem at the time, and "seek" our Father in Heaven in humble supplication, study his words, allow ourselves to feel the atoning sacrifice of our elder brother Jesus Christ on our behalf, we will start to feel a peace, a sweetness, a hope, that "this too shall pass."

During these times of being in our "most sincere" persona, we begin to taste the sweetness of hope and of peace to the soul. Perhaps the effects of the atonement are felt more at this time than any other. We truly approach our loving Heavenly Father with a "broken heart and contrite spirit," asking from the depths of our soul to be saved, for mercy to be extended, and for the hurt to be withdrawn. He answers that his Son was sent to die for all, to absorb the hurt, to heal the broken, and to offer hope to the weary and downtrodden. If we will but believe... believe in Him, our benefactor, even our Savior, Jesus Christ, we will come to know that the sweetness we taste during the deepest of trials is His love for us... for me personally. He willingly took upon Himself this darkness I have felt. He bled for me that I might have hope. He allowed Himself to be nailed to a cross and to experience agony of the flesh so that during my own Gethsemane, I might taste the sweetness of His love and sacrifice for me.

One day, the bonds upon me will loosen, and I will once again experience the satisfaction of providing for my family... the cold night of nights will give way to a brighter, sunlit day. Hope and restitution will replace the emptiness and self-incrimination that have occupied my soul these many months. Yet, the belief in a brighter day has already produced a dread inside my heart that with the passing of trial, the natural man will replace the sweetness I now feel. But mortal life is all about experience... and with the passing of time, that sweetness of trial will take its place among the effects of previous trials that served to draw me closer and deeper into the loving arms of my Heavenly Father and my Savior, Jesus Christ. I will have survived another test... and my faith and hope still shining strong as a beacon to the world that they, too, will survive... to live again to taste the sweetness of trial.

Charles Patrick Malone "The Sweetness of Trial" – A published article in Mormon Times, June 19, 2010.

***

I wrote these words in the above-published article in 2010 after experiencing yet another tsunami of trial—wave after wave of devastation in its path—leaving me confused, disoriented, and without significant income for over two years. At the time, I felt anything *but* sweetness from the trial my family and I were experiencing. "I had not yet learned the value of trial as a catalyst for change," and allowed myself to accept fully the blame for the condition that left me so vulnerable and unable to care financially for my family.

As the sole breadwinner for my family, I had no one else to blame for my financial losses and often found myself second-guessing my decision to leave a comfortable job with sufficient pay and benefits in meeting our growing family's needs, for a selfish desire "to be my own man – chart my destiny – see my name on the door."

I am being fully transparent here—I use the word "selfish" to describe my choice to change careers because of how things turned out. If I had become victorious in my early attempts at becoming an entrepreneur, I would have used words like "smart" or "wise." But I threw a negative connotation at you in describing the failure to meet my expectations because that is what I was trained to do by my self-talk, reflecting my low self-esteem and lack of understanding of the purpose of opposition and setback.

Now, don't get me wrong. I'm not saying I didn't read about trial in scriptures and books on motivation; for a while, I even pursued a degree in psychology during my time at University. However, I didn't comprehend how to proactively look at trial as a condition that could be changed. Instead, I viewed it as an "object." I took it personally. I let it define me. I ran from it–hid under the bedsheets as I did as a child when confronted with inescapable nightmares. However, when I awoke each morning, my nightmare was still present, its tentacles digging deeper and deeper into my weak resolve to fight back.

I will share a few "high altitude" details of my various business failures because I want you to know this book was written from the author's personal experiences in the trenches and not merely a collection of inspiring stories commonly found in Reader's Digest© and that I do know what it is like to fail and want to stay down and not get up again to fight another day.

I "do" know the feeling of losing all material wealth and financial security, not once, but several times, all while raising five active children. And I "do" know the feelings of despair, panic, and grief, which commonly follow the trail of destruction caused by self-incrimination and blame, as if the loss of worldly wealth was not enough.

<u>I also know that without these setbacks and failures, I never would have gained an understanding and appreciation of how to "fail forward" in the ring of life</u>, bringing to my awareness the oft-hidden "sweetness" of our Lord's admonition to "be still and know that I am God" (Psalm 46:10).

"Over the years, I have tried to define the 'sweetness' that comes from trial. I know that for me, it did not come easily or soon. When the trial first hits, it seems to come as a thief during the night, unexpected

and swift. We are often confused and lost, unable to find a bearing to give us hope. But if we are able to stand firm in the faith ... however impossible it may seem at the time, and 'seek' our Father in Heaven in humble supplication, study his words, allow ourselves to feel the atoning sacrifice of our elder brother Jesus Christ on our behalf, we will start to feel a peace, a sweetness, a hope, that 'this too shall pass.'" -Author, as quoted in *The Sweetness of Trial*.

I want to build within you a brighter hope that even if trial is upon you right now, pressing you to the limits of your endurance – "this too shall pass!" And I sincerely pray my words of encouragement and sharing of very personal and somewhat painful experiences will fuel a brightness of hope within you, to burn even brighter, as you learn to not only endure trial... but win to become.

Winning in any endeavor generally takes skill, practice, timing, and even a bit of luck, along with education, persistence, endurance, genetic disposition, and acquired understanding. Whew! No wonder I failed so many times (LOL).

Winning, as the world defines it, is "coming in first" or being judged on the merits of accomplishment over another.

In this book about trial, I have chosen to define the word "winning" a little differently from the worldview, aligning more with how our Savior, Jesus Christ, views winning: "In the world, you shall have tribulation (trial). But be of good cheer! (Take heart!) I have overcome the world"(Winning) – See John 16:33.

In this scripture, Jesus assures us that even though we will experience trial and tribulation in this earthly phase of becoming, we should not fear... because He has already won "for us" by taking upon Himself the sins of all humanity and the only thing He asks in return is that we "be of good cheer" (aka have faith) and live our lives to "become" as He is (paraphrased).

To His Apostles, Jesus instructed: "[Come], follow me, and I will make you fishers of men" (Matthew 4:19). Following Jesus is having faith in Him sufficient to want to "become" like Him; is this not also "winning?"

Jesus asks that we adopt "winning ways" in our becoming: learn from His character, develop knowledge and humility, become charitable, learn to love, be obedient, and have faith and hope in all things. He stands ready to assist in our becoming. All we need to do is "keep His commandments" and "be of good cheer" (think positive). He is with us every step of the way.

In this book, I share seven "Winning Ways" I have used to help me recover from the depths of despair and depression over many failures and opposition(s) in my life to move forward–to win. Each chapter will focus on one winning way principle to help prepare you for the next battle with opposition–to not only endure the trial but also win!

Winning Way #1 is appropriately titled "Call Upon God."

Where do you turn when trial strikes? Because I am a Christian and profess my faith and belief in the existence of a living God, I should position Him as my number one call. Whatever your chosen faith or acknowledgment of a higher power, we both tend to "over-think" when it is appropriate to contact the One who loves us beyond our ability to fathom and sees us more clearly than anyone else in our life, thus, perhaps unintentionally, choosing to walk the lonely road of trial alone.

Trial is non-denominational

Trial knows no barrier, including choice of religious conviction. We may have different and unique ways of expressing our faith, but we each share at least one common denominator in life–and that is mortality. We each arrived on planet Earth the very same way (birth) and will each leave this mortal life the very same way (death), with few exceptions. How we handle this mortal experience will determine our legacy. How we respond to trial will likely affect many generations after us.

What defines a trial? I gave you a few examples in the first paragraph of the Introduction. I love the one definition when used as a noun: "A test of the performance, qualities, or suitability of someone or something, such as… the product is undergoing clinical trials." I could have fun with this definition, especially the part about "the product" undergoing clinical trials.

Is the "test" referred to in the above-referenced definition an actual trial if it doesn't hurt? Of course, some will oppose my answer because, as my wife contributed when asked this question, "What may be considered a trial to one may not be of concern to another."

So humor me on this one, and let's agree that if it is personal and hurts in some way (emotionally or physically), it is a trial within the context of this book. Now, before you close the book after reading this definition because you haven't experienced hurt in your life... just wait. It would not be planet Earth if you have not, are not now, or will yet experience opposition and hurt at some point. And I genuinely believe the winning ways featured in this book, using trial to win and not just endure, will become a blessing to better prepare you for when trial does strike.

So please hear me out. Why not make the most of your time on earth and become your absolute best? Why go it alone? My God–your God, is extremely interested in your becoming an asset to society. My Savior, Jesus Christ, encourages me to: "Be ye therefore perfect, even as your Father which is in Heaven is perfect"(Matthew 5:48). This scripture has set the bar high for me to become even as He is... to become "all" that I can be. And because I lived with Him before coming to this earth (See Jeremiah 1:5), He knows me better than anyone... and knows my potential to "Win" better than anyone.

Why would I not want my first call to be to my Heavenly Father when facing trial?

Why would I not want to know what I am to learn from this trial?

Why would I not want to lessen the pain and hurt by infusing hope and vision?

God doesn't require more than a particle of faith to believe in His word, and I believe that particle of faith is exercised "when we ask!" (See Alma 32:48).

Picture yourself receiving a call from an adult child you have not heard from for a while... maybe even a very long time. You may have rejected the call or even let your pride get in the way of regaining a relationship by reminding your child how long it has been since their last contact. Does that sound like you? Probably not, but pride does get in the way of mortal relationships, even to the point of dividing families.

God would not be God if He chose favorites, played the "pride" card when we failed to call upon Him for a while, or refused to take our call because He was "too busy" or "too tired" to listen. He is God–and He will listen.

But how do I get the most out of my prayer time with God? First, I think of Him as my Heavenly Father; He is, after all, the Father of my spirit. It helps me see Him as someone I can approach–a friend and a Father who loves me.

The Book of Luke in the New Testament relates an experience Jesus had with two sisters, Mary and Martha, which might benefit our understanding of how to make the most of our prayer time with God the Father (Luke 10:38-42).

In short, Jesus was invited to the home of Martha. Martha had a sister named Mary. Upon entering the home, Jesus began teaching, and Mary positioned herself at the feet of Jesus, intently listening. Martha, the hostess, was busy in the kitchen, "distracted" with much preparing and serving when she noticed Mary was not helping.

Martha went to Jesus, interrupting His teaching, and said, "Lord, do you not care that my sister has left me to serve alone? Tell her then to help me." But the Lord answered her, "Martha, Martha, you are anxious and troubled about many things, but one thing is necessary. Mary has chosen the good portion, which will not be taken away from her."

It might help when we pray to visualize God anxious to hear what we have to say. We enter His room, aware it is our turn to speak. Are we distracted over what is top of mind at the moment? Or do we pause, maybe take a deep breath, and allow our mind to clear and our mind's eye to focus on He who loves us "before" we speak?

Martha was clearly distracted with the duties of a host, and sometimes we cannot avoid similar distractions when we attempt to have some prayer time. But Jesus sends a clear message that when we have the opportunity to "Call upon God," we should set aside our distractions and duties, find a quiet place, clear our minds, and open our mouths.

There will be time for speaking, and there will be time for listening. Your Father in Heaven wants to hear from you. It could be while you are in the shower in the morning, just giving "thanks" for all your blessings and not really having anything deep to discuss, or you might have just been sucker-punched with a trial and need some direction. Just remember that He is there for you. You have knocked on His door, and it will open as soon as you are ready, no matter the reason.

We don't always have to have a life-or-death reason to pray. But this is God! He knows your needs better than you do. And yes, He loves to hear when things are going great, but if you believe Jesus is sending a message to us all with His story of Mary and Martha, of the importance of pushing away the trivialities and distractions of life to call upon God frequently, then start today, and apply Winning Way #1 by "Calling upon God!"

Would there have been David without a Goliath?

Consider for a moment, please, where you would be today without trial or opposition opening a door for you or perhaps after closing one on you.

My family and I suffered the loss of our business income every 10-year cycle for almost four decades; after spending nine years growing it, it only took one year of trial to take it away.

If you are feeling sad for me after reading this personal insight, please don't! Earth life was not designed to get rich, retire at age thirty, and live happily ever after "without paying the price of mortality." This means life, as we have come to know it, is more about "becoming" than it is about having "arrived."

"Becoming" is a fluid condition, not a fixed state of being. Although I would have chosen not to experience what it felt like to be without significant income for over two years while our thirty-four-year-old daughter and family came to live with us to help in her battle against cancer, I would not change the effect of my "becoming's" as a result of it.

I was raised to be a problem solver, and asking for help is not in my DNA. Do you think my loving Father in Heaven knew that? I feel very confident He knew the stress I was under, as much as He knew of my unrealized potential as a writer lying within me. He knew I would need to fail in order to win… and as painful as it must have been to watch my family suffer over my stubbornness, He waited.

I will not know in mortality the reason for God's timing in answering prayers; I only know He would never ignore either of us… you, the reader, or me, the sinner. Yet I did not realize at the time that those impressions and thoughts of "re-inventing" myself at retirement age would lead me on a field trip to success, beginning with my answering an ad for a copywriter, hoping to find a way of earning some much-needed extra money, after experiencing the pain of seeing my real estate development business come to an end during the real estate meltdown of 2008, after still another ten-year run of entrepreneurship.

It was the call back from a publisher of a regional magazine that opened the door more fully to my future love of writing; it was being published several times along the way, which increased my faith and belief in myself as a person of worth, restored confidence in myself, and subsequently led me to come back to my roots in residential real estate. While I might have labeled that move in my profession more "desperation" rather than "inspiration" at the time, my vision of His hand in my life over the years has become even more visible; more on that later in the book.

Once we start the process of asking for help (even if it only starts with "help!"), that exercise of faith the size of a mustard seed is sufficient to be labeled "a knock" on the door of the One who wants us to win. It takes faith to begin the climb to win, and it will take even more faith to win... but by "asking," we have unlocked the door to the "Master Trainer" to assist us along the way in our pursuit to not just endure trial, but to win.

Winning through trial is more than just getting through the pain, discomfort, emotional stress, and inconvenience associated with the trial. This state of one's being is readily accepted by the world and defined within the pages of the book you are now reading as "enduring trial." I suppose the norm among most of us may even refer to this state of endurance as winning, but as I have reflected upon the many trials I have been privileged to endure over my advancing years, one thing stands abundantly clear: In my case, when trial struck, and I discovered I was still alive–I, therefore, had "choice" of how I would respond. I could stay down and pretend I was dead... or rise, dust myself off, and start over again. This would prove to be a lesson experienced over and over again.

`"Problems are not stop signs; they are guidelines." — Robert Schuller`

Choosing our response to trial is what this book is all about, so of course, I will devote at least one entire chapter to "Choice." But in the introductory chapter of "Winning," I chose "Call Upon God" as Winning Way #1–your first move toward using opposition as a catalyst to win–because I believe it sets the foundation for winning.

Bringing God into the picture so often and so early in this book will surely label it as another of those Christian preachy books by some, but I am convinced after enduring some significant trials in my life that without God as my co-pilot... (I've been waiting so long to use that reference.) I would not have continued to get back up–to win!

Asking you to ask God assumes a lot, I know. Having to decide how, what, when, and even where may stop you before you even get started.

So let's make this simple–if you reach a point in your life where you feel one or more of the following feelings: empty, alone, afraid, mad, angry, resentful, confused, disoriented, prideful, stubborn, hateful, hurt, pain, stress, hopeless, lost, blinded, or any other "natural man" condition I may have neglected to mention, it has been my experience that God stands ready and willing to help you heal: "God is our refuge and strength, a very present help in trouble." (Psalm 46:1) He even gives you direction on how to obtain that healing: "If my people, which are called by my name, shall humble themselves, and pray, and seek my face, and turn from their wicked ways; then will I hear from heaven, and will forgive their sin, and will heal their land."(2 Chronicles 7:14)

Did you notice in the list of all the "natural man" feelings I listed above, there is no mention of "humility?" Maybe it's not natural to recognize feelings of humility within us as a condition of "healing" after experiencing one or a combination of feelings associated with failure.

Maybe we have become "blinded by the craftiness of men" (Doctrine and Covenants 76:71-80) and refuse to see or feel anything but punishment for ourselves when trial is upon us. Humility is not a standard description of one who has set their sights upon winning. Humility is often considered a weaker trait than a leader or director. Yet this scripture in 2 Chronicles 7:14 cited above teaches us that humility is "key" to gaining the Father's attention through prayer. And if we can access the Father through prayer, doesn't that enable us to become the recipients of legions of angels at His command (Matthew 26:53) to bear up our sorrows, troubles, hurts, and pains? Does that sound like "weakness" to you?

Winning Way #1, "Call upon God," is the entry portal to winning; it was our first call when my wife and I learned our daughter had cancer. It was my first call when I finally realized I could not self-cure my chronic depression. It was my first call–once it became "somewhat" clear that I needed help beyond my stubborn, independent nature to fix it myself. Did you catch my subtle confession about "when" I made that first call? Frankly speaking, the "sooner" you make that first call to God, the better.

Suppose you are new to prayer or used to praying from a prayer book or reciting memorized prayers you learned as a child, as I did with the Lord's Prayer, or praying through the intercession of saints as your advocate to the Father, etc. In that case, you may find my use of the "Five W's" (Wikipedia) helpful in better understanding this sometimes confusing process called "prayer." It is pretty simple if you think about it. And using the formula mentioned earlier of the Five W's should make it even simpler (here's hoping):

<u>Who am I praying to?</u> We discussed this earlier in this chapter, but more clarity won't hurt. All prayers, no matter the chosen faith or manner of worship, will ultimately be heard by the One who made us all. In the Sermon on the Mount, Jesus prayed, "Our Father which art in heaven" (See Matthew 6:5-13, see also 3 Nephi 13:5-13). If you read the accounts of the ministry of Jesus Christ in all revealed scripture, you will see how sacred the Son of God treated the name of his Father in Heaven.

"But what if I want to pray to Jesus Christ? Is that wrong?" Good question! My faith in an unseen God was built upon the feeling I received when I studied the life and mission of the "Son" of God. That "feeling" has only grown in depth and understanding as I have aged and have taken advantage of His sacrifice and absorption for my personal sins, failures, mistakes, natural man choices, etc. That feeling for Him who carried me with Him upon the cross of Calvary, that fateful day of crucifixion–is "love." And the more I study about Him and pray to the Father to help me become more "like Him," the more Jesus Christ becomes part of my prayers.

We talked about not being distracted in our efforts to pray, but I have found that reading sacred scripture a few minutes before prayer puts me into a better frame of mind to converse with God–so you might try that if you have trouble getting started.

But it is worth reflecting that in the Great War in Heaven (Rev. 12:7), Lucifer, the son of the morning, wanted all power and glory for himself (See Isaiah 14: 12-20). Still, as revealed to Moses, it was Jesus Christ the Son who sided with "Father, that 'Thy' will be done, and the glory be 'Thine' forever" (See Moses 4:1-4 in Pearl of Great Price). And that "glory" referenced above starts with acknowledging God the Father as the Father/Creator of our spirits, with respect and love as a son or daughter would give their earthly parent.

There is great counsel in Colossians 3:17, "And whatsoever ye do in word or deed, do all in the name of the Lord Jesus, 'giving thanks to God and the Father' by Him." Address the Father in your prayers, and thank Him for His goodness, and all things asked for… and praised upon should be done "in the name of Jesus Christ, Amen."

<u>What am I praying for?</u> My first thought was to tell you to "make a list"… as tongue-in-cheek humor, but I have found that if my list of "needs" is preceded by a list of "thank you for…'s," it sets a better tone… kind of like a child telling a parent how much they are loved and

appreciated before asking for the keys to the family car.

Remember that your Heavenly Father is God, not Santa Claus. My youthful, immature prayers must have been side-splitters when I prayed to take away a pretty classmate's agency so she would start liking "me" instead of some other boy. That is more like "wishful thinking."

Sincere prayer would contain pleas for help, pleas for permission, thank you for blessings, and requests for opportunity and understanding. Heavenly Father loves prayers asking how we can serve Him and our Savior. How can we help build up His kingdom (the body of Christ) on earth? Begin by praying for your immediate family, neighbors, friends, worldly conditions, etc. You get the idea. There is just something transformative when we leave our personal island to serve someone else, even if it is only a moment of thought and prayer for their welfare and happiness.

One of the secrets I found while digging my way out of chronic depression was to "serve" others. In time, I could feel that grey cloud of despair beginning to be replaced by love for those I was serving.

<u>Where should I pray</u>? Again, given your choice of faith practices, there are many avenues to consider, but I have found the most effective "where" to pray is wherever it is most convenient.

If I am behind the wheel of the car headed for an appointment and find myself running late, I pray (not with my eyes closed, however). And if you feel, as I do, that finding a private place in your home the first thing in the morning works, then pray. If you feel good about praying in a restaurant before a meal, then pray. If you have a loved one and want the most spiritual experiences, gently hold their hand when you pray. No matter the where of prayer, God hears your sincere supplication (See Lamentations 3:55-56, also 1 John 5: 14 and Psalm 34:17-18, etc.), but remember the experience of Mary and Martha, and our discussion about treating your time with God as sacred "opportunity."

Having said that, we should also remember in Matthew 6: 5-8, where Jesus counsels His disciples to "not" pray as the hypocrites, for they "love to pray standing in the synagogues and the corners of the streets, 'that they may be seen of men...'" And He further reminds them to "not use vain repetitions, as the heathen do; for they think that they shall be heard for their much speaking" (See also 3 Nephi 13:5-13). Well, that gives us a few things to think about when praying, doesn't it? But if you are sincere and honest, I believe God will hear and bless you no matter "where" you pray.

<u>When should I pray?</u> How about this... Pray "always!" 1 Thessalonians 5:17 teaches us to "pray without ceasing," but remember that prayer doesn't always have to be about "wanting." I find that praying with "thanks and gratitude" leaves me fulfilled and happy. Try giving thanks, asking nothing, for all God has given you, and see how it makes you feel. I think you will be pleasantly surprised. Although our first call to God in trial is a given, why not also build a "gratitude" call into your faith? The next time things are going "great," why not make a call?

I also find that for "me," praying the very first thing in the morning is the "safest" time to pray because the household is *usually* quiet, and no one *usually* breaks in on my special time with God. I leave my phone in another room and have found our "guest room" to be a private place in the morning to begin my day by telling my Father in Heaven how happy I am to be on earth to learn what He has to teach me about "becoming."

If you don't have a guest room, maybe there is a "corner" somewhere that is occupied by a comfortable chair, out of sight from most household activity, where you can sit and petition the Lord in private prayer–that works, too.

How about a stairwell in your home, usually cluttered with "stuff?" I call those "Harry Pot-tah" rooms; simply perfect for a person who wants to feel surrounded by angels in a small environment as they pray.

How about while you are sitting in your car before heading to work in the morning? If you can focus your mind to not think about what lies ahead on the freeway, this would be a great place and time for private prayer.

I could go on, but hopefully, your imagination is at work now, thinking of your own "special prayer place" where you can begin your day supplicating to God.

<u>Why should I pray?</u> Probably the first answer we all think of is, "Because I 'need' something, duh!" But then you experience what most of us have experienced when asking for something without regard to what is best for us, or we ask and then wait impatiently before giving up. "Who is God, anyway?" you ask. "I can't see Him, and He never answers my prayers [in the way 'I' want them answered]. But ask yourself this question: "Why did Jesus pray?" Some say the answer is, "to set a proper example for us," and of course, one only needs to read Jesus' Sermon on the Mount (Matthew 5-7) to understand how true

that is.

On one occasion, Jesus Christ "was praying in a certain place," and "when he ceased, one of his disciples said unto him, Lord, teach us to pray" (Luke 11:1). Jesus taught what has become known as "The Lord's Prayer."

My mother taught me the Lord's Prayer by reciting it with me, as I think her mother had done with her. Although I could, and still can, recite the verses in the prayer, I didn't come to know the "meaning" of the prayer until I started praying on my own.

It was during what could have been a tragic mistake by a young boy of ten that I first prayed a simple plea-prayer to God to "help save my life!"

I loved participating in the barrel race competition at the County Fair in my hometown. I thought of myself as quite the horseman, but this one year, my horse was ailing, and I was without a ride. My cousin Buzzy offered his horse, named One-Eye, and my sister's boyfriend Pete loaned me his most prized possession–a pair of spurs given him by the closest father figure he had.

It was during the warm-up, just before being called to line up for the barrel racing, that I noticed with horror one of the prized spurs missing from my left boot. I looked everywhere I thought I had been, but there was nothing but sagebrush and dirt. In the distance, I kept hearing the call for barrel racers to line up, but I couldn't stop looking. Then, a feeling came over me to "pray." While on the horse, I bowed my head and offered the most selfish prayer ever offered, I'm sure: "Dear God, my sister's boyfriend will kill me on sight if I lose that spur. Please help me find it!" And then I started looking again, panic-driven.

I don't remember what it was that caused me to look in an area opposite of where I was looking, but I do remember second-guessing myself that it would be a waste of time to look over there because I didn't remember even riding in that direction, but that is where we went. After a few frantic moments of searching, I sat back in the saddle, hopelessly resigned to being put to death by my sister, if not her boyfriend–and found myself folding my arms, with head bowed, not even caring if anyone could see me or not, and uttered the most sincere plea-prayer ever spoke, with tears and everything.

When I opened my tear-filled eyes, with my head still bowed, a sharp reflection from something caught my eye, dead on. I jumped off the horse, ran over to the bush, and there–hanging off the top of this bush–was my lost spur. I quickly grabbed it to be sure it was "the" spur, and while thoughts of "how?" raced through my mind, my legs acted on impulse with a sense of their own as my boots smoothly entered each stirrup. With the trophy spur in hand, I raced to the check-in area, tears drying onto my dirty face as I gave ole' One-Eye plenty of rein to run. Yep, he was blind in one eye, I later learned.

And no, I didn't win a coveted ribbon that day, but something better came crashing down upon me when God sent "someone" to help a little boy in distress. I knew from that experience that God knew me and that I mattered–and I knew God knew that I knew it. And to make certain He had my attention, He had the lost spur relocated to an area I hadn't been in. That's how He knew "I" knew. This was just the beginning of other unique experiences to come into my life.

In summing this all up, it probably matters less about the where, why, or what–and more about the "who and when." If you pray with a humble heart, asking for... whatever troubles you, you will have God's attention. If you are consistent in prayer, you will develop a love for both the Father and the Son and hopefully want to become like Them and live your life according to Their words and deeds.

There is such power in prayer!

I may have neglected to mention one other minor condition and one not-so-small condition in the 2 Chronicles 7:14 scripture on how to achieve God's attention through prayer.

"Seek my face" when praying (Vs.14) seems to be clear advice. I need to know/see to whom I am speaking. Any conversation with another is enhanced by actually "seeing" the person you are trying to converse with–look at the emergence of video conferencing, Facebook Live, FaceTime, and ZOOM on your devices. Just use the image that comes to mind when you think of Him as your Father in Heaven, deeply rooted in your well-being and interested in your success. Can you feel the warmth of His love for you? Something extraordinary pulses through our body when we envision the personage we are praying to.

Jesus told Philip, "If ye have seen me, ye have seen the Father"(John 14:9). Perhaps if we seek to emulate the faces of our Heavenly Father and our Savior Jesus Christ in our own countenances, it won't be so hard to envision a radiance beaming back at us when we pray.

Maybe a trip to the local Christian bookstore to find an artist's perceived likeness of Jesus Christ is in order so we can make it a part of our home. If we can envision the likeness of the Son of God, we will most certainly see the image of the Father in Him.

I know I may have assumed a lot over the last few pages of Winning Way #1, and to be perfectly transparent, I can still remember periods of my life when I was so down on myself, angry at the world, kind of down, that trying to envision the face of Deity listening to my ranting was not accomplished. I know there are many of you right now hit by the ripple effect of post-COVID-19, only to be hit again in 2021-23 with supply-chain disruptions, labor shortages, rising inflation, and interest rate hikes... and have lost so much. I hope you realize from reading this book that "no one can take away your faith in becoming!" You can still possess "hope." You can still pray and be heard. You can still "Win!"

The other not-so-small condition the Lord of the Old Testament asked of His people was to "turn from their (our) wicked ways" as a condition of prayer. Does this mean that only saints will be heard when they pray? What about us sinners? Aren't we all sinners, saved only through the atonement and grace of Jesus Christ?

Perhaps the answer to my question above lies within the "intent of the heart." Few of us are like the "wicked witch" in the story of Snow White, but how many of us have adopted "wicked ways" by our actions toward others in the form of abusive behavior, bullying, intolerance of others, road rage, contentious and hostile social media posts, etc.? Certainly, our participation in such behavior can't be pleasing to our Heavenly Father.

No matter the exact definition or application of the term wickedness, as referenced in the 2 Chronicles scripture, if we are to solicit the aid of our Heavenly Father in guiding us safely through our trial, we need to be of the mindset that although He loves us and wants to help us, it is up to each of us, individually, to "prepare ourselves to hear His voice."

Ever tire of a straight road, endless in its promise of arriving?

I was born experiencing trial and lived to tell about it; my slightly older brother did not. Although born a year or so apart, we both possessed a rare blood disease that in the 1940s required a transfusion of old blood for new. I have often wondered how my parents survived that trial of losing their first baby boy and then finding out their second baby boy had the same diseased blood condition, requiring them to temporarily move in with relatives living in Hawthorne, California, so I could be close to a hospital in Hollywood, California who had developed new procedures for treating babies born with "blue baby syndrome," also known as infant methemoglobinemia. In this condition, a baby's skin turns blue. This condition occurs due to decreased hemoglobin in the baby's blood. Hemoglobin is a blood protein responsible for carrying oxygen around the body and delivering it to the different cells and tissues.

And yes, I got my start in life as an entertainer! My stage was a cold, sterile delivery room in a Hollywood hospital, and my supporting cast of "real" doctors and nurses were there to ensure this would not be my last gig.

My mother, Dorothy Malone, was not "the" famous actress by the same name, although she was as beautiful. Speaking as one who would be a constant source of trial to my parents, I would not have survived without her strength and love constantly in my corner.

When I took a hammer to the family car headlights at the age of five years old, during a quick trip out of town to visit family–preventing us from returning home that night for my dad's work the next day–my mother was heroic by not following her emotions to give me away. However, my later actions growing up would only prove she should have.

I was the one child every parent asked, "Why me, Lord?" I don't think I was a "bad" child; I was just... curious and a bit disobedient!

I am also known for "getting religion" in me quite early when my Methodist Sunday School teacher had quite enough of me using her class time as my platform to launch my stand-up comedy career. I never saw the Holy Bible flying as fast as the one leaving her hand... and then–blackness surrounded by stars!

More trials would follow as I proved myself quite unreliable when following Mother's orders to "not" go horseback riding on a Sunday following a rainstorm. I can only imagine her horror when she received a phone call at work to come to the hospital immediately because I had been in an accident–involving a horse.

That little exercise of poor judgment on my part would result in more pain and misery for both parents and child than I care to remember. My mother bravely fought against the surgeon's recommendation to remove my crushed arm, resulting in four surgeries and a month-long stay at St. Joseph's Children's Hospital in Phoenix to save the severely crushed arm.

I could fill up the pages of this book with similar stories throughout my life, but you get the idea. Trial would not stray too far, no matter where I lived.

It wasn't until years later that I had matured enough to become somewhat aware of the trial my disobedience had caused my parents. Lost time at work, the stress of losing one child, unexpected expense–now this?

Marriage, raising a family, work, obtaining a skill or education to provide for oneself, health challenges, human relationships, accidents, loss of income, and growing old all contain a measure of trial possibilities for each of God's children. Rarely do we get to be old without having sufficient family stories of trial and opposition to fill the pages of a book.

So, where is the fairness in trial? Where is the sweetness?

Trial is not designed to play fair if you haven't already noticed. Trial is designed to hit you where you are least prepared, when you least expect it, and with all the unfairness possible so that you "feel it!"

Although several definitions of trial are already mentioned in this writing, can we agree that within the context of this book, if it is personal and hurts, then it is trial? That definition can also apply when trial strikes someone we love, and our grief for them hurts so badly that we, too, mourn their hurt. In fact, to feel that deeply for someone other than yourself is truly the essence of the second great commandment–to "love our neighbor as ourselves," the first being to "love the Lord, thy God with all thy heart, and with all thy soul, and with all thy mind."

The Sweetness of Trial (2nd Half)

Trial is designed to open the door to greatness within you.

Some will look at trial as punishment, but do you remember the scripture in Hebrews 12: 6, "For whom the Lord loveth He chasteneth?" Paul, the apostle, taught the Hebrew saints that being chastened is a sign that their Heavenly Father loves them as a Father loves and chastens his children.

In Proverbs 3:11-12, we also read: "My child, do not despise discipline from the Lord, and do not loathe His rebuke, for the Lord disciplines those He loves, just as a father disciplines the son in whom he delights."

My father and mother were extremely strict with me (For good reason). My older (mostly perfect) sister cried whenever I did something stupid and tried to hide it from my parents, often resulting in a bit more than a "rebuke." At the time, all I could think of was how unfair my parents were in their means and severity of "chastisement." Still, looking back, now with a 20/20 vision, I am ever so thankful they were strict, given my curious nature as a boy and being a bit weak at resisting the natural man [boy] within me.

Our "correction" by the Father of our spirits is not usually as immediate as that from our earthly parents and not as easy to detect. When trial happens, we have a choice in how we will react, often assessing "blame" elsewhere and usually slow to look in the mirror first. Yet, when we are the recipient of "blessings," are we not quick to take credit?

There is a scripture in the Doctrine and Covenants that lays the foundation for our possible understanding of trial and blessings: "There is a law, irrevocably decreed in heaven before the foundations of this world, upon which all blessings are predicated–and when we obtain any blessing from God, it is by obedience to that law upon which it is predicated" (D&C 130:20-21).

When I first read that scripture many years ago, I thought it meant that if I were "good," I would never have anything significantly bad happen to me. Boy, was I in for an awakening? This scripture teaches that there is order in the universe and that by adhering to certain principles of cause, there would also be an effect because of that particular law of the universe. One that I can think of is "gravity." The law of gravity, simply speaking, promises if an object is lifted, it can certainly be expected to fall... unless it is a balloon filled with air, but eventually, it too shall fall.

Another prominent spiritual law is taught in the Old Testament book of Malachi, Chapter 3:10, promising the windows of heaven to open and bestow a blessing upon you for following the Law of Tithing. I can personally attest to the truthfulness of this spiritual law, but it doesn't mean you won't be subject to trial. And it certainly does not mean you won't lose your job or retirement savings. You are probably asking, "Then what does it mean?"

Moses brought the Ten Commandments to the Children of Israel to bring them a measure of happiness if followed. They didn't, and the outcome is history.

I am sure you can think of other examples of spiritual laws which promise a "measure" of blessings. Did you notice I didn't say anything about "guaranteed" blessings? Why not, you ask? Do you remember the oft-repeated saying, "There is nothing guaranteed in life except death [and taxes]?" And there is a reason for that saying. Even following the rules of crossing a street in the marked crosswalk, with the light blinking "OK to proceed," doesn't guarantee you won't be hit by a car running the red light from another direction. You see, that is where the principle of agency comes in. That is why trial cannot be removed entirely. That is why trial is non-denominational and even happens to "good people."

I had another "spiritual law" cross my path lately, twice, actually–while pondering over this section of Chapter One. The Law of the Harvest was taught on one of the podcasts I was listening to while walking one morning... and then on another, a reference to the Law of the Harvest was made from Stephen Covey's famous book, "Seven Habits of Highly Effective People." With such powerful "coincidences," I couldn't resist diving into a better understanding of what this spiritual law means about achieving greatness.

The "Law of the Harvest" (Galatians 6:7-10) is a biblical principle that states very simply: "You reap what you sow." But this principle is much deeper than the simple law infers, with much to learn from an analogy using farming techniques to explain how trial brings out the greatness within us.

So please bear with me while I try to connect the dots using principles of "farming."

In our analogy, the farmer's field (dirt) represents you and me. The farmer is our Creator, who wants to bring out the greatness within us. He starts by preparing the soil to receive nutrients so that when the seed is planted, it will grow in fertile ground.

At first, the dirt is hard, unyielding, and closed to change... to becoming. So the farmer "breaks the ground" (trial) by plowing and tilling the soil down to root level, which is about 6-9" Inches below the surface, where the "humus soil" is located (humus is a root word for "humble" and also as "grounded" – see Wikipedia) where rain and irrigation water pushes the nutrients. As the hardened soil is broken up, turned over, and mixed with the humus soil underneath (life happens), seeds are then planted in the enriched soil (open to change), which is watered, fertilized, and in time the new growth appears (becoming).

Many individuals, me included, have been "hardened" by life's ups and downs, twists and turns, only to find ourselves resistant to change. Like the hardened soil, we needed to become humble (humus) enough to accept change (seeds) when it is necessary to reach our full potential in "becoming" (new growth).

Chapter Five in this book is titled "Seek the Best Gifts, Discover Hidden Talents, and Look for the Miracle;" a mouthful, I know. But the Law of the Harvest has a connection with that chapter if you look at each trial as a season of growth in becoming.

This is where "Call Upon God" comes in, to ask for help and assistance in recognizing "opportunity" in each trial to produce hidden talents and gifts that otherwise would not have bloomed. Like the real-life farmer, Our Heavenly Father will assist each of us in fulfilling the measure of our creation. Chapter Five will help you better understand the potential for greatness within you and how to "look for the miracle."

Are "any" of us the same after a severe trial? Think about the last "shake and bake" trial you had. You did have a choice on how you would react to that trial. Take a moment and think about how you have changed because of that trial. If you don't like how you see yourself, put down the bat and "choose" to change.

The Christmas Miracle in the Life of Henry Wadsworth Longfellow

Life is hard and sometimes unfair, yet the heroic version of each of us is often born of fire amid adversity and struggle.

Such was the case of Henry Wadsworth Longfellow, a famed 19th-century scholar, poet, novelist, husband, and father. Young Henry was born into a well-established England family on February 27, 1807. His father, a prominent lawyer, had anticipated early on that Henry would follow in his footsteps, seeing that he attended the best private schools, attending Portland (Maine) Academy, then Bowdoin College, also in Maine.

Henry was indeed a bright student, growing proficient in foreign languages. Upon graduating from Bowdoin College in 1925, he was offered a position to teach modern languages.

In 1831, Henry married Mary Storer Potter, a childhood friend from Portland, Maine, also from an established family. The couple settled in Brunswick, although both were unhappy in this environment.

In 1834, Longfellow received a letter from Josiah Quincy III, president of Harvard College, offering him the Smith Professorship of

Modern Languages... but with the stipulation Henry spent a year or so abroad, studying the languages of European culture. This would mean Henry and Mary would be separated for a lengthy while, but ultimately, the sacrifice was made. While in Europe, Longfellow studied German and Dutch, Danish, Swedish, Finnish, and Icelandic.

Longfellow enjoyed such a catapulted beginning to his career and life that one rarely notices the clouds of trial beginning to gather until it is too late.

While Henry was on his sabbatical to Germany, immersed in learning the language and culture, he received word in October 1835 that Mary had a miscarriage about six months into her pregnancy, resulting in an extended illness that ultimately took her life.

Terribly devastated by her death, Longfellow wrote, "One thought occupies me night and day. She is dead–She is dead! All day, I am weary and sad." However, three years later, he was inspired to write the poem "Footsteps of Angels," about a lonely figure who encounters deceased persons from their past and finds personal inspiration in the idea that these people are now "saints and angels in Heaven," exposing the writer's deep faith in religion and spirituality, but not requiring that the reader have such a religious feeling, but perhaps a "safe-house" to shelter against the wiles of the world such as loneliness and depression, inspiring thousands of readers to their own conclusions of what the story means to them in their own experiences with lost loved ones.

Longfellow's popularity as a prolific writer grew leaps and bounds as he continued to teach at Harvard, producing some of his best work, such as *Voices in the Night, Ballads and Other Poems, and Poems on*

Slavery, opening his writing mind to a multitude of current and past events.

Enjoying fame and the honors of dignitaries in Europe and America, such as Queen Victoria, Lord Tennyson, Oscar Wilde, and many others, one would think that trial and heartache would never leave their mark upon this remarkable man. But that was not to be.

In 1843, Longfellow married Frances (Fanny) Elizabeth Appleton, whom he met while they both were touring in Switzerland. Fanny, as her friends knew her, was a well-educated and traveled young woman–the daughter of a wealthy merchant. She and Henry enjoyed (or endured) a long courtship, over which time she managed to calm his troubled soul over losing his first wife and child, finally agreeing to marry him.

I love this expression of Fanny for her husband, written in her journal just twelve days before the birth of her first son, "How broken and incomplete when he is absent a moment; what defines peace and fullness when he is present. Can any child excite as strong a passion as this we feel for each other?"(Encyclopedia.com)

How could anything come between such a happy and perfect union, producing two sons and three daughters and a strong bond of love between their parents?

On July 9, 1961, Fanny had taken a lock of her daughter's hair, as was the custom to preserve such memorabilia, by heating sealing wax to enclose the packet containing her child's hair, when the sleeve of her light cotton dress caught fire somehow, and she was immediately engulfed in flames.

Running to find her husband, screaming frantically, she was severely burned; she died the next day. Henry was so severely burned as well in his attempt at saving her he was unable to attend her funeral.

Having retired from teaching at Harvard in 1961, Longfellow had a tough time emerging from this trial of losing his second wife and caring for their four children. He worried that he would go insane, begging "not to be sent to an asylum" and noting that he was inwardly "bleeding to death."(Wikipedia)

On the night of December 1, 1063, Henry W. Longfellow received a telegram as he was enjoying dinner with his family. The trial comes when least expected, as a thief in the night, sparing none and taking no prisoners when you thought it could get no worse.

Henry's son Charles had run away from home and enlisted in the Federal Army in Washington, D.C. He was patriotic in his desire to serve his country and felt this was the only way to ensure his duty in life could be fulfilled. He excelled in training and became a commissioned officer, serving in the 1st Massachusetts Calvary unit.

As Henry struggled to open the telegram, all eyes were on him; it was as if all air in the room had been sucked out as Henry read the dreaded words. The telegram informed that during a conflict on November 27, 1863, Charles took a bullet, entering his left shoulder and exiting his back, but not before clipping the spine. The wound was profoundly severe and might cause paralysis, it was noted.

Not always present in trial is the word "good news." Three more surgeons looked after Charles and soon that evening sent a more favorable report that "Charles will be long in healing," but he will live and should recover completely. However, his injury was significant enough to end his military career.

What most people don't know about that Christmas Day of 1863 is that this gifted poet, immersed in personal trial, rose from the ashes–and with feelings of despair filling his soul with such "trouble and anxiety," took pen in hand and wrote what would become one of the most beloved Christmas carols ever written.

Henry Longfellow's poem, "Christmas Bells," had its beginnings in the roots of the American Civil War. Longfellow was so filled with the scars of personal trial that the lines of this Christmas carol carry within it the despair and feelings felt by its author as he sat to write his feelings on that Christmas Day in 1863, impacted by all that had happened to his wife, his country, and now his son.

With some modifications to the original, which eliminated reference to the war, this beautiful carol is sung by millions every year as family and friends gather to celebrate the season of giving and love, the words of one Henry Wadsworth Longfellow ringing loud and clear in mind and heart of each of us, to dispel the feelings which trial often brings into the lives it touches – "Christmas Bells."

And in despair I bowed my head;
"There is no peace on earth," I said;
"For hate is strong, And mocks the song
Of peace on earth, good-will to men!"
Then pealed the bells more loud and deep;
"God is not dead, nor doth He sleep;
The Wrong shall fail, The Right prevail,

With peace on earth, good-will to men."

There will likely be a serious debate about how much success gifted individuals like Henry Wadsworth Longfellow would have attained without trial. Longfellow was born with visible talents, but history will confirm that there is a depth to each of us that will never be achieved without the pain associated with breaking through to the humus (humble) level of our hearts.

This brings up a less-understood spiritual law that operates within the principle of agency. <u>Without trial in our lives, we can never truly become "all" we are capable of becoming.</u> But even during trial, it is our choice (agency) to open our hearts to change. That agency is exercised when we decide how we will respond to what trial brings our way.

Trial "may" open a portal to our heart in which a level of humility "may" be achieved, which opens our mind to search deeper for alternatives and answers to life's challenges. I use the word "may" because we are all subject to the principle of "agency," remember? This law is in motion when "choice" is exercised. If anger is our choice of reaction, fueled by blame and pride, we are less likely to achieve this desired state of humus.

A lesson in physiology may be in order. When trial enters our lives and often brings us to our knees, our hearts can open to vulnerabilities that can change our character to become more Christ-like. This change in character is the key to unlocking the greatness within each of us. My friend, it was planned that way from the beginning.

Adam and Eve's choice to fulfill the measure of their creation to "become" was exercised in their partaking of the forbidden fruit, which ended their residency of perfect 70-degree weather in the Garden of Eden. Had they remained in the Garden, God's plan for earth life would have been "frustrated." And our earthly "first parents" would never have known joy or pain... or the experience of winning!

It is the "being knocked down" part of life that truly puts us in a position to "Win." Because Adam and Eve were thrust into the "lone and dreary world," carnal and worldly-mindedness were also allowed to exist, and the natural man state within us was born, that we might learn to co-exist and be "in the world" but learn to <u>not</u> become "of" the world. This is the "test" of the trial. This is the "purpose" of this "second estate" called earth life–a probationary period to learn, grow, experience, develop, and prepare to meet God.

The Sweetness of Trial (2nd Half)

Without Trial, there is no "Win!"

There is something about the physical nature of trial, acting as a "key" of sorts, immediately connecting with our nervous and neurological systems to "unlock" access to our deepest emotions. I suppose over time, most of us create "walls" around these deep emotions to protect ourselves, showing control under stress and pressure. Some may enter professions that require the presence of these walls as a means to remain clear-thinking when a weapon is pointed their way or when the need to draw from stored expertise on how to save a life is called for. But for most of us, we approach trial as something that will "take" rather than give. This is where our thinking and prior-formed reactions to opposition need a facelift.

If it were possible to gain these "proposed" new understandings and definitions of trial just by reading and studying the concepts of each Winning Way presented in this writing, I would be so happy for you (and me). But that is not how this "key" works.

There are "levels" of trial that occur daily, to which the body's complex systems respond. Let's call these trials, "irritants." Some days, you feel like no matter how hard you try, you can't "get a grip" on life as it passes by. And checking your social media every hour doesn't help. You feel like a failure sometimes and wish you had stayed in bed. Or am I the only one who has those types of days? Those days, when they occur, are merely irritants to our "becoming."

While in the act of earning a living, these irritants happen. We may fail at making a sale, receive a bad review about our performance, arrive late for an important meeting, or any number of opposing forces that make us feel like losers. But the body is designed to "fight back" when an opposing force threatens your well-being. After a night of rest, you are usually good to go the very next day. This type of trial is generally replaced quickly by countering the next day with a right hook to the jaw of your "stinking thinking," and all is forgotten because a friend invited you to lunch or you received a box of cookies for just doing something nice for a neighbor.

Clinical studies have shown that our bodies are equipped with built-in "error-driven" correction systems, which, when we make minor errors in movement each day, these errors are used to adapt our future movements. This would qualify as one of those "clinical tests" I mentioned at the beginning of this chapter, defining trial. Our body manages this "irritant" trial level by storing/recording each reaction to help us through the next irritant assailant. In time, if we maintain the proper attitude about trial, we become stronger and less impacted by these daily irritants. This constant exposure to trial and opposition is designed to condition us to live in a world designed to test us in many ways, not as punishment for the sin of Adam and Eve being cast out of the Garden as is preached by some, but rather as a means of preparing us for more significant challenges, which if overcome could have the power to unlock the greatness within each of us.

These more significant challenges, a higher level of trial, are what I call the "shake and bake" level. These hurt… and they hurt for more than a passing day. And their hurt usually doesn't get better with sleep; in fact, they keep you awake, worrying about "what if" and "why me?" This level of trial can potentially rock your boat and your world. I experienced such a trial after receiving a tax audit many years ago of my various business and personal finances, resulting in having to take our appeal to tax court for interpretation. Even though we were successful, the pure "hell" we were put through extended over months and months of meetings and late nights searching for documents, ultimately leading to defending and receiving a fair settlement. It didn't feel like a win, but it could have been worse.

This book's definition of "Winning" might not be what you think!

Don't be misled by the title of this book. "Winning," as defined within these pages, is not going to be like when you were in high school, and after coming out on top of a tough-fought football game, everyone met at the local Pizza joint to celebrate. That is the world's definition of winning, which we all love to celebrate when "our" team scores the winning run.

But my vision for this book is to help you see the larger picture regarding trial in developing character... including spiritual strength, deeper faith, discovering hidden gifts and talents, greater perseverance, and gaining character-building resilience to better see yourself as an achiever in "becoming." Unlike the game ending with the home team scoring the highest number of points, the winner in a trial is the one who gets up to fight another day, with an awareness of a positive change to become better, not bitter. This is "Winning" through trial.

Although I have written a former book titled "The Sweetness of Trial," I wanted Chapter One of "this" book to continue where "Sweetness" left off, digging a bit deeper into the purpose of trial, the opportunity to choose better over bitter and provide actual personal-improvement Winning Ways to better equip you for the subsequent trial.

"After battling depression for several years, I found that I felt better when I immersed myself in helping others." -Author.

Attorneys often call me to represent their client in a divorce when selling a home, and dividing the proceeds between the separating couple is needed. Divorce is a shake-and-bake type of trial, often resulting in anger, distrust, and over-the-top emotions, which last for days, weeks, months, and sometimes years.

I initially begin as a spectator, doing my job as the laws and statutes of the land provide. But it doesn't take long before I become a protector, a mediator, a witness at trial, a diplomat, and a negotiator, all in the form of service to my client.

I market the home, consult with the attorneys, solve issues as they develop, and assist my client with legal paperwork to ensure their rights are preserved, all within my fiduciary relationship to my client. Other times, I even appear in court on their behalf to testify and, as a result, find myself "attacked" by the opposing attorney on any number of fronts. Through this process, trust develops between me and my client. I become a sounding board, a listening ear, a gentle voice amidst a storm. I can feel and share the pain of life and become a friend.

There is someone near you right now going through a trial of their own. No one is immune from trial, no matter how perfect their lives look on social media, but everyone could use someone to share their trial—to be in their corner when things get tough—someone who can be a friend.

I don't want to sound like the neighborhood "welcome wagon" driver because I am far from that. But I can say with conviction that when I have reached out to help another during their trial, no matter the depth of help or amount of time or resources involved, I have always felt "better" about myself afterward.

Life hands us more than enough red checkmarks that when we lend a helping hand or provide a bit of comfort to another, even if it is only by a visit or a meaningful hug and words of encouragement, it creates change in us.

Don't sell yourself short, thinking your sincere actions and words of encouragement to another aren't important enough or needed. We all need something more than a "Like" on social media. Pick up the phone and dial the number of someone who just experienced loss or received terrible health news. They may not answer, but if they don't, leave a message that you care. Drop off a homemade goodie plate of something "chocolate." I have accomplished miracles with chocolate. Be a friend to someone with trial.

The "sweetness" referred to in this book can also be felt when serving others.

So far in this chapter, we have made numerous references to the feeling of "sweetness" felt during trial. My reason for taking up your time to discuss a physical feeling you likely have felt before is that maybe you didn't have a name for it or understand "why" you felt that way.

Maybe you are like me and didn't have the scriptural background to know where to look for an explanation for such a feeling, so you just passed it off as a "hunch" or a feeling, or in some cases, a simple "assurance" that all would be well. Maybe you even felt peace at some point in your trial, but it definitely "felt" the strongest when your time in the ring was beginning to take its toll on you–the outcome not looking good at all, and maybe even without realizing it "you reached out to God" for help.

Let's turn to the scriptures, to the Book of John in the New Testament, which chronicles the life and teachings of Jesus Christ to His disciples, for a little more insight into this "feeling." On His last night with His disciples, in the Upper Room, Jesus explained that He would soon leave them so that the "Comforter" could come and teach them "all things." Jesus taught that this Comforter was the Holy Spirit, the third member of the Godhead. Next to God the Father and His Son, Jesus Christ is the Holy Ghost, or Holy Spirit, as He is also called.

The account of Jesus teaching His disciples about the Holy Spirit is referenced in quick succession in several chapters and verses in the Book of John (See John 14:16, 14:26, 15:26, and 16:7), highlighting the importance Jesus Christ placed in their (and our) understanding of this Comforter who would be sent to teach.

In John 14:18, Jesus assures His Disciples that He will not leave them "comfortless." This assurance reveals "another" role of our Savior as Redeemer and Advocate with the Father–He is also in our lives to comfort and to assure.

As I contemplate the disciple's thoughts and fears after being told the "Master" would soon depart from their midst–they would once again be alone–my mind reflected on a time of trial when I, too, was feeling very isolated and deeply disturbed over not able to find substantive real estate work for two years, and then a phone call from our daughter brought another wave of trial to our doorstep in the form of cancer.

I had read in scripture that God sent us trials to strengthen our faith in Him. I remembered reading in 1 Corinthians 10:13, where Paul declares that God is faithful and… "will not suffer you to be tempted [tried] above that ye are able…" but that is precisely where I found myself after the phone call from our daughter–I felt overwhelmed, unable to stand, unable to take one more hit–so I knelt by my wife's side and did the only thing I knew to do at that point… I prayed to God with all my heart and soul. And there it was–the rest of God's promise, that even in the darkest of nights where there is no light, the hope of a brighter day having been washed away by tears, God promised He shall… "also make a way to escape, that ye may be able to bear it."

In John 16:33, Jesus declares: "These things I have spoken unto you, that in me ye might have peace. In the world ye shall have tribulation: but be of good cheer; I have overcome the world."

Jesus Christ came to earth as a mortal, experiencing pains, temptations, betrayals, and even abandonment by His friends. He came to overcome spiritual death so that we might live and pave the way for our resurrection, having paid for our sins with His blood on the cross at Calvary.

During my moment of utter despair, I was joined by my wife and mother of this sweet daughter to plead for our daughter's life as we had never before pled. At that moment in time, we had reached a crevice, unable to move forward on our own, unable to bear even the thought of losing our daughter, a mother of five small children with so much to live for. Yet, if it be not so, what choice did we have but to believe in the goodness of God?

I have devoted an entire chapter of this book to "choice." Here is an exercise for you: Try defining the word "choice" without using the word itself to describe it. Not so easy, is it? It took me a while to think of the word "right" as adding some definitive meaning to it, but my other attempts ended up with only "descriptions."

Choice is indeed a right, as is agency. But perhaps agency is also a choice, as choice is agency. What makes choice such an explosive, defining, life-changing, potentially dangerous word is the question, "What if…?" What if I make the wrong choice? What if my choice leads to unhappiness? What if my choice leads to trial? It can be paralyzing.

As grieving parents of a child stricken with an uncompromising disease, we could have assessed blame. We could have "chosen" to blame

God for allowing this trial to reach our door. Or we could have chosen to believe that no matter what, we would not give up trying. No matter the outcome, we would do our best to "try" and then leave the rest up to God.

When does the Comforter show loving compassion toward a devastated parent, fearful beyond comprehension of losing a child? When does one feel the "sweetness" in trial? I think it is different for each of us, depending on a wide array of circumstances and perhaps needs. Some fear they are not strong enough to withstand the coming tornado, but they somehow do… expressing the deep appreciation of feeling strength in the Lord afterward… and the sweetness of the Comforter felt as dew falling from above, as confirmation that all will be well.

Others, perhaps surprised by their lack of strength, find themselves unable to cope and turn unashamedly to their Savior, pleading for His presence as the sweetness of assurance builds within them. This, too, is experiencing sweetness in trial.

After our daughter's call, my wife and I joined our faith together to contemplate a plan of action. We discussed what we knew about the disease, but mostly, we just wanted to hug and protect her.

I can't remember experiencing the feeling of "sweetness" until a bit later in the night after I had cried my eyes dry and found a quiet place in our big house to seek refuge. Wrapped in darkness but seeking light, I once again dropped to my knees and pled with God to hear my prayer.

The Holy Ghost is a spirit so he can come into a person and "move" them to change their nature, or to open their minds to possibilities, or to obey God's commands (See 2 Peter 1:21; 1 Cor. 12:3; John 14:26);

or, in my case, to comfort my being with a feeling that washed over me that I could only begin to describe as a "sweetness," however short that description may fall.

During the next two years, I would experience this indescribable feeling I call "sweetness" over and over again; impressions would come telling me how to teach my daughter positive affirmations to guide the chemo and radiation into the tiniest of crevices where this invading cancer might find to hide. I, in turn, would follow these promptings by recording my voice with positive affirmations for my daughter to listen to each night as she lay motionless before drifting into a fitful sleep and during the quiet time of each day.

The mind is such a powerful computer, designed to affect thoughts, feelings, attitudes, beliefs, memories, and imaginations, which in turn intimately affect the physiology and biochemistry of the body. I have also seen and believe in the power of faith and have seen with my own eyes how the combination of faith and a positive mind can achieve wonders (See Chapter Three – Attitude Begets Behavior), as Napoleon Hill wrote in his landmark best-selling book (Think and Grow Rich), "Whatever the mind can conceive and believe, it can achieve."

While I am not promising the same positive results as those having blessed my daughter, and I am certainly not offering medical advice in "any" form, I can say with such humility and belief that for me and my house, we shall be eternally grateful for the successful medical treatments our attending physicians were "impressed" to recommend, and to my Heavenly Father and His Son, Jesus Christ, for sending the "Comforter" to guide and direct me to assist my daughter in her miraculous healing.

While these "outcomes" were fantastic and appreciated in their own right, I still remember with such clarity the spiritual feelings of being "impressed" to follow what I now have come to understand as the presence of the Holy Ghost, being manifest by the Father in response to my faith and prayers for our daughter to be healed.

While I would love nothing more than to promise you similar outcomes by following this step-by-step recitation of inspired affirmations, I cannot, nor would I want to rob you of the spiritual growth you will find from applying your faith and prayers to solve personal trials.

I think I shall go to my grave not understanding why some prayers of the faithful are answered in visible ways, and others seem to have not been answered at all. I do, however, have faith in my Heavenly Father and in my Savior, Jesus Christ, that "all" prayers are heard. But there are so many different forces at work in our lives, where God sees the big picture, and we only see what is hurting at the moment. Faith is required to accept what is dealt... and to then move forward in becoming.

In this chapter, we have identified "sweetness" in trial as a feeling, a condition, or state of being, generally initiated by trial of some magnitude, as a means of bringing us closer to God. You will notice that I did not say "trial" was absolutely the means of bringing us closer to God. It takes a heap of growth and understanding on the part of each of us to see trial anything more than, "Uh oh, here comes trouble!" But as we have already discussed trial "can be" a means to accessing personal growth never before thought possible "if" we have the proper mindset and humility to be taught.

I have found that life generally moves at warp speed most of the time. But I can still remember as a kid growing up in a small town, feeling such boredom when summer days went by so slowly! We had three months of summer "vacation" back then. I think it was one month of vacation and two long months of waiting for school to start again. But even now (my wife will definitely not agree with this statement), I occasionally long for a little slack time.

If I am not careful, I allow the day to absorb me into its routine of checking social media, answering texts and emails, heading out to the gym, trying to get in a few paragraphs of writing done for my next book, reaching out to past and current real estate clients, or responding to some emergency business call that totally disrupts any resemblance to an organized daily plan–and before long I have forgotten my promise to check in with Heavenly Father in personal prayer that morning "before" giving myself to others.

We were children at one time, you and me. Can you remember how anxious you were for your father or mother to come home from work so you could do "show and tell" from the day's activities? Build within yourself that same excitement of looking forward to doing "show and tell" while on your knees each morning, and I promise your life will change for the better.

Winning Way #1 teaches us to "call upon God" when trial strikes.

However, if we wait to pray earnestly to Heavenly Father until we are knocked down to our knees, we are only building one side of our relationship with God. I love the feeling of just replaying in my prayers all the good in the world and how thankful I am for the good in my life, trying hard not to throw in my "expectations" and needs. However, if you are like me, it took some actual practice not to go away from prayer feeling a little cheated that I had that time and didn't address my "needs," as if He didn't already know them.

I'm not saying that every prayer is just about what's good in my life, but I do try to put some balance into the heavenly relationship so that when the good times have rolled on, and I need some TLC, it doesn't feel like "here I am again Father… why does this always happen to me," kind of prayer?

As I mentioned earlier in the writing, our "attitude determines our altitude." If our attitude smells from stinkin'- thinkin,' guess where the altitude is in that prayer? The fastest way to extinguish "any" relationship is to be known as a bottom feeder, always looking at the water glass half-empty, placing blame on others for your misfortunes, and developing caustic responses to others' attempts at friendship. If you think you might fall into that category occasionally, this chapter is for you cause there's no "sweetness" to be found in anger, justified or not.

I have also found that a contentious spirit (Romans 12:6-21) often stands in the way of receiving personal revelation from God and creates a closed cavity to the heart, unable to recognize any form of sweetness in trial. Contention is one of Satan's tools of defense against building spiritual relationships with our Heavenly Father and our Savior,

Jesus Christ. Think about it–do you usually feel "prayerful" after a contentious discussion with someone?

But this is life, and we are prone to occasionally give way to our natural man/woman instincts. Are we really expected to be perfect "all" the time? I can feel your smile at that one (LOL).

Several years ago, I was given a lifetime responsibility to serve as a Patriarch for my Church (in a specific geographic location) and was given the admonition in my ordination blessing to "avoid contention" in my personal and business life. I had to laugh as I thought, "Didn't you do a background check on me? I am in the real estate business! I am in the middle of contention all day long." But I must admit, I have toned it down a bit since realizing firsthand that developing a mindset for personal revelation (aka recognizing impressions, feeling the sweetness of communication, seeing God's hand in your life, etc.) takes work.

So, let me add a little grown-up perspective to my "who–what–where" instructions related earlier in this book. The first step toward building a successful relationship with your Creator is to devote regular personal time to Him. The next step is to develop a proper attitude in your discussions, and a third step might be… "be thankful." What a great start toward creating a healthy relationship preparing ourselves for a "Sweetness" experience.

But what about "my" needs, you ask? If I tell God nothing but what I am grateful for, how do I get my needs addressed? Well, start your morning prayer with all that you are thankful for, and if you have anything left at the end, go ahead and ask! Yet Heavenly Father does want to be in the details of your life, so try to keep a proper balance between Thanksgiving and Christmas.

I also think in developing a relationship with our Creator, we need to be aware of "His" needs. What? Yes, you heard me right. Our Heavenly Father has needs that He would love some help to satisfy. But couldn't He send a heavenly angel to do whatever He needs? Sure, and He does, at times, send angels. But where is the growth for us human angels if heavenly angels have all the fun?

So, how do we get our instructions to know who to help? That is such a great question; I'm so happy you asked!! And that is the answer... we "ask!"

In your daily visit with Heavenly Father, include your honest desire to help Him and His Son accomplish whatever needs to be done in your home, neighborhood, city, or country. You may receive impressions to send a note to someone you haven't spoken to in years or call a friend you know is going through a divorce or family sickness. Maybe there is someone who needs a plate of cookies. You are learning to communicate with a Supreme Being; each assignment builds more faith and desire to serve within you. In return, you will begin to hear and feel more clearly when God speaks. One might even compare those feelings to a "Sweetness."

This humbling experience of Sweetness is most often felt while in the ring with trial and not during times of plenty. It can be sought after but generally only received after having done all you can, including prayer and fasting, to overcome the opposition that overshadows you.

It was in the attitude of complete submission and acceptance of Jesus

Christ as my Savior and Redeemer that I first recognized this serene feeling of peace, comfort, and assurance that all would be well… "<u>But if it isn't,</u>" this is where the development of faith kicks in, leaving us in complete submission to God's will, accepting whatever outcome occurs, not bitter–but better, no matter what!

After receiving the heartbreaking news from our daughter that she had aggressive breast cancer, my wife and I "called upon God" to enter the ring of trial with us, to guide our decisions, to bless us with peace and understanding of this vicious enemy we were about to attack, not just defend against it.

It is through the depths of humility, a broken heart and contrite spirit, brought upon us through severe trial and opposition, that we are brought to our knees to acknowledge the bitter cup before us, a symbolic gesture of oneness with our Savior.

We will each fall short in our own personal suffering to adequately experience the cup of bitterness Jesus Christ endured and then drank in submission to God's will, showing us the way. However, there is nothing sweeter than to experience the feeling that we are not alone in our trial, nor do we have to drink from the bitter cup as He did. When we accept His atoning sacrifice for us, He promises: "I will write it in their hearts. And I will be their God, and they shall be my people" (Jeremiah 31:33).

The "Sweetness" of trial comes as we acknowledge in our suffering that we are His people. We are His sheep. He is our Shepherd and cares deeply for every single one of us. We are not alone in our trial, for He has paid the price and willingly submitted to the cross so that you and

I could find rest and protection in His arms. Is that not a sweetness of trial endured?

Satan would have us think trial is punishment–retaliation by God for our abuse of a commandment; or to cause us to believe that "life [just] happens…" and if there was a just God who loves us, why would He let such horrible things happen?

Sometimes, trial strikes through no fault of our own, nor as "chastisement" from our creator, but instead as a result of "agency" from our choices or those of others. The Great War in Heaven was a conflict over the right of agency. We fought "for" it. But when someone exercises their right of agency over us, many blame God for not preventing it. It does get complicated, doesn't it?

This is where the exercise of "faith" is once again introduced, even a particle of faith to believe that no matter the intensity of our trial, we are still under the watchful eye of a loving Savior who has atoned and absorbed and experienced "everything" we have felt, are feeling, or ever will feel–so that He would know how to succor us in times of need.

This particle of faith, aligned with the hope that "this too shall pass," will set the framework for how we may achieve greatness through trial and opposition, <u>opening the door to hidden talents and abilities, and character traits that may bring us closer to becoming all we can be toward fulfilling the measure of our creation.</u>

History books and religious scripture alike are filled with inspiring accounts of everyday ordinary people achieving greatness through trial and opposition. In fact, I would say that "most" famous people we read about in such records overcame overwhelming adversity along the way to becoming exceptionally known for their achievements:

Walt Disney overcame poverty.

Albert Einstein had a speech impediment until the age of nine. He had a rebellious nature and was expelled from school and refused admittance to others.

Abraham Lincoln overcame chronic depression

Franklin D. Roosevelt overcame polio and paralysis

Hellen Keller overcame the loss of sight and hearing

J.K. Rowling's short-lived marriage ended; she was jobless and nearly homeless, counting herself as one of the biggest failures she knew.

Steve Jobs was fired from the very company he founded.

And to quote Michael Jordan's words: "I've missed more than 9000 shots in my career. I've lost almost 300 games. 26 times, I've been trusted to take the winning shot... and missed. I've failed over and over and over again in my life. And that is why I succeed."

And, of course, there are many others...

But what about all those people who "didn't" achieve stardom or become listed in "Who's Who" in whatever? What about all those millions and millions of just "ordinary" people who still fought through their trial to stand another day, like me? And maybe you?

Growing up, I didn't see myself as a future writer and author creating content for his fourth book, but ever since I can remember from my youth, I was a "comeback kid," not because I am some superstar Tony Robbins or anything like him. But I "am" a child of God, sent here to earth to learn how to deal with agency, natural man instincts, carnal mindedness, temptations of every kind, failure, success, and every other type of opposition that would help strengthen me into becoming "like" Him and my Savior, Jesus Christ.

Please don't get me wrong over my statement in the preceding paragraph of being a "comeback kid," as if I possessed something you don't. I have said more times than I remember, "I take absolutely no personal credit for where I am today." By that, I mean my level of maturity growing up and penchant for making incorrect choices often led to corporal consequences for me, and severe trials heaped upon those who tried to teach me how to function in society without injuring others. I was indeed just a selfish kid.

I certainly didn't see myself as a "winner" growing up. I knew my parents loved me, but because I challenged them every step of the way, they were focused more on "keeping me between the lines" than perhaps helping me realize the greatness within me. For that, I suppose I should be eternally grateful because my curious and worldly nature more often led me to make decisions that led to trial.

So, how did I survive this phase of growing up? Well, for one thing–I didn't blame God for my mistakes. I didn't know at the time that I was keeping the door open to receiving more Heavenly guidance; this is one reason I can't take credit for my becoming who I am today.

I hope you caught my statement two paragraphs above about my parent' "not" helping me realize my greatness. That is a little ploy writers use to accentuate a principle they want to explore without actually putting it in BOLD letters with a flashing red light.

Of course, as parents, we want to help our children realize the greatness within them, but not at the expense of "not" learning to control the body's carnal appetites and natural man instincts, the lack of which [not learning to control] contribute to the overpopulation of jails and prisons all over the world.

Parenting! What a responsibility to be entrusted with greatness in the form of a child who hasn't yet learned to walk or talk. The challenge for a parent is not to get so carried away with teaching a child how to "walk a straight line" that they forget to build some tolerance for exploring. It is in the exploring that we develop interests and inborn talents I call "gifts." See Chapter Five for more about seeking and developing gifts and talents through trial.

But Winning Way #1 should also inspire parents to "Call upon God" in the development of greatness within their children. To do that, they must allow God to "co-pilot." My parents were strict, but in truth, they never stood between me and something I wanted to try, whether they thought it was a good idea or not.

I wanted to play the trumpet growing up. My sister was a drummer in her high school Drum and Bugle Corp, and besides wanting to be a cowboy, I was also attracted to music–and sports. My parents let me try the trumpet. I never put it down all through junior high and high school. They sacrificed for years so I would have the best trumpet lessons our little town had to offer. Unlike my character concerning most things while growing up–I did not quit.

One day I brought home a set of drums and explained to my parents that while I was at work in the town music store, I heard this fellow talking to the owner about his need to find a drummer for their upcoming dance in a neighboring town. I have no idea what possessed me, but I bravely walked over, interrupting the conversation, and announced, "I am a drummer!"

When the fellow walked out of the music store, I had agreed to an audition when he came back through town in four weeks. I had time to learn "how" to be a drummer.

Although my parents may not have been as close to God as I might have wished, God knew me and knew my potential. He also knew I would one day need to draw upon my developed musical skills to help pay for my college education. My parents never questioned my intentions, or that I had no drumming skills whatsoever, or that they couldn't afford more music lessons.

I never took drum lessons nor possessed superior drumming skills–but in four weeks, with the help of a radio tuned to a country western music station, I managed to learn a few beats that enabled me to pass my first audition to play drums, on stage, at a dance, in front of people... and actually get paid for it. This experience would one day prove to have been inspired.

Maybe this is a good time to relate the "Parable of the Runner."

One night, many years ago, a loud knock at the door was followed by a neighbor friend standing in my foyer with a paper in his hand.

"I need ten dollars to register you," he said as I walked over to shake his hand in exchange for the paper. A quick glance at the paper showed a group of runners breaking through the finish line and a bold headline reading "1st Annual Fiesta Bowl Marathon."

"What's this?" I questioned, afraid of the answer that was sure to follow.

"We are running a marathon," he quickly responded as I looked behind him to see who else was standing with us in the foyer. There was no one else.

"I've never run a marathon," I responded, trying to end the conversation and return to my paperwork.

"Well, we have six weeks to get ourselves ready," he answered as if that would satisfy my concerns.

"No, what I mean is, I have 'never' run more than a 10k," I belted out a little louder than needed as I felt the pen in my hand signing a name–my name.

"No problem, I'll see you at the track tomorrow at 4 a.m.!" And the door closed, the signed paper in my hands now gone.

"When the trial first hits, it seems to come as a thief during the night [or as a loud knock at the door], *unexpected, and swift. We are often confused and lost, unable to find a bearing that will give us hope."* -The Sweetness of Trial.

When the alarm went off the next morning at 3:45 am, I have to be honest–I might have muttered something that would have caused me to contribute to the "naughty word" jar... again! But somehow, I found my shoes, put them on the right feet, and hobbled across Southern Avenue in the dark and through the gate that led to the rubberized track at Mesa High School to begin a training regimen that was supposed to put my body in shape in just six weeks to start "and finish" a twenty-six-mile (26.22 to be exact) run.

We (my neighbor running partner and I) repeated that scene every day (Except Sunday) for six weeks, and then we ran the marathon race and finished in record time... except that we didn't.

You see, even when you have a plan, life isn't going to just lie down and fall in behind you. Sometimes, it will hide in a dark corner and wait for you to get comfortable and then jump out and scare the bejeebies out of you; or, in my case, wait until we did our long run on the Saturday before the meet, working up to twenty miles, and leaving my legs so heavy on the way back home that my shoe caught on the train track, and I went down, flesh connecting with asphalt.

Why me, we ask? Why now? When trial hits, don't we sometimes find ourselves second-guessing the timing of the latest trial, often assigning blame to someone else for our unfortunate circumstances? Even blaming God? When you think about it, trial is never welcome in our lives, no matter the possibility of experiencing "sweetness."

A quick diversion–A real estate client of mine, a father of three boys, married to a wonderful wife and mother, all active in sports, great Christian people trying to live their lives in harmony with God's teachings... one day found out his wife had developed stomach cancer and within two weeks it had progressed throughout her body, causing her to be intubated because she could not breathe. Today, they removed the tube, and amidst grief and pain, she was placed in God's hands to come safely home.

How does one feel "Sweetness" from such an experience, you might ask? Indeed, my client would be qualified to ask such a question.

Another client of mine recently discovered her husband had been having a long-distance affair for the past nine years. When she discovered his infidelity, she spray-painted the words "Cheater!" on his car before taking a hammer to the windows. There would be no "Sweetness" felt that day.

Then how/when does it come?

Let me continue my marathon story, and I will tell you.

I made it home that fateful Saturday, blood still oozing down my shin from missing knee tissue, and finding no one home to share in my agony. Where is the justice in that? There was "no one" home to even make a fuss or have stomach convulsions from seeing the blood now being absorbed by my white sock. So I just sat there at the kitchen table, thoughts of quitting filled my mind, feeling very sorry for myself... until the sound of the garage door prefaced sounds of happy feet and cheers of "we won!" instantly chased away any thoughts of being a bad example to my children and wife as I sat there with a big grin on my face waiting to be showered with love and concern by my adoring fans as they assessed the carnage. I was not disappointed.

I did want to compete in that race, but when I woke up the next day, I could hardly walk. We are all going to experience opposition in our lives. Sometimes, we will fall short of accomplishing our goals because "life happens." But on that Sunday day of rest, I was praying for a miracle.

Have you ever been the recipient of a miracle? I have, more times than you would believe, or that I ever deserved, if you could ever "deserve" a miracle. But I was about to experience another.

On Monday morning, I awoke at 3:45 am, put my feet on the floor, and stood up, feeling stiff but no pain. I was going to run in the race. Prayers had been heard... and answered.

My training partner and I trained low-key for the remainder of the week, careful not to pull anything, fall, or over-exert. We took Friday off and prepared for the early morning drive to Scottsdale, where the race would begin.

The morning temperature at the race was quite cool, causing the more experienced racers to sport black garbage bags to keep their muscles from stiffening due to the cold chill. But other first-timers, like my partner and I, were so much in awe of the sheer enormity of the event... helicopters flying overhead, reporters, cameras, vendor displays, free water, carb stations, and such that we barely even noticed the precautions being taken by many runners. I was sporting my new running shorts and custom racing shirt–so proud of the number pinned to my chest, separating me from the bystanders who came to serve or to cheer on their favorite runner. I was going to run a marathon, just like the Greek runners of old. But I had never run 26.22 miles. And I had no idea how hard this day would be.

Would you believe that even novice runners need a race strategy? My partner and I were no different. Phase 1 of our race strategy was "position." We knew that when that gun went off, the runners at the front of the pack would start running, followed by the next wave, followed by the next, and so on. If you happened to be in one of the waves toward the middle or even further back, you would likely be waiting a while before you could get up to a fast walk.

So, with that strategy of positioning ourselves near the front, we "casually" mixed in with the runners ahead of us, moving slowly and pausing frequently to fake a stretch or tie a shoe, then move another space forward, and so on. For the most part, the runners were engaged in stretching, talking, and remaining somewhat oblivious to our movement to position ourselves to gain an advantage.

Have you ever felt exposed and vulnerable when you knew something and thought no one else knew it? But you knew it was only a matter of time before they did know? Well, this is how we felt, right there on the "second" row from the very front of the pack. No way were we going for the front... but the second row, you bet!

The gun went off, sending the first row and everyone around me forward like being shot out of a cannon. My legs were so light I almost fell, grabbing my partner's arm to steady myself before plunging ahead, laughing like two kids who had just stolen the flag and raced to bring it home.

It's funny how you feel once the adrenaline wears off. Gravity seems to pull you back, your legs start to feel rubbery, and you can hardly breathe. Then we realized we were trying to keep up with the lead pack and wouldn't last another mile unless we adjusted to our training pace. Boy, you should have seen the sneers and occasional muttering from those passing us–and we thought no one noticed!

I have been asked how a person gets into the proper mindset to feel the "Sweetness" in trial when it can be so destructive, as in the cases of my two clients. I have found only one other experience from which to draw a comparison; it is a "runner's high."

This condition of elation, peace, or euphoria is sought-after by long-distance runners because of the "zone" you can find when you achieve this sometimes-elusive condition. I would run the farmer's roads behind my house every morning before the US60 freeway was extended east of Dobson Road–and when I wasn't being chased by blackbirds protecting their young, I might settle into a steady gait and allow my mind to kind of "zone out" and not feel the pain or stress associated with running steadily for a length of time.

One who carries the burden of trial can also experience this feeling of peace, even a euphoric sense of removal from the burden carried when a state of complete brokenheartedness is reached, aided by a contrite spirit and humility that you have done your best, only to fall short in understanding "why."

In my sincere attempts at finding work during my life's chapter titled "two years lost in the wilderness," I found quiet supplication to be the portal to communicate with God, often just sitting in the car under a shady tree or taking my camp chair with me to show houses and finding a park-like atmosphere to be alone. With five active children, my private time with God had to be either early in the morning as I ran or late at night.

Even now, after evening family prayer with my wife, I have a small "garden nook" in our home that I slip into to enjoy time with my Heavenly Father and my Savior, clothed in complete darkness and silence. Although this time is precious to me, I often have to address whatever looms larger than life over me to finally experience the sweetness of knowing my prayers are being heard.

I am somewhat impatient in waiting upon the Lord; my mind is usually filled with details of that day's unfinished business, thoughts of what "might" go wrong, and even the occasional appearance of the "boogeyman" out of nowhere. "Where did 'that' come from?" I ask myself, trying to create an image of a patient Heavenly Father and His son sitting at His right, waiting for me to begin.

Patience is another "key" to opening the portal to experiencing Sweetness within trial. When it happened the first time, I remember thinking, "I just felt something!" It was peaceful, warm, tender-sweet. But when I later tried to recapture the feeling, I felt nothing. It is as though it comes as a "gift" and not as an entitlement to effort.

I am certainly not the only human to wait upon the Lord's timing for a blessing or answer to prayer... or to experience the Sweetness of trial. Job lost everything over many years, but toward the end, God restored to him double all he lost.

Abraham, the Father of many nations, was promised posterity numbering as the stars in the sky, but he was 100 years old, and his wife Sarah was 90 years old before they were blessed with Isaac. (See Genesis 12)

Joseph (Coat of Many Colors) was sold to Potiphar by his brother (See Genesis 37) and had to endure significant trials before God's promise of power and responsibility was answered. Joseph never lost his faith in God.

I can't promise you will taste this Sweetness on your first attempt or even after another, but I can tell you that if you are filled with anger and resentment, choosing to assign blame, you will not achieve the sweetness of which I speak. Job, Abraham, and Joseph all shared one common denominator: they did not blame God for their misfortunes or having to wait upon the Lord.

Likewise, a runner's high will not be achieved very quickly if the runner's head is filled with thoughts that dominate their attention rather than allow the mind to drift away from the stress, emotional thoughts, decisions to make, or other like-detractions. The mind must be free, as the body maintains a steady pace for some length of time, allowing the release of "happy chemicals" into the body. I believe achieving a runner's high may have more to do with a proper mindset than how "hard" the runner trains.

THE PURPOSE OF THIS BOOK is to help you, the reader, prepare your mind to not only endure trial when it comes but prepare you to choose what your reaction will be by replacing your "natural man/woman" tendencies of reacting to opposition and conflict with proven exercises and a proper mindset of "Winning Ways" I have personally used in overcoming many of my own trials along the way.

But it is time to get back to the race...

After the crowd of somewhat perturbed runners who felt we were in their way had passed us by and moved on, my partner and I settled into our own training pace, searching to find our zone and perhaps experience the elusive runner's high and enjoy this challenge without feeling the stress competing with others seemed to bring. However, that was not to be. The first ten miles were quite fun. Although runners constantly passed us, we also passed others who had perhaps been carried away by the excitement of it all to run faster than they had trained.

It was around mile fifteen that I began to feel winded. I managed to make it another five miles, and then it hit. "It" is called "The Wall" by marathon runners whose glycogen supply of stored energy within the body's muscles is depleted. Although reactions vary, those who experience it use the term "wall" to describe the feeling that brings many to their knees or, at best, to a walk.

My partner and I had put a few feet between us from mile fifteen when I started feeling something unexpected. By mile twenty, he was almost outside yelling distance, but I managed to attract his attention by yelling his name and then waving him on. He knew if he stopped, he would likely not get started again, so he continued, looking back only once. I was on my own.

The road we were on at that point was a paved road leading to the finish line at Scottsdale Community College. There was a curb, and I barely made it there before my legs gave out, and I sat down somewhat hard. There was no sound in the air other than an occasional patter of running shoes walking or running past me. By now, my mind had also given in, and I was a mess, wondering how I would call for a taxi to pick me up this far out from nowhere. My wife and kids were at the finish line, and I was thinking about how to hail a taxi to drive me to meet them. I began second-guessing my decision to even try this crazy run. What was I thinking?

It is amazing what goes through your mind when you have reached your limit and gone the distance… but it wasn't good enough to get you across the finish line on your own. I didn't make a call to God, then. I hadn't achieved that kind of relationship yet, I suppose. But somehow, another miracle was about to happen. And it wasn't in the form of a yellow taxi.

With my head bowed between my knees, I sat lifeless on the curb–the sound of another set of runners then reached my ears. Expecting to see their shadow cross in front of me, I was startled to see an actual pair of skinny legs in what appeared to be "big tennis shoes" jogging in place right in front of me. I raised my head to see who it was, but the sun was so bright behind her that all I saw was part of her gray hair underneath a hat pulled low over her face, and I heard the words: "Come on, Sonny, you can do it!" and she was off. I have thought so often how many times I have heard those words over the years following my first and only marathon when trial hit again and again, and I found myself on some curb, figuratively speaking, and I heard these words: "Come on my son, lean on me and I will give you rest."

There is no trial, test, or opposition of any kind that can outmatch the love Jesus Christ offers us if we will only reach out to Him with a broken heart and contrite spirit of humility, after all we can do to become.

I was looking for an answer to how I would get home, but I did not expect it to come in the form of an "angel of light" with gray hair and skinny legs sliding inside big tennis shoes. Yet I found myself trying to stand up, allowing my shaky legs to calm down a bit before raising my head above my self-inflicted cloud of despair and desire to quit.

Little did I know that one day I would be standing before hundreds of people retelling this experience, and the words "pick yourself up, dust yourself off, and start all over again" would fill the auditorium, followed by cheers and clapping for the man on stage who "decided" to get back up and try again.

My eyes looked down the road to the horizon before me. I saw nothing but a paved road as far as my eyes could see, but I started reciting positive affirmations to spark some energy and hope into my tired body. Then this thought came to me: "Just start putting one foot in front of the other, and don't look any further down the road except where you will plant the next foot."

My left foot went first, followed slowly by my right, then the left, and again the right foot followed. I checked my watch and set a goal of walking for one minute at a time without stopping, then three minutes, then five.

My hips were so tired, as they rotated turns, lifting each leg, followed by sore feet hitting the pavement, time and time again, but I did not stop. In fact, within fifteen minutes, I was walking at a faster pace until I managed a very slow jog.

Falling is part of life, as it was designed in the pre-existence, but staying down was never part of the plan.

Life can be quite difficult at times; even when we think we can't take another step, we can… Just take an hour at a time, then two, and then take a breather. Repeat the process. This is precisely what I did to regain my energy, fueled by laying eyes on the goal ahead.

I have preached and been preached to all my life about the benefit of having a goal, but on that day, I was never so happy to see what appeared to be the rooftops of Scottsdale Community College in the distance. My setting of small, achievable goals was the beginning of success. And once achieved, they were replaced with another goal far enough ahead to stretch me. The key was setting another goal the minute I achieved my distance goal.

I can remember like it was yesterday what it felt like when I reached the turn into the college parking lot and caught sight of the huge banner that seemed to fill the sky. It read: FINISH.

With my eye fixed on the words "F I N I S H," I picked up the pace, my head up, shoulders squared, arms pushing like ninety-degree pistons, toward the crowd screaming and clapping as each runner passed the finish line… some falling into the arms of someone, or onto the grassy field next to the parking lot.

It was all a blur at that point: familiar voices, hugs by small humans, then recognizable faces, someone helping me into the back seat of our Chevy Suburban, feeding me something cold and colorful; my mind beginning to clear a bit as I remembered setting up an appointment with our family Chiropractor to meet at his clinic after the race so he could put me back together. It was the wisest decision I could have made in my effort toward recovery.

So, there it is, the Parable of the Runner, a real-life reminder that life, with all its ups and downs, curves, and boring straight lanes, might take you down occasionally, but it is within your greatness—your internal flame as a son or daughter of God, to not only survive your trial, but to once again stand, dust yourself off, and win!

I can't remember "when" I adopted the "failing forward" (See chapter six) mindset. I have read many self-improvement books and been inspired by the greatest comeback stories ever since my first failure in 1985. But reading about those great heroes and believing I could do likewise is a bit like reading the story of David slaying the mighty Goliath with only a rock and sling and visualizing myself as David the Conqueror. The thought of slaying a Goliath in my life didn't make the ten o'clock news until I saw myself "failing forward," gaining experience... and even in failure, I was becoming!

My fear of trying something new that might result in failure seemed to weaken with each attempt until it was not strong enough to keep me from "trying." **It is in that spirit of "striving" that we win.**

I use stories of my own failings and successes because they were given to me to better connect with you, the reader, building a belief that if Chuck can do it, there is hope in failing forward for you also, rising once again to win.

Remember our definition of "winning" in this book? It is to continue along the road of "becoming." A win is not always a finite condition, as taught in my Parable of the Runner and as defined by the world's standards. Yes, I did cross the finish line, but not ahead of everyone else, yet "I won" because I fell and didn't stay down. I got up, dusted myself off (removed the negative thoughts from my mind and replaced them with positive ones), and took one step "forward" and then another. <u>This is what winning is all about–failing forward in the process of becoming!</u> I sincerely hope you can grasp this truth; it will change your life.

Chapter One could be a primer all by itself, but I wanted to set a strong foundation for you as we move into Chapter Two, the second most important concept and Winning Way #2 in this book, teaching you "how to prepare yourself" for the next trial–conditioning!

When you are ready, please take a deep breath, hold it in for a few seconds, then let it out and turn the page...

Chapter Two

When Trial Strikes

"The richest place on earth is the graveyard. Because in the graveyard lie inventions that died with the deceased, that the world was never exposed to; ideas and dreams that never became a reality; hope and aspirations that were never acted upon." -Les Brown

The most impactful deterrent to winning in life is not lack of talent—but one's "reaction" to trial.

Trial comes packaged with as many variations as one might find under a brightly decorated Christmas tree—different sizes, colors, values, and impact upon the receiver. Don't get me wrong—trial is not a Christmas present wrapped in colorful paper intended to bring joy and happiness, at least not initially. But if we can change our attitude about trial, at least gain a personal understanding of its purpose in life, and build within us an internal plan of action to not only endure... but to win, we will one day look upon our trial(s) with a measure of gratitude and peace knowing we did not let opposition destroy us—but instead, we grew to overcome how the natural man within us would have responded.

Winning Way #2 – Proper Preparation Prevents Poor Performance!

A fighter does not get into the ring without *preparation*. He prepares physically and mentally, using developed strategies to expose his opponent's weaknesses.

When we get into the ring of life with trial, we are rarely prepared with a plan "or" strategy. Most of us hardly give one idle thought to how we would react to trial–so when it strikes, we are often caught blindsided, with no defense or plan of attack. This chapter aims to prepare you to face your worst nightmare in the ring of life... and "Win."

Let's begin your preparation with a training exercise. This exercise is to put you in the proper frame of mind to face your opponent:

Exercise: Think about the worst trial you have faced thus far in your life's progression. Don't dwell on it, but reflect honestly on these questions:

- Did you live through it? (Easy answer if you are reading this book.)

- Nothing else matters! (Not a question, sorry!)

Despite the beating we may receive, the only way trial can win is if we quit fighting (refuse to get back up).

NO MATTER WHAT LIFE THROWS AT US, WE STILL HAVE AGENCY (CHOICE) ON HOW WE REACT.

"Men Go Off to War... they are forever changed," a personal

story of bravery, choice, and overcoming—as told to the Author for use in this publication.

Over the years, at this time of year, I would always withdraw and go to my mental cave to hide from everyone. I know what the date March 23rd means to me and how it messes with my mind and my heart, and my ghosts and my closet of fear, doubt, and worry. This year is different for me. I don't find myself wanting to go hide from the date... I want to embrace it and know that as bad as it was back then, this coming March 2020, I celebrate the fact that I came home 49 years ago from Vietnam and I met for the first time the woman whom I chose to marry. The past 49 years of my life have changed for the better because of that time; the mistakes, the regrets, the loss, and the grief have each shaped who I became as a man – a man who loves life so much more as I was given a 2nd chance. Today, I choose to celebrate the man who made it possible for me to still be here, sharing my story.

March 23rd is the day I landed in Vietnam 50 years ago as a 20-year-old snot-nosed kid who was so scared. I got off the plane with no gun no nothing... and the week I land they have already lost over 450 men for the week. Three days later I am going on my first ambush patrol... it is a pitch-black night with no moon... I am appearing fearless, but my knees were knocking, and I can hardly breathe, my mouth was so dry. Here we go a walking in the area around our base camp setting up to catch Charlie and blow him away... suddenly, we are getting hit and fired upon... I forgot how to cuss for if I remembered I would have used every word I knew... the guy next to me sees me frozen in place and he pushes me down and takes a gunshot wound to his side. My bullet... he screams out, "I'm hit! I'm hit! I crawl over to him, and I turn on his flashlight and mine so I can see what I am doing. Big mistake, now everyone is shooting at the idiot with the two flashlights on, but they stay on so I can see. I put myself between him and the bullets that are hitting all around me. God must have been watching out for me, not to get shot. I find an entry wound and put a bandage on him and turn him over, looking for an exit wound, and there is none. By this time, the shooting has stopped, and I don't even know how to call in Dust-off (I am that new). They send out a duce and a half truck to come pick us up. I make up a makeshift stretcher out of two connected ponchos, and we load him up. It is then I notice that I have pissed in my pants. I am almost hyperventilating at this point. I hold him up next to me so that my body will take most of the bumps and not hurt him so much. He asks me if he is going to die and I tell him no. I ask about his family, and he tells me of his wife and mom and dad and brothers and sisters from Alabama.

We finally get him to the dispensary and the Doctor looks at him and has him taken to the Evac Hospital which is on our compound. I go see him a couple of times in the hospital. However, on the 28th day, I get word that he passed away from liver failure. I lost my first casualty, and his death has always haunted me, did I do enough, why him and not me, why did he push me down? His name is Benny Dale Cash, and his cause of death is listed as Misadventure. How can this be a misadventure... we were shot at by the South Vietnamese at an Outpost who thought we were the Viet Cong.

Years later, I contacted Benny's family who were very kind to me, and I explained to them what had happened to their son, brother, and uncle.

They went all those years not really knowing what happened to him. His parents had passed away before I could talk to them, but the other family members were happy to know he died protecting Freedom.

I wrote a poem about experiencing doubts, fears, and worries many years ago in order to deal with those feelings of loss and facing challenges and overcoming:

THE OLD MAN AND THE MOUNTAIN

Along life's journey, I had to learn a thing or two;
Sometimes we got to climb a mountain to overcome our fear
or it will get the best of you.
I met an old man on the road one hot day in the Sun
He said to me, "Son you look mighty troubled"
I replied, "You can see that clearly huh?"

He told me it was in my eyes… was a sure give away.
All he could see was the pain, the hurt, and agony.
"If you want true healing you need to face it today."
"True healing comes from overcoming the ideas called
'Could have' and 'Should have'," he told me soft and low.
"In Vietnam, you did your best. You did not fail or fall."

"See that mountain straight ahead; it contains all
the answers that you seek." I turned to ask a
simple question, but he was gone, his name I started to call.
I began to climb the mountain, and I heard voices begin to say
"Go back." It wasn't safe even for them.

I replied, "Nothing would stop me from finishing today."

As I reached the mid-way point, I heard someone cry
It was doubt. he had been discovered, faced head-on,
he was such a coward; he began to fade and die.
I thought to myself: that was too easy, he seemed stronger,
he had been my partner for the past 50 years or so.
I usually gave in to him but not today, not any longer.

Renewed in self-confidence I began again to climb
then I heard the evil laugh of the twins, fear and worry;
their voices in the clouds did chime.
I climbed faster now I knew I could not stop
for I had to take them to the task, to rid their life in mine.
I knew what I had to do – throw them down from the top.

I reached the top and there they were ugly to my sight.
We began the struggle to see who would win today
They taunted and they screamed as we began our fight.
"You can't win; we have controlled you far too long.
We know your every weakness." I was bound
and determined that in my life they did not belong.

I grabbed Worry by the throat and shook him with all my might.
I squeezed the very life out of him and tossed him off the side.
Then it was Fear's turn; I hated him most of all.

*It was me or him that would win today. I glanced
into his big brown eyes, and there I saw it. He was terrified!*

*He tried to run away. He tripped and fell off the side,
Falling to his death, and now I knew I had another chance.
To begin my life over without worry fear or doubt.
I know that Vietnam is a part of my life and will continue
to be. But now I can live my life finally pain-free.
©Copyright 2001 by Kerry "Doc" Pardue*

I know that it is good that I talk to other medics about what I am feeling inside. They know the loss and grief I have losing my first patient, particularly because I didn't get down fast enough and he got shot instead of me. Over the years, I used to beat myself up over this and blame myself. But in the past couple of years, those feelings aren't there anymore. Benny died doing his job; it was his time to go. I know this now more than ever. He died, and I was able to make my life a better one because of him… I learned how to be a better soldier and medic because of not knowing all that I was supposed to do. I was able to become someone's husband, father, and grandfather and live a life that has meant more to me than it would have without this challenge. I know that Benny is looking down and I know that he smiles, and he tells me that it is okay because he is with Jesus and he is with his mom and dad. He is glad because he is remembered by a medic who tried to help him, and I won't let his memory die for anything…

Benny, thank you for that night, thank you for pushing me down, and *thank you for allowing me to have the joy of being a father, husband, and grandfather. Life has meant more to me because of you... I didn't take it for granted. Yours is the first name I touch when I go to the WALL... every time I talk to a group of Junior and High School kids in history classes I talk about you.*

Thanks, Benny.... I finally made it all of the way home!"

©Copyright 2018 by Kerry "Doc" Pardue (Printed with permission)

Most of us will never be tested to the degree Medic Kerry Pardue was tested on the field of battle that day when an unknown soldier stepped up, maybe just out of impulse–maybe out of training and preparation, and took a bullet meant for another.

You may be thinking, however, "Wait a minute, didn't you mean the way the unknown soldier was tested? It was he, after all, who gave his all in the fight. Isn't that the supreme test... to give one's life for another? Are any of us prepared enough for that?

Of course, to give your life for another would be considered the supreme sacrifice. On that fateful day, Benny Dale Cash was prepared–perhaps out of instinct, duty, or love, to throw it all down to protect another, giving no thought to the price Lady Luck would demand. Kerry Pardue's benefactor would no longer be tested on Earth, having progressed to his next estate to join in the reunion of loved ones. But the earthly struggles of one left behind to face the self-doubts, self-incriminations, and trial by a jury of one was just beginning.

My sincere hope in writing "Winning Thru Trial" is that you will come to understand that whatever happens during your time in the ring when trial strikes (however long or short), it will eventually pass and afford you the opportunity of choosing "what's next?" You can still win–IF YOU *CHOOSE* TO WIN. That is "preparation."

The scriptures teach of "preparation" against trial: Noah didn't wait until the rains came to build the ark (Book of Genesis); "If ye are prepared, ye shall not fear" (Doctrine and Covenants 30:38), and perhaps one of the best known "preparation scriptures" is found in the book of Matthew 25: 1-13, as Jesus Christ taught His disciples the "Parable of the Ten Virgins," in which five of the attending bridesmaids awaiting the arrival of the "Bridegroom" at night, were prepared with oil in their lamps, and five were not. It was a sad reality to the unprepared to be locked out from attending the celebration.

Likewise, in the Book of Luke, a similar counsel to the "men," in Chapter 12, is to "Be dressed in readiness, and keep your lamps lit. Be like the men waiting for their master when he returns from the wedding feast so that they may immediately open the door to him when he comes and knocks..."

The Disney Character "Scar" in the classic movie *Lion King*© sings a war cry to his band of hyenas, to... "Be Prepared!"

As a Boy Scout, I was taught the Scout Motto: "Be Prepared."

I recently listened to a podcast of an interview with Kieth Merrill, writer, author, producer, and director of motion pictures. He is a member of the Academy of Motion Picture Arts and Sciences and the Director's Guild of America. He is a two-time Oscar Nominee and winner of an Academy Award for his film The Great American Cowboy (https://en.wikipedia.org/wiki/Kieth_Merrill). He is also the father of eight children thirty-three grandchildren, and a devout Christian.

Kieth Merrill made his "mark" in the motion picture industry during the 1970s when he surprisingly won an Oscar for his work. In his own words, during the interview, Merrill referred to himself with a bit of tongue and cheek as a "hot property" during his career. He was sought out to produce new work and soon had to hire an agent. In the contract, he clarified the types of material "he would and would not do" (decision). As if the agent didn't read that part of the contract, one of the first projects he was presented contained almost "every" would-not-do listed in the contract. Because he was "prepared" by already deciding what work he would produce, "Kieth only had to make that decision once." He didn't have to endure the agonizing process of considering temptations and undesirable solicitations, no matter the potential of the financial brass ring.

Even at one point in his career, Kieth Merrill was offered $500,000 to produce a project, with the stipulation he would denounce his affiliation with the Church of Jesus Christ of Latter-day Saints because the benefactor did not believe that the church, which bears the name of Jesus Christ was Christian. Again, Kieth was prepared in his beliefs, and not even the promise of a very fat paycheck caused him to contemplate this decision, "even for a nano-second," quoted the producer.

Winning Way #2 is centered on the understanding and attitude that life ebbs and flows in cycles. What may appear to be a disastrous condition in your life today will undoubtedly cycle through and offer a different perspective–days, weeks, months, or even years from now. This condition, this trial, will surely pass, offering an opportunity to choose how you will let the trial affect the next chapter in your life.

You can either become better or remain bitter when adversity strikes.

Which attitude will you choose? Are you prepared to choose "better" over bitter?

It was about 6 pm on a beautiful spring day in Northern Arizona, as my wife and I made our way over the Mogollon Rim from Payson, AZ, to our destination in Lakeside, Arizona, to pack up our belongings stored in our recently sold seasonal home.

My nearly new Chevrolet Silverado pickup truck was humming at just over 60 miles an hour, showing no hesitation when confronting a steep incline–the deep-blue metallic paint finish still catching the last streaks of departing sunshine. I loved that truck... 20" custom tires and rims, leather bucket seats, extended cab, Bose sound system pumping out tunes that could alter my mood, depending upon the selection. And it was "paid for!"

That day, with my lovely bride of 40 years sitting shotgun in the comfortable bucket seat next to me, the satellite radio tuned to a favorite old-time series, Fiber Magee and Molly–my last thought as we rounded a gentle curve was how "perfect" the day had been, and...

"Bam!"

There was no screeching of tires nor the smell of hot brake pads applied with the strength of Hercules, just a violent meeting between nature and machine. There would be no declared winner here, only carnage.

The challenger, a twelve-hundred-pound trophy elk of the forest, carrying an antler set wider than the truck bed and posed to kill, had wandered onto the highway just as the warm Arizona sun had set and was immediately confronted by a familiar intruder with yellowish-white flames of light protruding from its mouth. There would be no backing off now.

The impact between man and beast was surely heard deep into the surrounding forest, carrying a message of doom to those who cared. Tragedy had struck with the speed of lightning and without notice or warning. A magnificent life was taken, and a treasured personal piece of machinery was eliminated.

Obviously, I lived to tell this story, as did my wife, thankfully... yet I had a choice to make. I could become better–forgiving, accepting, thankful; or I could become bitter–angry, cursing, accusatory, hateful, depressed... even blaming God or the state of Arizona for allowing this to happen.

When we internalize Winning Way #2 into our being, it sets the stage for when the next trial hits and how we will respond.

Let me break down for you the physical impact of choosing "bitter" over "better:"

- Negative thoughts affect your body's defense system. You lose energy, creativity, and bounce. The body becomes more vulnerable to sickness.

- Negative thoughts often lead to anger and frustration, opening the door wide for anxiety and even depression to enter.

- Harboring blame toward others clouds the mind to opportunity. When we become bitter over "one thing," it doesn't just impact that one thing. Instead, it covers the whole playing field. It follows us to work, home, church, and to bed. When we choose bitter, we tend to see the glass of life "half-empty."

- Choosing bitterness is like trying to succeed in life and relationships by adding a 300-pound gorilla on your back. Life is hard enough; why make it even harder? Let it go!!

I experienced this "condition" of mind and body not long ago when I "allowed" myself to react negatively to a perfectly valid mistake while under time pressure to prepare a real estate contract for my client to purchase a home. This contract took a good hour to prepare, demanding research and confirmation of facts before sending it to my client for approval. The hour was late, and I was exhausted from a full day of activity, looking forward to a little "me" time before bed. It only took a nano-second for trial to hit–just a tired look at the screen monitor furthest from me, and without even focusing on what that little blue square on the screen said, without hesitation, I placed my cursor on it and "clicked!" What happened next both surprised and horrified me as I gazed at the blank screen.

I had mistakenly deleted "everything" I had entered into the contract template. When the reality of the significance and far-reaching depth of this mistake reached my brain, I instinctively reacted like a volcano spewing out hot lava over all within earshot, which happened to be my wife. Even recalling my (re)actions that night sends chills down my neck as I remember all too well the now-embarrassing fit of anger I displayed. Yes, even at my age, I tend to react to trial much like I did as a child when the string to my treasured yo-yo broke, sending it into the street to meet a swift death under the tire of a passing neighbor's car–maybe I reacted even a little worse. Gratefully, I had grown enough to be able to control my speech, but I was not prepared for the fit of rage I displayed from beating myself up over making such a time-sensitive mistake.

Wait! You say... That wasn't trial I experienced; it was merely childish behavior out of control, like road rage. Well, that may be what it appeared to you, but remember there are two parts to trial: (1) the act itself–what caused the pain? Did it hurt? And (2) how we react.

While we can't always see trial before it hits, we can be prepared for how we will react. And yes, it does take more work than just " reading" about the need for preparation in a book. It takes a change of nature – "my" nature, "your" nature; it takes a desire to change your heart. For most of us mortals with some age, it takes a bit of reprogramming.

My wife's reaction to my outburst flipped a switch in my brain to "want" to change. Maybe you experienced such rage when someone cut in front of you while in line with other parents taking their kids to school. Without thinking, you slammed the steering wheel, and all the pressures of a busy, overworked schedule the day before came spewing out your mouth, lips tight, and fists prepped to slay the dragon. For you, it might be seeing your child strapped safely into the harness of his seatbelt or car seat, eyes open wide with fear after seeing and hearing his grown-up parent display a fit of rage in front of him. And we wonder why little Billy grew to handle his aggressions in a similar fashion.

Please don't throw this book into the trash thinking, "This is just what I need–one more thing reminding me what a terrible parent I am!" I promise you this is not my intention... and as one who suffered from depression for years of beating up on himself, I know what you are feeling. But this book was written for you "and" for me–not to add defeat to our lives or add additional guilt to our already full basket of self-incriminations–but rather to help us "win" in the ring of life, becoming more like the man or woman we hoped we would be. Perhaps take on more Christlike attributes in becoming.

Choosing to see trial as a finite condition, with a beginning and an end, allows the brain to focus on "solutions" rather than occupy its time with what I call a "treadmill mentality." When we focus our time and energy on something, someone, or some condition or past event we cannot change, "it is as if we are running on a treadmill at the gym, expecting it to take us home."

The treadmill was not designed to transport us to another location, no matter how fast we ran. Expecting to achieve success in life and relationships by clouding our brains and emotions with negative energy is a form of treadmill mentality.

I chose "Proper Preparation Prevents Poor Performance" as Winning Way #2 because I believe it sets the foundation for every other principle taught in this book. We have to set in place how we are going to react to trial or surely become driven by the natural man (See 1 Corinthians 2:14 and Mosiah 3:19) within each of us, subject to the senses of the flesh (if it feels good, do it–or if hard, don't do it!). Even the laws of the land cannot protect us from ourselves when acting under the influence of the natural man.

An author's "worst nightmare!"

A few birthdays ago, my wife, who always seems to think of gifts I didn't know I wanted, surprised me with a brand-new iPad-Pro© with a keyboard feature so I didn't have to use my thumbs when writing a book. But since I write mostly while at the gym, on the treadmill, elliptical, and stationary bike... I figured I wouldn't be using the new iPad much. Little did I know that life as we know it would soon change (COVID-19), and in a matter of hours, my (and yours) favorite gym would be deemed a "non-essential," and I would lose my writing platform for who knew how long.

So, fast forward a couple of months using my new iPad. It soon became my go-to iPad of choice, and two months of writing was quickly added to my new tablet.

There is often no warning when trial strikes, and such was the case late one night as I was on a roll, pounding the keyboard and trying to capture fleeting thoughts on the screen before they disappeared like a mist in thin air, which seemed to happen more and more as I have aged (LOL).

I still cannot recall what/how it happened; it was so sudden–a distant memory of leaving the page I was typing on to cut out content from another, to paste it into another file–to come back to where I was, only to find... only to "not" find it. I was confused, disoriented from being at it for so long, and suddenly unable to find my way back to the page I was working on. Everything looked unfamiliar, not current; heat started rising from my shoulders and neck.

I have already disclosed my (former) lack of control of the natural man when presented with an unexpected trial, and as the heat began to rise within me, surprisingly, thoughts of how I was going to react 'actually' appeared in my mind, causing the heat to slow down a bit while I processed just what had happened.

I had lost weeks of writing content, trying everything I knew to retrieve it–but it was gone. I entered a few writing sites to see how other authors have handled the loss of their manuscripts; maybe they discovered a secret recovery method I didn't know about. What I found scared me. One author wrote about his period of grieving, which lasted five years before he could get back into his writing.

"Grieving?" Was that the depressed feeling I was experiencing after several days of searching with no results? Was that why I could not even "look" at my tablet without this "empty" feeling in my stomach? I was indeed experiencing loss and the grieving process that accompanied it. I wondered how long I would feel this grief, which brought up feelings of depression because I realized it could be the end of my writing if I could not come to grips with this.

I decided to apply the Winning Ways taught in this book to my experience with trial.

... and I called upon God.

It was during prayer that a thought entered my mind about how the young prophet Joseph Smith, in 1828, must have felt, trusting 116 pages of his work in translating the Book of Mormon to an associate, Martin Harris, only to be lost. I realized that Heavenly Father was sending me a message that what I was feeling was natural but not life-ending. The thoughts I had captured in my lost pages would likely not be recovered, but new ideas would be forthcoming if I could clear my head and allow God's spirit to regain control.

Opportunity—look for it!

<u>There is opportunity in trial if we will just look for it.</u> Through my experience with losing manuscript pages of "this" book, I could connect personally with someone I look up to with the utmost respect and love and catch a small sample of how he must have felt after being trusted with such sacred work but then lose it anyway. I will never read the account of the "lost 116 pages of manuscript" again without experiencing a level of grief that I now share as a pure connection to this great man, Joseph Smith. This was my newfound "opportunity" from experiencing trial.

And to give me a little love... I did "not" give in to the natural man's disappointment enough to hold me back from pushing through the hurt I felt from having to replace the lost content in Chapter One; neither did I throw anything (LOL).

"Your present trial, and the one following, has both a beginning and an end." It is so crucial that you believe this principle... because it is true! You may not have become immediately aware of when the trial started because it was disguised as a mere inconvenience or concern. But when the inconvenience or concern turns "personal" and "hurts," it becomes trial.

Likewise, the end of a particular trial does not always immediately become clear until time has passed, and something clicks in your mind that you are "alive," and somehow you survived the trial to live another day... maybe not without blemish or change in lifestyle or status (or having to re-write your lost manuscript) - but you are alive! And with life, there is hope. We must never lose hope. With hope, there is a chance for a brighter tomorrow.

This belief (in hope) was further underscored in a 2017 Marvel® Movie titled "Justice League." A quote by the Lois Lane character hit me like Superman himself: "<u>Darkness, the truest darkness, is not the absence of light. It is the conviction [loss of hope] that the light will never return.</u>" She says later in the quote: "Our darkness was deep and seemed to swallow all hope."

There will be times when trial first strikes like a punch from Superman, when you may feel darkness so void of light that you cannot find any trace of hope. Winning Way #2–Proper Preparation Prevents Poor Performance–should become a "light stick" in your 72-hour Emergency Preparedness Kit, bringing to memory how you prepared for this trial and should at least bring a ray of hope into your heart, adding a spark of fire to your belief that even this trial has an end... and the sun will once again shine.

As you read these words, are you beginning to sense some movement in your attitude... for the better? Even a seed of belief is enough to crack open the spiritual portal between you and your God, a loving Heavenly Father waiting with open arms to connect with you.

Winning Way #2 should remind you of the atonement of Jesus Christ, who suffered and died for all. Our first earthly parents, Adam and Eve, brought trial upon themselves by partaking of the forbidden fruit. Although some may see this as an act of weakness on their part...

had they not partaken, there would have been no posterity—no Savior—no opportunity to be tested, to grow, or to win. Their placement on earth would have had no meaning. Yet, they did act unselfishly so that you and I would be born into this world with agency to experience both trial and joy, both the bitter and the sweet.

This act by Adam and Eve opened the door for the need for a Savior to atone for the sins of humanity. Otherwise, they would collectively, without exception (because we are all sinners), die spiritually as well as physically, "for no unclean thing may enter into the presence of God" (Revelation 21:27). Only one person could do what needed to be done. It took the Only Begotten Son of God to lower Himself as a mortal, to experience trial, and in the act of pure love, accept the role of Redeemer for every sin ever committed so that you and I might have a way to be cleansed from our mistakes and poor choices, our pains and our sorrows, and our addictions and worldly appetites. He suffered them all.

Jesus Christ experienced what you are now going through so He could comfort you in time of need: He was prepared to fill His role as Savior. This belief should at least provide a measure of reassurance when trial strikes that your Savior—my Savior, is right there with you, knows exactly how you are feeling, and stands ready to provide comfort if you will but let Him into your heart. He is prepared, are you?

"How can you and I expect to glide naively through life, as if to say, 'Lord, give me experience, but not grief, not sorrow, not pain, not opposition, not betrayal, and certainly not to be forsaken. Keep from me, Lord, all those experiences which made Thee what Thou

art! Then, let me come and dwell with Thee and fully share Thy joy!'"
-Neal A. Maxwell

Although most of my writings of trial are based upon my own time in the ring of life, I love to underscore the principles taught as my beliefs and principles of doctrine that have spiritual roots. From my scriptural reading, I believe that all earthly creatures and occupants were first "spiritual" matter, and physical forms were added. I also believe that truth is truth. It always has been and always will be. It is humanity who distorts truth into something else. But true principles have " power " if we strive to understand them.

"True doctrine (principles of truth) **understood, changes attitudes and behavior..."** (Boyd K. Packer, CR, Oct. 1906, p. 20)

In addition to understanding true doctrine, we must "strive to put into practice that which we learn and understand." It is also from the "doing" that attitudes and behavior change.

Reading a book on how to lose twenty pounds is only half the battle. We must internalize what we read and then practice what is taught. Simple enough, yes?

So here is your "action assignment:" <u>Whenever the next trial strikes, you are to write down the following truth principle immediately:</u>

This Too Shall Pass! This Too Shall Pass! This Too Shall Pass! This Too Shall Pass! ... *as many times as necessary.*

Believe it or not, this exercise is the "doing" part of changing behavior. By scripting in your handwriting (not on the computer or other electronic device), you are reprogramming the brain to think differently. Do this exercise every day for 21 days, or however long the trial lasts, if less than 21 days.

As you reflected on this experience, didn't you feel a sense of relief just reminding yourself that this trial will end at some point and the sun will once again shine in your heart?

I will be very transparent with you for the remainder of this section of Winning Way #2 by sharing "another" personal experience to back up the truth principle I just taught.

"I allowed myself to become depressed." I will defer the details of the how and why to later sections of this book, but I want you to know that "I know" what it feels like to live in a gray world where the sun rarely shines. Yet, what I learned about how to change that condition changed my life.

I studied human programming in psychology classes at Arizona State University (ASU-go Sun Devils). Here, I learned that the human brain could be programmed while in the ring with a trial. In my case, negative thoughts led to low self-esteem, which opened the door to depression. The challenge soon became how to dig out from under the grey cloud that followed my every move. Even my psychology studies didn't prepare me with principles on how to deal with this personal trial.

Here is a truth: "If the human brain can be conditioned to believe negatively, it can also be conditioned (reprogrammed) to believe positively." If you internalize Winning Way #2 as a personal belief principle, it may act as Popeye's can of spinach to give you a boost when all looks dark and dreary. Remember, when faced with a personal trial, "This too shall pass." But in the meantime, let's prepare your mind to do more than withstand the lasting effects of your current or next trial... let's prepare to "Win!"

Preparing to win in any sport, business, or personal fitness goal generally begins with the mind. If you don't "believe" you can win, at least possess a particle of belief–the odds are stacked against your success. Sometimes, it takes overcoming self-image issues before you can even see yourself winning, so I started reading time-tested book classics such as Dale Carnegie's *How to Win Friends and Influence People* and Lewis Timberlake's *Born To Win*. From these timeless self-improvement books, I began to feel some inspiration that I, too, could become better. Reading the inspirational stories of how others overcame their trials and circumstances caused my brain to begin considering, "What if?"

The experts in my psychology studies taught me that it takes at least twenty-one days to form a habit–good or bad. Your challenge is to fill your mind with positive information designed to change how you look at trial, no matter how long it takes. This book is not about a get-rich scheme promising limitless achievement by just reading the pages herein and sending in a donation of $99.99. Instead, it promises guidance through your current and future trial with "Winning Ways" to not just endure opposition, hurt, and setbacks–but to use those conditions as a catalyst to open doors to personal growth that otherwise may never have opened.

Please take a moment and close your eyes (Not yet! Wait for me to finish my instruction) and think about a trial you are currently experiencing, however insignificant. Got it? Now grab a 3x5 card (or piece of paper, napkin, or large sticky note), and write the following:

"I will win from this trial of... (describe the nature of your trial), by preparing my mind to recognize opportunity when it comes."

Here is what most people don't understand about trial: It can be a catalyst for change! Now, if you caught yourself saying, "What a dummy! Of course, there is change with trial... I just lost my job, you fool!" Then, this book was written for you. If, on the other hand, you responded by saying, "Change begets opportunity–how do I discover opportunity while going through my trial?" This book was "definitely" written for you.

I will admit that I do not know what it feels like to lose a child to death, expected or otherwise. The thought of seeking "opportunity" in the face of such a loss may appear initially cold and without feeling if we restrict the use of the word "opportunity" as the world may define it–the means to gain an advantage over another or to experience gain at the expense of another. <u>But in this writing, the word "opportunity" may also describe a condition of opening our minds to the possibilities of personal growth and spiritual advancement.</u>

Suppose I seek through this trial the opportunity to be loved by my Heavenly Father in a way I have never felt before, to experience the healing "sweetness" of the atonement. Would that not be an acceptable use of the word "opportunity?"

I would never trade the life of a loved one or wish I could have a devastating trial so that I could benefit by experiencing the Lord's healing influence in my life. We do not seek trial. But when it seeks us, it then becomes personal... and a planned approach on how to "prepare" to not just defend ourselves but to come out the other side more grateful, more faithful, more charitable, more empathetic, and more determined not to give in to the natural man within us seeking revenge, or refusing to forgive. Is that not accepting opportunity to change? Because in my way of thinking, if I do not prepare myself to win by using trial to become more like God, then I willingly submit myself to a chance that I will do the right thing... in becoming all I can be.

One does not need to look far from home to find examples of trial used as a catalyst to win. Here are just a few that come to mind:

- Harland Sanders was a cook with little promise of a secure future. At the age of sixty-five, he was broke and decided to retire. However, Harland Sanders would not remain retired due to the economic conditions of the Great Depression and his meager social security check (aka Trial). Harlan was "forced" to put himself on the road to sell the only asset of any worth–his recipe for fried chicken. 1000 (+/-) rejections later, Harland made his first sale, which led to one of the first franchise companies in the USA. You might have heard of Kentucky Fried Chicken.

- Walt Disney was told he lacked creativity.

- Bill Gates watched his first company crumble.

- Steve Jobs was fired from his own company.

- George Steinbrenner, the famous New York Yankees baseball team owner, also owned a small basketball team called the Cleveland Pipers in 1960. By 1962, as a result of Steinbrenner's direction, the entire franchise went bankrupt. That stretch of failure seemed to plague Steinbrenner when he took over the Yankees in the 1970s, as the team struggled with several setbacks and losses throughout the 1980s and 1990s. However, despite public fear and criticism of Steinbrenner's controversial decisions, eventually, he led the team to a fantastic comeback, with six World Series entries between 1996 and 2003 and a record as one of the most profitable teams in Major League Baseball.

Remember this: Success is not controlled by the clock–or age.

Although citing examples of famous individuals who succeeded in the face of failure has likely elicited a response from you, like: "Sure, he succeeded despite trial and opposition; he is George Steinbrenner, or Colonel Sanders, after all." Or... "Bill Gates succeeded; he was a billionaire and could afford to fail dozens of times."

We sometimes fail to realize that a "trial of faith," and often "risk," are required to pursue a dream–both common denominators among the few examples I have shared.

Each of these examples used could have reacted differently to trial, as many do. They could have given up, cut their losses, and moved on, perhaps letting opposition define them and their future success instead of using trial as a catalyst in becoming the success we know today. There is that "choice" word again. Remember agency? Our lives–our legacies–are defined by our choices, and even more importantly, our reaction to trial and even our successes lead us back to *choice*.

You have a choice right now in reading this book. You can choose what to do with the principles of truth being discussed here. Simply speaking, you can choose to ignore them, scan through the pages looking for something that stands out or entertains you, and close the book with no thought of picking it up again. Or you can *ponder* over each paragraph you read, looking for answers to your particular reason for picking up the book in the first place. Whatever your choice, I encourage you to, at the very least, choose one of the "Winning Ways" contained herein to focus on as a matter of self-improvement.

You have already invested a few bucks and some time, hoping to find relief from whatever is still burning within you. That is why you were drawn to this book, isn't it? You still want to win in life, yes? Then, before you choose to close this book to that possibility, "please" use Winning Way #1 and choose "Call Upon God," asking for some clarity of thought in what choice you should make. Then, as my wise mother would say: "Charles, listen to your body!" She was so spot on; even though she didn't attribute that "feeling" as God's way of showing He cares about you, she was right about there being a feeling within, IF... you will listen (quiet your mind–turn off the noise plugged into you for a while), and "ask"- ask God to help you know; ask for direction. Then be patient, and wait upon the Lord to confirm the feeling–the presence of the "still, small voice" within you. Google that phrase if it is unfamiliar to you. We can't force the spirit, but we can choose to "invite" that comforting feeling, that breath of peace, into our minds and hearts in our preparation to win. I promise you will know it when it arrives, for you had it within you before your earth life–a topic for another day.

Yes, there are plenty of other books to read about the climb to success by famous people if that is your only goal in selecting this book... even Joe Ordinary has stories in Readers Digest of escaping from the jaws of death to become an instant success on the public speaking circuit. This book, however, is about "you"– your trial, your preparation... and your success at becoming all you can be–and winning!

Winning doesn't always manifest itself in dollars and cents or national recognition–true happiness and self-fulfillment have little to do with worldly wealth and position or title.

Perhaps in your story, you experienced trial early in your marriage, but somehow, you worked through those issues together to celebrate over fifty years of marriage. Or perhaps you didn't, for whatever reason(s), but moved on to find the love of your life. Within the definition of "Winning," as defined within the pages of this book, you Won!

Life's trials will come in many shapes and sizes, and it is impossible to address every one of them in this writing, so let's agree that "Winning" through your trial is not an absolute but rather a moving target. Life was not intended to be easy or defined. If you can be patient with me as you read on, keeping your mind open, I hope to build a different mindset about trial within you. It won't take away the pain of making mistakes or the hurt from a failed relationship–but if you practice these "Winning Ways" and incorporate them into your being, you will experience trial as few others can.

Timing...

How does a parent respond when the call comes in the dark of night that their 32-year-old daughter, and mother of five children, was diagnosed with aggressive breast cancer? Panic–grief–fear–thoughts of young children being raised without their mother. I promise you there was no thought in our minds at that time to "look for opportunity." They had no job, just finished law school in another state, no money, and no insurance–but for her mother and I, there was nothing to consider except how to get our daughter and her family home... and under the care of a cancer specialist.

Not even the fact that the nationwide real estate industry was experiencing the beginning of the 2008 meltdown could distract us from seeing that our loved one received the best care possible. However, I had just completed my last retail project for a client and was, at that moment, out of significant work myself–a condition which would exist for another two years, during which time we battled our daughter's cancer.

To our credit, "our first call was to God." The minute the first punch was thrown, we did go down–down on our knees. There is something magic about kneeling when trying to attract the attention of our Heavenly Father. Of course, He hears your every prayer–standing, sitting, or kneeling... but for me, it's when I kneel that I feel most reverent when calling upon my Heavenly Father.

Grief is a natural reaction to loss and is necessary as part of the healing process. Winning Way #2 in no way suggests that experiencing grief is a weakness to be subdued or replaced with some form of mind control. In fact, from my notes taken in a psychology class at ASU, the body may experience as many as five stages before healing is complete–denial, anger, bargaining, depression, and acceptance–representing the various stages of recovery. The trap, however, for many who grieve is getting stuck in one or the other stages before healing is achieved. I believe this is where the Five P's (aka Winning Way #2) will be of great value.

As unique individuals with different temperaments and personalities, we will likely react to trial and opposition differently–even as members of the same family. May I suggest you consider taking a personality insights test to gain at least a surface understanding of your personality makeup? Or, I suppose you could seek out the local Fortune Teller at the next County Fair... but from one who was married for twenty years before I understood, by accident, that my wife did not see things in the same way I did, nor did she react to trial the same way–I believe you will benefit from a little study on this topic as part of your "Proper Preparation **to** Prevent Poor Performance" action plan when confronting trial.

Here is a simple test to start you off evaluating your personality profile: Do you consider yourself outgoing or reserved when engaging with other people? Are you task-oriented or people-oriented? Everyone has some of all four of these tendencies at different levels. So what, you ask?

My previous experience with personality profiles could have been more extensive, even after taking several psychology courses at ASU. But, many years ago, when I attended a lecture by Christian self-help author and public speaker Florence Littauer–who was promoting her new book, "Personality Plus," I was confronted with "four prominent types of personalities..." one of which, to my utter amazement, described my wife perfectly. The realization I had been unfairly judging my wife through "my" colored glasses came crashing down upon me and has served to enrich and prolong our marriage, which is still going strong at 56 years as of this writing. I would say my time attending that lecture was a significant investment with eternal dividends.

I later became acquainted with a more detailed and layered approach to defining one's personality strengths and weaknesses, called the DISC Personality Types system–similarly breaking down the prominent personality types into four distinctive behavioral differences. Learn more about your particular temperament by searching the term "DISC personality assessment" online. You can take a simple, getting you started, fun test at www.123test.com/disc-personality-test/ for FREE.

The more we understand about ourselves, the more prepared we can become when trial strikes.

Do you understand the difference between personality and attitude? If not, you may spend the first twenty years of "your" marriage trying to change the one you love. Personalities are mostly stable... as a semi-permanent reflection of who we are. Attitude, on the other hand, is changeable and can influence behavior. Although this book mainly focuses on the study of attitude, it is imperative to learn at least the fundamental differences in human personality and know where you fit in.

I have learned a bit about myself through the study of personalities. I am assertive in *some* things but a self-starter in most. But my

Achilles heel in responding to trial comes from my closely influenced sub-dominant personality type–I am detail-oriented, with a propensity to overthink things. I like organization and seek control in my life, but I chose the field of entrepreneurial real estate as my life's professional pursuit–go figure? I am artistic, but not exceptionally so, but very sensitive, and I take life "very" personally. And here is the attitude contribution to my personality mix... I struggle with low self-esteem. Even when positive affirmations from others validate me or my actions, I tend to "humbly" dismiss their opinion as merely being kind, still struggling with the feelings that I still "lacked" in my performance.

Because I have become aware of my personality strengths... and weaknesses, I can work on changing my attitude about trial... and myself, thus changing my behavior from what would usually be influenced by my low self-esteem.

If you were to come into my home office, you would find the following self-talk(s) taped onto the front of my computer console: "Without Challenge, There is no Change."

I recently added my rendition of this reminder to better coincide with this book: "Without Battle, There is no Win!" And, of course, to coincide with Winning Way #1 – "Have You Prayed About It?"

Consciously and subconsciously, I absorb these "attitude shorts" (my term for them) designed to prepare me for the next trial. They condition/prepare me to remember (i) there is a beginning and an end to trial, and (ii) challenge and opposition produce change. And I recently added a fourth "attitude short" as "Opportunity–Look for It!"

I believe you will benefit from knowing which personality type you are most closely aligned with because only you know what motivates you to act. Or are you like me and have yet to give it much thought? Then wake up, my friend... and let me elevate your awareness to another level. This one may be worth the entire price of this book–times 100.

So, let me continue... What motivates you? Do certain personality types react differently to motivation? Are some easier to motivate than others? What causes you to react? How do you know you are appreciated? Loved? How do you show appreciation? Love?

The second level toward understanding ourselves is found within the pages of the book "The Five Love Languages," written by Author Gary Chapman in 1995. The book's subtitle is "How to Express Heartfelt Commitment to Your Mate," but don't let the title fool you, men! The real gem in this book is in the main title. I had no idea what a "love language" was before reading Mr. Chapman's book. However, I found the awareness of different love languages to be as insightful into understanding behavior as my study of personality temperaments provided, giving me a much clearer picture of who I was dealing with each morning when I confronted his face in the mirror.

Within the pages of *Love Languages,* you will be asked to take a test to help determine what makes you feel loved–appreciated–and motivated. Said in another way: "What turns your crank?" If, like me, you have never really thought about it until now, hold on...

Are you a "gift giver?" Do you find yourself going out of your way to find tokens of appreciation for others? Are you a great "listener?"

Prone to sit for hours listening to someone confide their feelings to you? How do you feel when someone compliments you? Are you usually the one in the group giving others compliments and encouragement? Are you the one who cleans without being asked? Looking for an opportunity to relieve a burden from another?

Maybe you are the first one to volunteer at the homeless shelter. How do you feel when someone goes out of their way to bring you a homemade goodie or mows your lawn when you are away? How do you feel when someone you love reaches out to touch you for no reason other than to express appreciation?

These questions give insight into which "attitude shorts" might be more effective than others in preparing "you" for when trial strikes.

The Five Love Languages, as described by Mr. Chapman, are:

- Gifts

- Quality Time

- Words of Affirmation

- Acts of Service

- Physical Touch

After reading this book together, my wife and I discussed which of the Five Languages we thought matched the other. I was so wrong in my selection of "Gifts" as her love language. And to be fair, she chose "Physical Touch" as mine, but not the kind described in the book. Yes, I am responsive to physical touch by my beautiful wife of 56 years–but "words of affirmation" drive me to succeed.

My wife yearns for "quality time" from me, our children, and our friends. She judges her worth by a spontaneous phone call from one of her daughters or a neighbor friend, inviting her to lunch. I tried cleaning up the kitchen to reach out to her, but that often had the opposite effect–making her feel she failed for not cleaning the kitchen to my standard.

We once had friends drop in one busy Saturday morning, and my wife dropped everything to sit with them in the living room while I finished my task of mowing the lawn in the backyard and swallowing an attitude of resentment for their "lack of consideration" for just dropping in without advance notice, no matter they had just come from California.

Are you following my line of thinking here? If you have a reserved/people-oriented personality whose love language is Acts of Service, you may want to use "Who Can I Serve Today?" as your Attitude Short. When trial strikes, and we become all consumed in our own needs, it is proven that serving others is the quickest way out of the grey blanket of depression and worry.

On the other hand, if you are motivated by "Physical Touch," you might write "Give 5 Hugs Today" as your Attitude Short. Although you need to be considerate of those you might want to hug, given post-COVID-19 effects on people, and… with all the ever-present attention to inappropriate touching, which seems to be featured prominently in the news, especially around election time, you may want to ask permission first? And you might want to consider the appropriate, gentle "side hug" rather than the full-body slam.

In the spirit of Winning Way #2 – "Proper Preparation Prevents Poor Performance," I hope adding these two books as part of your read list will help prepare you for much more than just how to respond to the next trial–I hope they will impact your life, as they have mine; maybe even "prevent" a trial? But it will now be up to you to research further–for we must move on...

When trial strikes, what is your anchor?

So far, in this writing, I have attempted to inspire you to start discovering "who you are," what makes you tick... and what causes you to "want." But trial is often like a storm at sea, disturbing the very essence of our foundation, and unless we are firmly rooted, we may be swept away into an abyss of confusion, depression, or even worse.

In my effort to prepare you for trial and win, you need to discover your anchor in life because it will likely be this anchor that sustains you and keeps you rooted when all others about you are being swept away. Trial is like that; it confuses and disorients and self-inflicts–often causing us to lose hold of precious ideals and dreams and forget for a time who we really are and who/what is most special to us.

Have you ever looked into the eyes of a person just ambushed by an unexpected trial the size of King Kong? What did you see? I'm confident you only saw King Kong reflected at you because that is all the recipient could see right then. It would take a very disciplined and prepared trial recipient to grab ahold of their anchor to get a bearing, to remain steady and firm in the face of such a monster, and to look for opportunity.

I am somewhat of a history buff and love to read stories of immigrants who left all they had accumulated for a chance at a better life for themselves and their families. Such is the story of the Utah pioneers who gathered from around the world and crossed the American plains on foot in search of a place in the West where they could build their homes and live without fear of religious persecution. Such is the story of my wife's great-grandfather, Edmund Lovell Ellsworth.

Edmund was born July 1, 1819, to Jonathan and Sarah Galley Ellsworth in Paris, New York, a town in Oneida County. Edmund's father was a carpenter by trade, and right before Edmund's birth, he and his brother (Edmund's uncle) left for Quebec, Canada, to purchase a load of lumber to barge down the St. Lawrence River back to their home. The first wave of tragedy struck the Ellsworth family when Edmund's father came down with Yellow Fever during the trip and died.

The next wave of trial came from the uncle who accompanied his brother to Quebec. After the death of Ellsworth Sr., the brother informed the family of his passing and then asserted himself as the sole heir of his brother's property without a trace of proof. Yet somehow, the brother convinced the local authorities he was indeed the rightful heir, forcing newly born Edmund and his family to vacate the property.

Before long, however, Sarah remarried, and the children once again had a home.

Only a short time later, however–after the marriage to Thomas Merrit–the little family was once again displaced upon the untimely death of Mr. Merrit.

Nine years passed before Sarah married again. This time to Abram Hendrickson, who, according to Edmund's journal, "did not make a desirable home for me."

Around Edmund's twentieth year, he was working on the Mississippi River floating barges when he received word that his mother and her husband had joined a church called the Church of Jesus Christ of Latter-day Saints... or as they were nick-named–the "Mormons." Edmund had heard bad reports about these people and felt the need to return home and save his mother from the apparent delusion.

With arrangements made, Edmund began the journey, which took him right through the country where the church's founder, Joseph Smith, allegedly found gold plates containing a history of an ancient civilization who migrated to this continent from Jerusalem just before the fall and captivity by the invading Assyrians.

Edmund was prepared to gather all the negative information he could find about this new *cult* to disprove their claims and spare his mother the embarrassment and indignation of becoming a follower. However, instead of digging up dirt, he found much in their favor and was baptized a member.

Edmund's story does not end there... and his trials were only beginning as the popular opinion of neighboring towns forced this band of Mormons from one county to another, often leaving all possessions behind to avoid assault or death.

Upon the assassination of their Church leader and President, Joseph Smith, while falsely incarcerated in Carthage, Illinois, Edmund Ellsworth and his new wife, Elizabeth Young, the oldest daughter of

Brigham Young, successor to Joseph Smith as President of the fledgling Church, was assigned to the first company of handcart pioneers, departing from Winter Quarters, Nebraska, for what was to become a "promised land" for this growing band of believers, who professed that God Himself had preserved this western land for their inheritance.

Trial of one's faith often precedes the miracle, and the "call to Zion" to settle an untamed part of the world would take its place among the most impressive colonization efforts in history, with thousands of locals and overseas emigrants answering the call. It was no matter they had nothing but a few belongings in their possession upon their arrival at Far West; they would construct and pull those belongings in a handcart, without shelter against wind, rain, or snow–and the story of the handcart companies who trekked across the barren plains during the most bitter of all winters will long be remembered for grabbing hold of their anchor to make it through the ordeal which lay ahead. But as is often the case with trial, the legacy left behind in the wake of the loss of personal goods and often the death of loved ones served to solidify individual family anchors for generations to come.

"What a story it is," said former Church President Gordon B. Hinckley (1910-2008). "It is filled with suffering and hunger and cold and death. It is replete with accounts of freezing rivers that had to be waded through, howling blizzards, and the long, slow climb up Rocky Ridge... Hopefully, it will be told repeatedly to remind future generations of the suffering and faith of those who came before. Their faith is our inheritance. Their faith is a reminder to us of the price they paid for the comforts we enjoy." ("The Faith to Move Mountains,"

Ensign, Nov 2006, p84)

Names of pioneer children – newborns to young adults, were strewn across the western plains in shallow and often unmarked graves due to the extreme weather conditions, which caught the Willie and Martin handcart companies before they could reach their destination. Names of mountain passes, like Rocky Ridge, are noted in family journals as taking 18 hours to ascend amid a fierce snowstorm, as is the name Rock Creek, where the beleaguered company of Saints camped to rest following their ascent to Rocky Ridge, and where thirteen faithful emigrants died before morning–their frozen bodies buried in shallow graves.

Why would someone "invite" in a trial that can take a life or bring suffering to parents who lose their children... and children who end up without parents to care for them? Ask the millions of emigrants who have fled war-torn countries for another, more peaceful environment. Ask them "why" they fled, and they will likely tell you the same story–we wanted peace! We wanted a place where we could live without extreme control over us. We wanted to find a home where we could raise our family to love one another and not fear government tyranny and corruption. We wanted a place where we could worship where and how we wanted. We wanted to be free to move about the land without fear of imprisonment for leaving our home. We wanted to be free to work as much as we wanted and the freedom to choose what we did with our earnings.

Why did I leave a safe-haven job right out of college for an uncertain future as an entrepreneur? Because I was following the desires of my heart to "captain my own ship!" To see if I could become "all" that I could be without the bonds of safety, security, and the known. I love the "unknown" because of what it represents and what it offers–a chance to be tested. A chance to "Win!"

What would you describe as the early pioneers' "anchor?" How about the emigrants who fled from one country to the next? What would you describe as "my" anchor? "Oh, that's easy, Chuck," you say! "Your anchor is your ego!" (Ha-ha!!) Well, maybe it is, in a worldly sort of way. Don't most winners have an overstuffed ego that drives them to success? Only to discover that ego alone is insufficient to anchor against the severe trial of losing what you worked years to accomplish. Sometimes, it is that puffed-up ego that often turns on you in the face of such personal trial.

Early in my career of making it to the top, I was impatient because those who could influence my rise to management did not move fast enough to satisfy my need to rise–so I left the company to become the captain of my own ship. One might say I was ego-driven, and there was no doubt the ego-ingredient additive was mixed in with the high-octane goal of winning, but I think it was more about answering the call to "become all that I could be..." and I would never know unless I jumped.

The trek to my first real estate office of Malone Realty & Investments, located in downtown Mesa, Arizona, was different from the Mormon pioneer's trek up Rocky Ridge or the flight across the South China Sea in nothing but a small watercraft filled to over-capacity. And certainly, there was little chance I would be found by the side of the trail, in a frozen heap, or killed by sea pirates, or sunk to reside forever in Davy Jones Locker. But the need for an anchor was there just the same.

Maybe my first anchor was selfish, a desire to succeed. That anchor was not destroyed during my first trial of losing all I had worked ten years for as a co-owner of a local Home building company during the '70s and '80s. It might have become nicked and beat up, somewhat... but it was still strong enough to get me up off my backside, dust myself off, and begin looking for the next chapter of my life, where I could, once again, succeed.

You may not know at this reading what your anchor is. And I didn't know either, at first. You were probably surprised when I said my anchor was first the "desire to succeed," right? You probably thought I would say "God" was my anchor! That didn't happen until the third ten-year run at trying to succeed, which also ended in failure. Don't get me wrong or interpret my comment about the delay in bringing God aboard as my anchor. I was a "believer." I followed my heart, as Edmund Ellsworth did, and have tried to live my life worthy to be called a disciple of Jesus Christ–with Christ at the center. But it took many trials and failings to learn how to trust in someone I could not see–could not hear in the same way as mortals can communicate with one another. This trust and ability to see... and hear would come through faith.

When I had finally been beaten down sufficiently to see the Hand extended to me, my eyes and heart finally opened to accepting God as my anchor. Together, we would reach into the darkness to see what could be. Together, we would work to serve others and to make their lives just a little better. Together, we would cry when things didn't work out the way I had hoped. I would then ask, "Lord, what am I to learn from this failure?" Or from this opposition? Or from this trial of which I find myself in the crosshairs? And then, the keyword (or words) that unlocked the door to greater understanding came to my mind. "Heavenly Father, please help me see the opportunity!"

I think a suitable anchor to "any" trial could be to develop an "attitude" of seeking an understanding of opportunity, not in terms of using opportunity to rise to the top of the corporate ladder, necessarily... or to achieve personal greatness, although there are books and books written about individuals and companies who have risen above their trials to become great–and we shall also incorporate that interpretation into this writing as well. But within this discussion of Winning Way #2 in preparation for trial, let's explore a lesser-used understanding of opportunity, perhaps overlooked by many when overshadowed by personal gain.

It is the opportunity to "change internally" when confronted with trial.

Each of us has undeveloped talents and gifts embedded within us, which have laid dormant and unused until trial dug deep enough to create an attitude of humility so that those undiscovered gifts could come to the surface and be used to bless us and others. This process, often used by God, also helps define our efforts to "become," perhaps creating an opportunity to change our somewhat abusive nature and thoughtlessness of others in need. Maybe to become more forgiving, more tolerant of others, and maybe more focused on changing ourselves than changing others to our way of thinking. These are all "opportunities" in trial.

Trial can help us become gentler, more tender, and willing to see others for who they can become rather than who we think they are today. Personal trial connects you with others of similar experiences and opens doors that may otherwise never open. My wife and I became more aware of how many other families were experiencing the impact of cancer in a family member's life because of the experience with our daughter.

The last chapter of this book, titled "Be Mighty," tells the story of Mighty Jake, a young grandson of ours with autism and diseased mitochondria, with a terminal diagnosis to his young life. Jake's illness has built within my heart a gratitude for every day of life he is granted… and has enabled me to feel grateful for every new day I have been given–and experience still another chance to Win!

I have personally witnessed the effects of repeated trial in my life having a profound impact on my attitude, causing my behavior to change in areas I was not aware needed change. Without trial, I would likely not be writing these words–on my iPad, while on a treadmill at the gym–for you to read.

Without the loss of my first business and savings for retirement, I might not have been forced to temporarily work for someone else to supplement the support of my family. At the time, I considered it a blessing–a lifesaving opportunity from answering a well-hidden ad in the classified section of the Mesa Tribune Newspaper for a development and construction manager for a fledging gas and convenience store retailer–and a chance to work on my attitude.

"Why" things happen will often remain a mystery, usually until years later, but if we choose to connect some dots, we may find that doors to becoming who we are today–satisfied with the product or not–were opened, and all we had to do was walk through them. Since I am likely older than most of you reading this book, I can look back over eight decades to see how the pieces began to come together, as one door closed and another opened.

Follow the bouncing ball... and connect the dots.

I "allowed" the trial of losing the first ten years of acquiring wealth to gut-punch my self-image. This sent me looking for another source of income, which led me to a "slow" Fast-Food restaurant franchise, which turned into our receiving the Golden Cone award two years straight, but still couldn't make enough "money" to support my family–which led to answering the small ad referenced above, to put my real estate skills to work for a regular paycheck, which put me in a position to learn excellent contract and negotiating strategies directly from two of the three owners, which led me into learning about real estate environmental laws and contamination clean-up... and drew on my franchising experience to develop five Arco AM/PM stores for the owners, which ignited my understanding of recurring income, which led to the familiar and recurring desire to build a secondary income, which opened my mind to an opportunity to build a product distribution business–which started to make money after about ninety days, which led to an invitation to speak to a group of businessmen, which caused me to begin reading books on how to change my attitude, which caused me to become more successful in my product distribution business, which gave me more opportunity to speak to more people, which inspired me to join an early morning "Toastmasters" group to learn how to speak before people, which led to singing lessons to improve the strength and tone of my voice, which led to a lengthy run as a paid motivational speaker for years, which allowed me to negotiate a three and one-half work week at my "job," so I could travel more, which led to a larger business, which became so large that we (ourselves and other linked associates) became a threat to the product master distributor, who illegally cancelled our distributorship, which caused us to ultimately lose our fifteen year-old business and our second attempt at retirement.

Whew! Were you able to connect all the dots?

Here is the lesson I learned from the experience of one door after another opening and one door after another closing: "All experience is ultimately for our good," if we choose to make it so!

First, I had to fix my attitude.

Chapter Three

Attitude Begets Behavior

I *loved* this chapter, even before I wrote it, because there is so much already written about "attitude," which I have either read or experienced personally, and I couldn't wait to add my perspective.

What is "attitude," anyway? Cambridge Dictionary defines attitude as "how you feel about someone or something." Now, that sounds simple, yes? Except that it isn't. If it is as simple as it sounds, why do leading experts in behavioral science tell us that attitude can determine success in life? (See Inc.com article "How an Upbeat Attitude Makes Success Simple.") If attitude affects chances of success, then why isn't "everyone" successful?

Of course, the other question is, "What is success?" Again, the Cambridge Dictionary comes to the rescue. Success is "the achievement of desired results." I really like that definition. It is straightforward and covers a wide range of applications.

So, how's this? "Attitude triggers a feeling which drives the achievement of desired results." But if we are being honest, attitude can also "sabotage" the achievement of desired results. So, does this simple word, "attitude," still sound simple to understand? No?

So, let's try to simplify... attitude can either be "positive" or "negative." Now we're getting somewhere. And if we take this one step further–a "positive" attitude is essential to achieving success! Ha! Do you love it?

Is a positive attitude also essential to winning through trial?

You might be thinking, "I thought this book was about "trial?" And yes, it is about trial... but you don't step into a ring to confront an opponent without being prepared, do you?

Since we are on the subject of attitude, how does a person "prepare" for trial by preparing his attitude? Answer: by not allowing yourself to think "negatively."

The natural reaction to trial in the ring of life is to think the worst and allow negative self-talk in without throwing a few positive self-talk punches in defense. I believe what is to follow as we proceed in Chapter Three will help equip you for the fiercest of trials if that is what lies ahead.

Being in a positive state of mind will not protect you from having trial in your life, but it will definitely help you approach your reaction to trial in a more controlled and more productive way, helping to diffuse the stress associated with trial and learning to think more positively that this too shall pass.

Now, with that bit of exercise accomplished to help us better understand the "type" of attitude we should strive for in helping us succeed, I would like to share a few of my favorite attitude quotes, or as you know… I like to call them–***Attitude Shorts:***

• Attitude is a little thing that makes a big difference — Sir Winston Churchill

• Being sexy is all about attitude, not body type. It's a state of mind — Amisha Patel

• Each day, I come in with a positive attitude, trying to get better — Stefon Diggs

• Failure will never overtake me if my determination to succeed is strong enough. — Og Mandino

• If you don't like something, change it. If you can't change it, change your attitude. — Maya Angelou

• Fake it 'til you make it! — An English aphorism

What do we learn from some of my favorite Attitude Shorts? I hope you agree that… <u>the achievement of desired results is more often accomplished when we are in a "positive" state of mind.</u> This state of "being" is achieved by having a "positive attitude." If you don't mind a simpler definition of this, our attitude is the "heavy machinery" that builds the roadway to success in life, and the driver/operator is Mr. Positive. Our attitude drives our actions (Attitude Begets Behavior), and Mr. Positive follows the "directions" you give him.

Since we have to play fair here… there is also another driver who occasionally tricks his way into the driver's seat when Mr. Positive is not feeling well or doesn't show up for work that morning. His name is… You guessed it, Mr. Negative! And boy, can Mr. Negative tear up a nice straight road.

We're obviously having a little fun here… but can you see from this visual that either Mr. Positive or Mr. Negative can drive the heavy machinery? So the decision you get to make is, who do "you" want to be the driver that day? How do you want that roadway to success to look like? And how quickly do you want to arrive?

I choose Mr. Positive to be the driver/operator of my heavy machinery!

Isn't this fun? I really like the direction this conversation is headed.

Let's review... I am responsible for building a roadway to personal success (arriving at a happy place in life, etc.). I'm going to need some heavy machinery (personal attitude) to build a roadway that leads to my destination. If left alone, this heavy machinery can wreak havoc with my roadway... so I bring a driver/operator (Mr. Positive attitude) to follow "my directions" in building the roadway.

I won't get too complicated here, but let's say that my "directions" can include positive "self-talk," positive "affirmations," and even positive input from friends, etc. When I add "spirituality" to the octane that fuels the heavy machinery, mixed with goal setting and hard work, there isn't much that can keep me (and you) from building that roadway to success unless we let Mr. Negative drive.

But hopefully, this slight over-simplification opens your mind to how attitude (heavy machinery) plays such a significant part in the achievement of success.

What kind of desired results are possible with a positive state of mind? How about celebrating success by bringing onboard a new client at work because he likes how you are always upbeat and positive about getting things done?

How about when you are thinking positive thoughts, you just seem happier?

How about people like to be around you more when you are in a positive state of mind?

Thinking positively opens more doors to success than the alternative state of mind.

We could go back to that Inc.com article… "If you have a generally 'upbeat' attitude, you should at least achieve some level of success." And probably the opposite projection is also true… a "negative" attitude will most likely result in a level of success "lower" than hoped for or none at all.

And let's not forget the effect a positive state of mind has on the human body and mind. That's a door opener to a book all by itself.

"Alright, Chuck," you say. "Then just how does one get into that coveted state of mind called "a positive attitude?"

Adopting a particular state of mind generally signals a change in one's nature.

I believe to effect a change of nature, one needs to want to change so badly he will do the work to change it. It starts with "desire," followed by a change in habits. More often than not, that desire is born out of trial. Minds are open to change, new habits are put into play, and lives are changed.

One of the first habits required to effect a change of attitude is to feed it with proper self-talk. While the world is basically programmed with a negative slant toward local and national news, it becomes the duty and responsibility of each human being to determine "what" is allowed to be stored within, except that our mind is built like a sponge and generally accepts and stores everything fed into it.

When trial strikes, it is usually without warning and often catches us in a vulnerable state of mind, unprepared on how to react, so we usually react by blaming ourselves or others. Feeding our mind with negative self-talk can set in motion feelings of low self-esteem, loss of self-confidence, affect our sleep, eating patterns, and even our love life. I find nothing good about allowing my mind to retain negative self-talk, so I suggest you build within your skill set a method for countering those negative feelings when they first hit.

I love to start the day with positive input. I spend time with my Heavenly Father, giving thanks. Then, when in the car heading to and from the gym, I try to immerse myself in uplifting messages intended to insulate me from the day's typical negative information blitz. Then, I usually spend time on the treadmill, elliptical, and cycle machines during my exercise regimen, writing my next book. Over the course of ten years, I have written four books and several published articles while accomplishing more than one goal. My regular self-talk is, "If one paragraph is good, then two is better… but one is always better than none."

By the time I am showered and dressed for the day, my mind has been well fed on positive affirmations, hopefully serving to counter the negative of the day. Remember our goal of creating a positive state of mind? Choosing to start each day with a concerted focus on positive input will go a long way to initiate that positive mindset. When it becomes a habit, you will experience a new inner strength and confidence to help keep you on your feet when the next trial hits.

If you truly "want" to adopt a positive attitude mindset and are willing to form new habits that will reflect your positive attitude, you are going to need to walk the walk as well as talk the talk. Here are a few ways I stay positive:

#1 - <u>Learn to talk positively "to" yourself rather than listen to negative talk "from" yourself.</u> This sounds easier than it is, but it is genuinely the most essential change that needs to occur in your mind. It is indeed a change of nature, so treat it as such.

#2 – <u>Hang around people who have a positive influence on others.</u> This is another reminder that you will be the same in five years except for the influence received from the books you read (podcasts included) and the people you associate with, so choose wisely.

#3 – <u>"Decide" to lift others.</u> I truly "love" this one. Many years ago, I read a book titled, "Balcony People," written by Joyce Heatherly. This book taught me how to remove myself from ground-level self-talk and move up to the balcony where I could be heard by "lifting others" in word and deed. However, during political election years, I wished I could remove myself to another planet during the months before election day. It has become the norm for all parties to elevate themselves by calling out the weaknesses of their opponents rather than just focusing on what they can bring in the way of improvements. I try to counter this negative by finding occasions on social media when I can send a personal note to a friend going through hard times or send an uplifting message to a friend, citing a few of their admirable qualities. It literally "makes my day!"

#4 – <u>"Practice" seeing the world, your City, your neighborhood, and your home as a wonderful place to live. Look for the good around you.</u> How do you accomplish this when the neighbor's dog begins barking at 6am and doesn't stop until midnight the night before? You practice!

#5 - <u>Learn to laugh</u>. Now, this one shouldn't be too hard, right? Try it right now. Laugh!

Hmm! Not so easy, is it?

What's that, you don't have anything to laugh about? That's the point. Learning to laugh is a state of mind, not a reaction to watching an "I Love Lucy" episode. Since laughter is a physiological response, it can be learned. If you can learn to laugh, you can learn to react to trial without giving in to negative thinking.

Laughter is the fastest way to create a positive state of mind.

We will spend the rest of this Chapter discovering together how to achieve a positive state of mind, even after digging yourself quite deep into a state of depression.

Here are a few Attitude Shorts lining the computer monitor(s) in my office:

- Have you prayed about it?
- Trial has no power of its own unless you plug it in. — Author
- Without the Battle, There is no Win! — Author
- Opportunity- Look For It! — Author
- I Have Something to Prove! — Author

```
*Attitude is Everything!
```

Winning Way #3 – Fake it til' you make it! (Or "Behave

until you believe!")

Now, before you form a negative opinion of Winning Way #3 because of the use of "Fake," notice that I have included a sub-title using the word "Behave."

I invite you to look at your behavior during specific periods in your life when you "imitated" a happy persona when, in fact, deep down, you felt exactly the opposite. You didn't consider that behavior "fake," did you? You probably felt like you were acting grown-up — "because that is what grown-ups do," taught parents, teachers, and coaches your entire life. "Just suck it up!" was heard more than once around my home, school, and field of athletic pursuit.

Do you remember my reference earlier in this book about "garbage in, garbage out?" The mind is a beautiful thing (attempt at satire), but it can also turn "ugly" when fed garbage.

During my period of deep depression back in the day, I fed my brain on negative feelings of failure as a provider and allowed those feelings to affect my self-worth as a human being. I am not proud of that period in my life, but I am proud that I did not stay there. I can remember as if it were yesterday, running into a good friend of mine in a parking lot as I was walking to my car from my office in Mesa. He made the mistake, albeit out of natural reaction as part of a greeting, to inquire: "How are things going?" I remember spewing all over him every negative feeling I had built up. When I had finished unloading my baggage, he looked a little like he had been sprayed with something green and gooey out of a Ghost Busters movie as we parted ways, and I watched him try to find his car parked right in front of him. It was then I realized I had just spewed negative all over a well-meaning friend who had only asked a simple question as a gesture of friendship but was treated with green slime instead. "This had to change," I vowed!

This is how the door to change of behavior is opened—we reach the tipping point of our questionable behavior and finally admit to ourselves that we need to change. But it usually takes an episode or two, like mine, before we recognize a behavior change is necessary. You ask yourself, "How did I get here?" The silent answer is most often, "garbage in, garbage out." When we feed our minds with negative thoughts, we are prone to spew out negativity. I can attest to this from my own experience.

These days, when social media has become the information channel of choice, keeping a strong self-image while watching the lives of "perfect people" unfold before us is exceedingly difficult. If we don't do something to counteract the "negative in" from comparing our lives to theirs, we become like a ship lost at sea during a raging storm, taking on water with no bilge pump to remove it to stay afloat. It's just a matter of time before the ship is underwater.

Although I can't dedicate sufficient space in this book to cover every aspect of depression, I can call your attention to habits and actions that produce a breeding ground for either positive thinking or negative thoughts over time. We do have choice. It starts with desire, just like I shared in the paragraphs above. A willingness to change is essential in recovering from a case of the blues. That same desire to change is doubly critical in recovering from depression or any other type of addiction because of the firm hold it has over you.

My dear mother struggled with alcoholism. Before she passed away, I was left with a mental picture of her sitting on the side of her bed at the recovery center, her small frame stripped of any meat on her bones - slumped over, head hanging low. I tried pleading with her to stop drinking, start attending AA, and give up this life before it took hers.

Do you have "impact moments" in your life that you will never forget, no matter how old and senile you get? Like where you were when 9/11 happened? Well, I will forever remember my mother's answer to my attempts at convincing her to change. She said, with her head still hung low, her voice barely audible: "I will quit when I am '#@&%!' good and ready to quit, and not one minute before!"

When you read further into this book about "opportunity in trial," I want you to think about this experience with my Mother. Through her trial, she taught me an understanding of human nature, which would serve me well, even now... and for many years to come: "People will change their ways when their mind (and heart) is open to change, and not one minute before." I call that the "tipping point" to change.

Enter trial.

Trial is often the catalyst to affect change; at least, it can open the door to change, even if just a crack. Like faith, able to sprout from just a seed, change often requires the ground to be broken open before seeds of change can be planted.

Actual change doesn't occur as simply as I have described it as the planting of a seed, but when the heart finally "welcomes" or perhaps only "accepts" the need for change, it is most often the result of the kind of trial that "hurts" sufficient to humble us and open our heart to change.

I now understand that one of the purposes of trial is to "prepare the ground."

Stories abound in recorded scripture of individuals, families, and even entire peoples who have changed from their "wicked ways" after experiencing trial. In my five years serving (prison ministry), the inmates at the Arizona Dept. Of Corrections (ADOC) prison facility in Florence, AZ., over the years, I heard from many about how ironic it was that they had to experience "prison life" before their heart became open sufficiently to allow positive change. I witnessed time and time again an actual "change of nature" within several of these "throw-aways of society," as many of those who are against prison reform would call them. I know from experience and witnessing firsthand that change is possible in every human being who "wants to change."

It took a terrible experience while under the influence of alcohol, resulting in near death, for my mother to finally open her heart to change. And it took a desire deep enough to sink into my soul for me to finally seek help. I have come to see trial differently now; I now understand one of the purposes of trial is to "prepare the ground."

Please do not go looking for trial as a "cure for what ails you," a phrase my dad used to say. I have devoted the entire Chapter Four to "Choice" because trial does not "always" bring positive change and often does not because of the agency of man to choose how he will respond to opposition in all things.

Like my mother, I, too, did change! And thankfully, for the better. Not immediately, and not without many slips in the process, but I eventually changed because I "wanted" to change. My first call was not to God, as it should have been—it was to blame myself. I failed to accept the truth of Christ's atonement for "the one," even a sinner like me who fell but kept getting up. I could not pass the blame for my financial failures to anyone but me. I suppose I felt, without really knowing it, that I had elevated myself "above" the atonement.

Remember the scripture warning in Proverbs: "Pride goeth before destruction, and a [haughty] spirit before a fall…?" One writer defines pride as a turning away from God, specifically to take satisfaction from oneself. Is it possible to take satisfaction from the destruction caused by pride, you ask? I suppose, in some dark way, there is satisfaction in self-misery, a kind of "defeatist" attitude that sells the idea that you "deserve" to be caught in this fog of depression and continual grief. But the author of this type of thinking is not Jesus Christ, I promise you.

In the spirit of love, please take this chapter seriously. Attitude is so fragile. It can determine your course in life. It can influence your choices. It can be the difference between success and failure in marriage, career, or even destiny after life.

Attitude will [even] accompany you from this life to the next.

If you are currently struggling with feelings of hopelessness, self-blame, loss of interest in pleasurable activities, or profound and lengthy bouts of continued sadness, you may require the assistance of a trained professional to guide you through the healing process. I was so prideful in my battle with depression that when I finally admitted I could not win this battle on my terms, in my way, and sought help from a professional—I almost "ran" out of his office after slapping down a check for $75.00 on his desk, on my way out the door; not because I was cured, but that I could not see how in the world this man was going to help me. I could not see through my own selfish pride.

I ran to my car, sat behind the wheel for a moment, letting the frustration build within me... and then it broke. I am told that by hitting my steering wheel as hard as I did, I was fortunate the airbag didn't explode into my face. But at that moment, I didn't care. I had made the prideful decision that no one could help me but God–and I told Him so.

I sometimes wonder what God thought of me when I rejected professional help and just turned it over to Him. Some readers might consider it a sign of great faith to turn my trial over to God, but as much as I would love to think it was an act of faith, I am more inclined to give an honest assessment that my action was more of an attempt to punish God. My heart was just not humble enough to get on my knees and admit I couldn't crawl out of this hole, so I just sort of "threw" my problem to God and said, "Here, you fix it!" I do not recommend that type of relationship-building exercise at all.

Things did not immediately improve; unfortunately for my wife and family, things didn't improve for quite a while. Pride is like a bulletproof vest, protecting the soft spot within my heart from allowing the seeds of change to enter. I just got more frustrated with myself, and that anger was directed at my family. How does that song go...? "You always hurt the one(s) you love... the one(s) you shouldn't hurt at all."

Maybe my Heavenly Father got tired of seeing me about to destroy the relationship I had built with my wife and young, impressionable children. I don't have an answer for what happened next – or why. Perhaps He knows the "intent" of our heart much better than we give Him credit. I didn't want to lose my family; I think He knew that. But how could I be the kind father and husband I needed to be when I couldn't stop beating up on myself? Can you ever reach your potential when you hate the person you have become?

Growing up, I remember my mother telling me more than once that "no one can 'make' you happy!" And she would usually follow that up with, "You are in charge of your attitude; no one else is!" Although in concept, I agree with my mother's wise counsel, I must admit, a pint of "Rocky Road Ice Cream (and a spoon) goes a long way to bring a smile to my face. But to a person with depression, that brief reprieve generally lasts only as long as the last bite of their favorite dessert.

Those of us who have experienced depression and those currently experiencing it will likely agree there is a difference between the "Rocky Road" happiness and the emotional state of happiness that leads to "joy." I remember occasionally feeling periods of emotion resembling happiness, but they were just a "lighter" state of mind; a lighter "mood" definitely not the type of happiness a person could claim as a long-lasting change of behavior.

I remember making a $100,000 commission from selling a large parcel of land to a Homebuilder client of mine. After I picked up the check from title, I went to the bank, deposited my share of the commission, and went home to bed, feeding my depressed state. It was definitely one of the lowest points of my life, instead of being a fun celebration. What changed? Attitude drives (begets) behavior.

I hope the transparency of my personal failings and faults doesn't cause you to doubt the truthfulness of the concepts and Winning Ways taught in this book. When my walk on earth ends, I want my tombstone to read: "He just kept getting up!" That's attitude! And that's choice.

Chapter Four is all about choice. As I shared with you, I, too, believe attitude is a choice. Roy T. Bennett said, "Kindness is a choice. Giving is a choice. Respect is a choice. Whatever choice you make, makes you. So, choose wisely." But... I share the lowest parts of my life with you in this book to let you know that "I know" that sometimes you are so full of bad feelings about yourself that you can't easily "choose" to be happy. You want to... but you can't convince your face. Trying to act happy when your insides are sick with feelings of low self-esteem and disappointment is like trying to climb an icy mountain wearing roller skates. Something has to change! For me, it took a reprogramming of my "stinkin'- thinkin.'

Please don't get discouraged by my creative description of roller-skating the Matterhorn. Depression, low self-esteem, and feelings of hopelessness can be beaten, so can a negative attitude... but it's not going to be easy!

Now, where was I before my departure into Chapter Four? Oh yes, I was just about to tell you of my "miraculous recovery."

He really can't tell one story without losing himself in another, can he?

Fast forward to summertime and a much-needed family vacation in a rented casita on the beach of Lake Tahoe. But that didn't stop me from acting like a jerk. I had just scattered my family from my presence with a fit of anger and was left behind to "entertain" myself when a knock on the door startled me. I gruffly opened the door to confront the intruder, and there stood a man, all of about 5' tall, wearing a beanie hat, shorts, very colorful socks, and a golf club in his hand. I later learned he was warned that he might need it.

The interesting person at my door introduced himself as a friend of my brother-in-law we were traveling with and said he was told I was a "golfer." I nodded in affirmative and waited for his response, which was to invite me to be his partner in completing a foursome, ready to tee off at that very moment. What was strange about the entire exchange was my "attitude" in accepting a stranger's invitation to play golf when all I really wanted to do was stay in and feed my hurt pride.

We became acquainted as we walked across the street and down a couple of blocks to the first tee. And over the course of nine holes of golf, I learned that my partner was a Doctor in Sun City, AZ. His specialty? Depression!

I have taken more than enough of your time detailing, maybe in too much detail, my path to healing from depression... but it is so important to me that you understand that (1) you are not alone in your trial, and (2) there is hope that "this too shall pass."

This "chance" encounter with Doctor X led to me driving from Mesa, where we lived, to his office in Sun City (before freeways) twice a week for a few months while he assessed and treated my "medical" condition, as well as my "mental" condition. I mean, "who" does that? Where did this guy come from? How could he have been so prepared to diagnose my body's electrical system as being severely banged up due to the stress I was under, throwing my physical being into a near state of breakdown, and my low self-image so low it had no resistance to the negative self-talk I was feeding it. But he did know!

Choose to feed your mind a diet of positive affirmations.

We will talk more about the "reprogramming" of the mind that is often necessary to realize the greatness within each of us. If your personal goal is to lead a fulfilling, productive life, leading to "becoming" all that you can be… then your diet of negative self-talk must change, as did mine.

It is so amazing how the "silent" subconscious mind works like a sponge to store every bit of information fed to it from our eyes, tongue, nose, and ears–and we pay so little attention to it.

Would it surprise you to learn that according to scientific study, the subconscious part of your mind occupies "90%" of space in your mind-house… and your conscious mind, the part of your thought process most familiar to us, occupies only 10%?

Would it surprise you further to learn that this vast space in your mind-house can't tell the difference between fiction and truth? It has no logic base as does the conscious mind, so it essentially digests whatever you feed it. Thus, the saying, "garbage in, garbage out!"

In my recovery from chronic depression, I had to essentially "re-program" my mind to the extent of feeding it more positive messages designed to heal my troubled mind and low self-image. This knowledge might help you understand why you don't feel uplifted after scrolling through social media for hours. Do you know that no matter how fast you scroll through social media "stories, reels, etc.," your subconscious sponge still captures those images and feelings you transmit to it and sends the message to your body's nervous system that you don't measure up? "Everyone" is having more fun than you, looks better, makes more money, has more toys, takes more trips, etc. This is likely why we see repeated warnings to "limit" our impressionable children's exposure to social media. I wonder if there is a correlation between heavy video/social media non-reality immersion and teen suicides.

Imagine achieving a personal state of "happiness" whenever you want!

Even writing about depression and having to relive that very dark period of my life creates some downward pull to my heartstrings. Do you see how easily the infusion of certain information can impact how you feel?

The dictionary defines attitude as a "psychological construct," a physical and emotional entity that characterizes a person. Our attitude(s) are complex (boy, that's an understatement) and are an "acquired state through experiences."

What I love about this dictionary definition of attitude is the assurance it gives us that our current state of mind "can become whatever we want it to be!" (Music, please: "Celebrate!") I just asked Siri to play "Celebrate" by Three Dog Night, a favorite of mine back in the mid-seventies, and before I knew it, I was out of my chair (because my 'Smart Watch' had been telling me for 30 minutes that it was time to stand) and dancing to this "feel-good" music; all thoughts of my former depressed state now replaced with some positive vibe all through my body.

Can You "Really" Choose to be Happy?

When you "decide" to adopt a positive frame of mind, you open the door to all sorts of possibilities, one of which is achieving a state of "happiness!"

However, according to a recent podcast featuring Hank Smith, a highly sought-after, entertaining, motivational speaker and the best-selling author of many books and audio CDs, happiness is not "a" choice. Happiness is the result of "many" choices, often repeated.

Although I do still believe that the "pursuit" of happiness begins with a "choice" (better over bitter), I will concede that true and lasting happiness is the result of many smaller, incidental choices.

Happiness is often compared to a work of art. It is said that a beautiful painting is not accomplished because the want-to-be artist decided one day to buy some brushes, paint, and palette and set aside the afternoon to paint a beautiful picture. I suppose the intent of this comparison is to insinuate that attaining a skill to become an artist capable of producing a beautiful work of art is accomplished over time, with the artist developing basic art skills learned and practiced daily. Failure is experienced, faith is tried, and often, a mentor is called in to help, and once again, different brush strokes are learned, practiced, and internalized. In time, our artist might produce a painting worthy of hanging on a wall in a house of love.

While this comparison between attaining an attitude of happiness and learning to paint a beautiful picture may sound rational, even attainable–I must say that when I was in the depths of despair, the long road to happiness, as described above, would have discouraged me from even trying. I didn't have the faith to look that far into the future.

Thankfully, I learned a great lesson in my first-year college Psych Class 101 that changed my thinking about the power of the mind to affect attitude without actually "becoming" an artist to produce a work of art.

I have three such paintings as described above because I followed this exact formula my college professor taught me.

First, the motivation to even try: "You won't receive an A in this class unless you teach yourself how to produce a work of art," Doctor Cummings told her students on the first day of class.

Where do you get the power to change your attitude? It comes from a deep desire to become better. If happiness is your goal [and I suggest that few of us intentionally want to change our attitude from happiness to unhappiness], you must dig within to find a reason to change. I wanted an A in that class; no, I "had to have" an A to accomplish my goal of graduating. You must "have to want" to change.

The next step leading to an A for the class involved a #2 pencil and a blank sheet of paper. "Learn to reproduce a simple picture onto your blank sheet of paper, a line at a time... and use your eraser a lot, until you have created your masterpiece," read the instructions from Professor Cummings.

In changing your attitude, you must decide "who" you want to be. I decided I had had enough of "spewing green negative slime" over anyone unfortunate enough to ask, "How are you?" I "decided" I did not want to be that person any longer, and so I "chose" the word "Marvelous" as my subject to copy. Anytime someone asked me how things were going, or "how are you?" I would respond time after time, "Marvelous!" And you know what, just creating that word into my being (my etch-a-sketch) made me feel a tingle at first, and then eventually, I felt the power to change. Even today, decades later, when asked that same question, I respond in the same manner, "Marvelous!" And I mean it! It truly has become part of my nature and positive state of mind.

Each week, we brought our work to class to show the other classmates and the results were amazing, from pencil sketching to charcoal, watercolors, and oils. I admit to running into trouble a few times when my learning curve got a little too steep, but thankfully, my wife's mother had already mastered that learning curve many years earlier and could make up for my deficiencies by adding just the proper brush strokes.

As the semester drew to a close, the final exam was to show our work to the class. I was never so proud of my accomplishments. And I did receive an A in the course. But what was more important than receiving a top grade was the reality that I had done my best and that my mother-in-law had made up the difference between "my best" and my getting an A. If that statement sounds a little familiar to you, it's because we "all" fall short of receiving an A for our attempts at "becoming" perfect (Matthew 5:48).

Your journey to the world of "self-inflicted happiness" will not happen overnight. Yes, it does take time to become a true artist. Yes, it does take time to completely change your nature from one persona to another, to a place in your world where happiness "radiates" from your heart through your eyes, lips, words, and actions. But the "journey" of *becoming* is absolutely within your power to begin feeling different–happier the very first time you show your work (i.e., Respond with a positive affirmation -marvelous!), and it makes both the "giver" and the "receiver" feel good... and it only gets better each time you reach a new level in *becoming*.

SIDE NOTE: I have to ask–did you catch my reference a couple of paragraphs ago, when I told the story of how my mother-in-law added a few "experienced brush strokes" to my painting "after I had done my best" to complete the assignment?

I genuinely hope this resonates with your own story of falling in your journey toward becoming, only to fall short of perfection. Yet, your Savior, my Savior, makes up the difference by feeling every negative experience you and I will ever have. By His atoning sacrifice on the Cross at Calvary, He lovingly makes up the difference whenever we fall, repent, and get back up again to try harder. His "experienced brush strokes" show evidence of compassion and love toward us, no matter how often we make a mistake. I just wanted to bear my sincere testimony of a loving God, a forgiving Savior, and an experienced mentor who stands at the ready, with arms open and hands extended–and all we need to do is "ask."

Now, according to Hank Smith's podcast, as referenced earlier, there are twelve "Practice Strokes" every wanna-be-happy person needs to do:

1) <u>Happy people have happy friends.</u> I remember years ago learning

wise counsel in a seminar taught by Charlie Tremendous Jones... "You will be the same person in five years as you are today except for the people you meet and the books you read." I think I would phrase this sage council a slightly updated way: "We become like the people we most often spend time with and the information we feed our brain."

2) <u>Happy people try to be happy, even when they are not</u>. Your brain responds well to "happy thoughts." Take a break, and for two minutes, think "happy thoughts." Add that reminder to your smartwatch.

3) <u>Happy people use their "signature strengths"</u> – those activities that fill you with energy. Now, before you move on to the next brush stroke, take a moment and think about "Which activities make you feel happy?" What do you consider your "signature strengths?" Wisdom–Courage–Love–Humor–Happy–Adventurous–Thinker–Leader. Make your own list and name as many personal strengths you have now, and then make another list of strengths you wish you had. Spend time developing the ones you have, and have fun exploring the ones you wish you had. You will amaze yourself with the results.

4) <u>Happy people spend money–but it is most often for others.</u> I wondered about this until my wife and I were recipients of another person's generosity. We were overcome with gratitude. It genuinely inspired us to pay it forward.

5) <u>Happy people have in-person conversations</u> to build upon relationships. Oh, this is a good one! How do you feel when, after weeks or months, you attend a gathering of friends? I bet you can remember being "quarantined" from COVID-19, yes? That memory probably

doesn't make you feel happy, does it? Then think about how you felt to finally go outside and take a walk, waving to every car that passed by. How did you feel? Silly? But happy? Or to meet a friend for lunch and "catch up." Wasn't that the best feeling?

6) <u>Happy people laugh.</u> Children, on average, laugh 300 times per day. Adults laugh 15 times a day. My wife and I just finished watching one of the best Hallmark Movies made, which was more comedy than romantic drama, and we laughed and laughed for two hours. It is fun just to laugh. I remember times in my life, usually late at night, when I would get into a silly mood and start laughing… my laughter would escalate to a high C, and I couldn't control it, which got everyone else laughing. Like other muscles, our laugh muscles weaken without regular use.

7) <u>Happy people use music to make themselves happier</u>. Do you want your children to fight less? Play Classical music. There was a time when my wife and I would alternate picking up one of our grandsons from school, and I used to love it when it was my turn, and Tyler would get in the backseat, buckle his seatbelt, and ask: Granddad, could you please put on some classical music? I feel very stressed today.

This love for classical music started because we spent so much time together, and I would often have classical music on when he was with me. Other times, I would ask him what his choice of "tunes" would be, and most often, he would say, Classical! Now, remember, I was a self-taught drummer in a lounge, rock, and western band… so I like music with a beat (LOL).

8) <u>Happy people always seem to have something fun to look forward</u>

to. Put something on the calendar to look forward to, however insignificant. Celebrate National Doughnut Day–calendar a walk through the local city park with a friend. You can buy tickets in advance to see a new movie showing at the local movie theatre and invite a family member or friend to go with you.

9) <u>Happy people exercise and eat well.</u> There is scientific evidence that consistent exercise, coupled with healthy eating habits, has so many benefits that don't necessarily include weight loss, which seems to be on everyone's mind these days, with gyms full and fad diets alive and well.

"My" top ten benefits include, in no particular order... (1) Anti-depressant, (2) Reduces stress and anxiety, (3) Boosts creativity, (4) Strengthens the heart, (5) Stave off age-related vision loss, (6) Live longer - happier, (7) Every dollar spent on preventative health it saves $2.71 in future medical costs (APHA), (8) Improves self-esteem, (9) Helps get better sleep, (10) Slows down the aging process.

Don't forget these other benefits to healthy eating: pumps up the immune system, creates more energy, reduces cravings for bad-for-you food, enhances exercise, and lessens insomnia.

10) <u>Happy people go outside for at least 20 consecutive minutes (when it's cooler, of course) – or go to the mall and exercise (No, pulling your wallet or purse out and exercising your wrist by swiping the card doesn't count).</u> Eat outside, take a brisk walk, walk the dog, visit a neighbor, walk to the cluster mailbox, ride your bike to the corner gas station, or sit outside and "people-watch" as cars and neighbors pass by. Practice "happy waiving" (like you mean it). With COVID-19

quarantining entire communities to their homes for school, work, church, even shopping... there have been more "homebound" infirmities than ever. According to a report from the National Academies of Sciences, "social isolation has been associated with a significantly increased risk of premature mortality from all causes, including a higher risk of developing dementia and coronary heart disease, cancer, and increased risk of stroke (Article updated 04/18/2020, by Urology of Virginia).

11) <u>Happy people get enough sleep</u>. Although we are all unique individuals with different body and mind compositions, we all need sleep. According to an online article by *Business Insider*, "More sleep = a happier person." Studies show that our bodies thrive with more sleep. People who sleep between eight and 9.5 hours at night tend to wake up happier; however, almost nobody regularly sleeps over eight hours a night. Most of us get less than 7.5 hours of sleep a night, usually calling it a day around 11:00 - 11:30pm, and depending on your commute time, may rise and be in the car by 6:00am or earlier. This type of schedule, over time, will take a toll, I promise you. And the toll is often a steep price of happiness deprivation. So get some extra sleep for a month and just put it to the test. What's to lose?

12) <u>Happy people meditate and pray.</u> It doesn't have to be a religious thing; just practice sitting still and letting your mind focus on a single idea or thought for ten minutes (set a timer if it makes you feel better?). According to a 2017 Policygenius blog, "Meditation can actually 'change' your brain," not just subjectively make you "feel better." It can actually make you happier!

Often referred to as "mindfulness," the consistent practice of meditation was strongly related to a positive state of mind and stress reduction.

Praying is like having a private conversation with a friend. Who doesn't like the chance to visit with a friend... and do all the talking? But here's a switch-up for you: How about praying first... and meditating after? I think you may be pleasantly surprised at the outcome.

Be brave, even if you're not...pretend to be; no one can tell the difference.

I have laid out a lot of information, case studies, facts, testimonies, and other reasons to "choose" how to become a positive person, a happy person, a balcony person... but no matter how convincing it sounds, it all comes down to attitude towards change.

Let's "pretend," just between us... that you "are" happy. Can you think of something that "made" you happy? Maybe write down a couple of "things" you enjoy doing that cause you to feel pleasure. As a kid, I remember loving Saturday mornings because that's when my favorite cartoons were on, and after my chores of cleaning my room and bathroom, I got to watch Mickey Mouse cartoons. The expectation of being able to watch TV, even though it was black and white TV, made me happy. But when Mickey said, "See ya next week," my whole demeanor changed. I fell in countenance like a balloon that had just lost its air. I became grumpy and pouted when my mom gave me something else to do, like homework or more chores. My happy disposition changed once my happy time ended.

Now, fast forward seventy-something years or so... and I still love going to the movies today. I love the anticipation of going. I love to talk all week about what we are going to see. I love driving to the movie theater, the fresh popcorn smell and rush of cold air when I open the door to the lobby, and my excitement when I see a short line at the refreshment counter. Arriving early enough to watch the previews of upcoming movies is also a big part of going to the movies. Eating popcorn, a kernel at a time, with occasional sips of a soft drink while the countdown to the previews begins is such a pleasant experience. The movie itself was fun to experience, but then the walk afterward past the big trash container open to receiving my leftovers seemed to act as the portal to reality as I continued through the lobby, not failing to notice happy faces of anticipation lining up for "their" refreshment selection–and perhaps feeling a bit envious that they are about to experience movie magic and ours had ended; the feeling of anticipation satisfied and the weight of real life once again falling upon me.

It is at this moment that I have a choice: to either stay a little gloomy or "behave" like I am happy and maybe put on some happy music or force myself to laugh at something my wife says (No, I didn't mean it like that, sweetie! Ouch!).

What I have just described is how life is. We experience ups and downs all the time. We learn that being "happy" is temporary, just like my experience at the movies. Although we don't think about it, we were not meant to "always" be in a state of happiness. Yet the "natural man/woman" inside us seems to think otherwise. When I was young, I was hooked on "external means of achieving a desired state of happiness" every Saturday morning. And boy, if something got in the way of that goal, I really put up a stink.

As I grew older, I found that my attitude didn't change much–I still needed external means to fund my desired state of happiness. And I suppose I still do to some degree. But because I was designed to experience both joy "and" pain, life isn't always a state of happiness. By the time I reached adulthood, I was expected to stop throwing tantrums when life didn't turn out the way the Hallmark movies do. I had to learn that the guy doesn't always get the girl, and the promotion at work doesn't always come through.

If we continue to look for external causes for happiness as our "only" means of achieving a state of happiness (positive attitude), we will likely make ourselves and, consequently, those who love us very miserable.

Creating a positive state of mind within us should be one of our goals in life. You can call it what you think best fits your goal, but I have chosen to seek "an attitude of happiness!" I have seen what this attitude does for me and those around me, and I want this attitude to be one of my "legacy hallmarks."

This choice of attitude affects the subconscious in much the same way it picks up and stores negative information. My conscious goal, then, is to purposefully fill my subconscious mind with more positive than negative input to "feed" my brain with "healthy" information. A simple example of this would be a "daily practice" of seeing the positive side of life.

An example of practicing daily to see the "positive side of life" could start the minute you wake up by holding back a while the temptation to check social media or respond to an email that came in during the night and build into your plan to attain an attitude of happiness by first "feeding" your mind with "appreciation."

I have found that when I start each day on my knees in private supplication to my Heavenly Father, giving appreciation for even life itself, no matter the state of affairs at the time–it gives me more internal confidence to face whatever challenges might lie ahead. At first, it took a concentrated effort on my part to see a "visual" picture of how many "appreciations" I could come up with to fill the "positive" side of my brain... much like filling the gas tank on my VW Atlas at Costco. But in time, it became a habit to begin my day this way because of the way it made me feel. I felt happier and more confident knowing I wasn't alone to face the day, whatever life would bring.

One advantage of growing older is the perspective it gives you of the "now." You gain a yardstick of sorts with which to measure the days of old against the here and now. That, too, is interpreted by your attitude, but sometimes it just takes observation to see differences.

I remember the term "road rage" becoming a term used to describe how a driver of one vehicle would retaliate toward another because "something" set one driver off. They each used a moving vehicle to express violent anger, generally caused by frustration over something and the aggressive driver's inability to deal with it civilly.

We also have a similar condition as road rage displaying itself in our society, but this time, it uses social media as the vehicle of choice. Some call this attitude form "cyberbullying" because it usually happens in a public forum created online when someone makes a post, others comment, and someone disagrees, and instead of agreeing to disagree, this phenomenon condition of "if I don't agree with you that gives me the right to 'hate' you," plays out in words of anger and frustration against another. This condition might be exacerbated due to COVID-19, but it started way before the months and months of self-isolation as a means of curbing the spread of the virus.

Clearly, our society today has taken a few giant steps backward when it comes to politeness and civility toward others. Yet, many recognize this destructive behavior as an attitude that can be changed… and offer such remedies as "relaxation techniques" to help us gain awareness and control over our natural instincts, such as breathing techniques, healthy eating, exercise habits, etc.

One such technique for gaining control over mind and body is called "mindfulness" (Refer to #12 in the Attributes of Happy People discussed earlier). I love this term because it infers personal control over the mind to produce positive results within the body, such as reduced anxiety and stress and the release of hidden creativeness within us due to negative self-incriminations, etc.

Mindfulness is another term that has as its root a form of "meditation," such as one would encounter in a yoga class, where technique is learned on how to achieve a "oneness" between mind and body to gain greater control in reaching a state of peace, allowing the body and mind to heal from the stress and anxieties of daily life.

The term "mindfulness" can also be considered a "mental state" or "conscious condition of attitude" in which a person learns to become aware of their present state, and by using specific learned techniques may positively affect change. Although my solid bone structure makes an invitation to a Hawaiian Luau seem like torture, I have recently started with basic yoga stretching techniques and incorporated some mindfulness exercises to help clear my brain of yesterday's recorded negative self-talk.

Hopefully, this chapter on "attitude" will open doors to a higher awareness of how your thoughts affect your behavior and how to embrace attitude as a living, breathing condition, full of choice and opportunity to defeat any trial that may enter the ring of life with you at any given moment–but this time "you will be prepared!"

When trial strikes again, as it surely will, if you have attained some measure of the desired "attitude of happiness" (aka positive attitude), I suggest this state of mindfulness–a feeling of "choice" to come over you "before" you automatically react negatively to the opponent's presence. "Choose" to stay in your desired mental condition of happiness and refuse to allow this negative flow of information, anxiety, what-ifs, and second-guessing darts of fear to enter your mind. Instead, fill your mind with positive affirmations and see yourself overcoming this temporary condition with a positive outcome.

Consider the current state of our world affected by the pandemic known as COVID-19. It is not hard to find someone near you, even yourself, who has not been affected in some way by this disease, yours truly included.

Speaking frankly here, since the announcement of the wild spread of this virus throughout the land, my real estate business was impacted in more ways than just providing a consistent income over those many months. As negative as that may sound, however, I can say that I managed my outlook for the future "opportunity" to change and grow despite the impact on my business. I was able to remain steadily optimistic, without "external" influences to necessarily stimulate that outlook.

In fact, if I can recall my comments to my wife about our tentative condition, it was more like: "I am excited to see which doors of opportunity will open for us during 'this' trial!" Just having that frame of mind helped both my wife and I feel more optimistic about the future and opened my mind to greater possibilities. Couple that state of mind with your own prayers to your Heavenly Father, expressing gratitude for His blessings of mental clarity and awareness to recognize opportunity... POW! And down went your trial opponent.

*Here is an interesting side-note to the above experience during the COVID-19 days... I am currently experiencing a similar "state of the real estate industry" trial to the one during the COVID-19 years, which has been caused, in part, by the ripple effect on industry products, services, and inflation. And I am once again practicing my positive self-talk and mindfulness stretching exercises to see me through this recurring feast or famine industry condition I have lived with for the past fifty-three (53) years.

I am both a "visual learner" and a "verbal processor," which is why I feel the need to provide visual examples in my writings and "one" of the reasons why, at times, I seem to "wander" off-topic a bit.

A verbal processor needs to "express" his decision-making processes (even frustrations, etc.) out loud to someone... like his spouse. It took years of doing this before I realized the power my "often negative verbal processing" had on my wife. She was a natural "processing partner." Her dominant personality trait is "listening." And her Love Language is "quality time." She has that gift of listening and not necessarily feeling the need to outdo the speaker or verbal processor while still in the middle of a thought like many of us are prone to do. But I was devastated when she finally mustered the courage to tell me she felt like going to bed after I had finished "sliming her" with my often-negative thoughts and fears. I left her depressed, with feelings of hopelessness because she didn't hear an ounce of hope in my rantings. "I" might have felt better, but she was often out for the count!

Now, I contrast that experience with my earlier story of how my real estate business had been impacted, but instead of expressing fear and uncertainty, I expressed excitement for change and about the opportunity that would surely come. At that moment, I realized again the power to influence others with our words and tone of voice (attitude of happiness) expression.

Before we move on, please indulge me with one more attempt at convincing you of the "advantages" of developing an "attitude of gratitude" (aka state of happiness), as my longtime motivational speaker hero, Zig Ziegler, often called it.

People who think positively are usually healthier than those who think negatively. The mind has a strong effect on the body and health. And when you think positively, your immune system is healthier, and your body recuperates faster. I've heard this saying before, "It isn't our position but our disposition that makes us happy."

Your attitude and how you think (your thoughts) have much to do with how you feel about yourself. If you adopt a positive attitude and think positively, you will have a better opinion of yourself, which means a more positive, healthier sense of self-esteem. Don't worry about negative people and what they think and say about you. When you have a positive attitude toward yourself, the people around you will often have a better opinion of you and treat you with more respect. A great quote comes from Francesca Reigler: "Happiness is an attitude. We either make ourselves miserable or happy and strong. The amount of work is the same."

As we finish this chapter, let me provide you with "Five Steps to a Positive Attitude."

<u>Step One</u> — Desire to change!

The fact that you spent money to purchase a book that teaches Winning Ways to "win" through trial is sufficient evidence that you have at least a trace of desire to improve your attitude–so let's keep this train a-moving down the track.

Sometimes, we must cultivate desire by listing things we want to change about ourselves. Can you recall your last trial? Not necessarily the most impactful one, but an experience or condition that took your breath away. How did you react? Are you content with the way you behaved? Is there room for improvement?

What are the chances you might win at something if you don't actually believe you can? Your answer might be, "Well, I bought a lottery ticket, not really believing I would win, but I did win," you cheer. And then I might argue that you did believe, or you never would have spent your money to purchase a lottery ticket. Either side can argue these points with varying degrees of accuracy depending upon which side you choose to take, but in the end, those who win "most often" will attest to the benefits of training their mind to "think positive."

Let's continue our training...

<u>Step Two</u> — Accept responsibility for your actions.

My mother was a sage fountain of wisdom. Not the book-learning type of wisdom, but the kind that only time on earth filled with trial can teach. Growing up, she would often catch me down in the dumps because of what someone did or didn't do to me at school. She would say: "Charles, no one can "make" you happy or sad. It is you who choose to feel those emotions."

Or, another popular lecture topic of my mother was: "No one is responsible for your happiness but you!" My mother was a very smart woman.

So, if you find yourself falling apart at the mere presence of trial, remember this truth: "Trial has no power of its own unless you plug it in." (another 'Attitude Short') You are responsible for your actions, so let's keep working toward a positive attitude.

<u>Step Three</u> — Forgive yourself... and others.

This step may seem odd at first, but I assure you my years of assisting inmates incarcerated within Arizona State prisons to make their peace with God "before" they could change the personal nature that got them into trouble in the first place gave me a front row seat to witnessing the "power" forgiveness brings to the body and mind of the forgiver, who wants to change.

Holding back forgiveness for those who have offended you and holding back forgiveness of ourselves only adds weight to the heart and cankers the soul. There is no freedom of spirit when one is carrying the weight of non-forgiveness. If you focus on what you can change and leave the rest to God, you will free yourself up to feel the peace and calmness of spirit that comes when we forgive.

<u>Step Four</u> — Avoid being *slimed* by other people–Hang out with people who reflect a happy vibe.

Do you want to know what you will be like in five years? Consider the books you read and the people you hang out with. We are heavily influenced by those with whom we associate, and what we read programs our mind for the good–or otherwise.

Let's pause for a moment to give you time to complete this exercise. With pencil and paper, write down the names of the last three books you read and the last three people you spent time with. Are you filling your mind with information to help prepare you to become all you can be? Are you spending quality time with quality people who are headed in the same direction as you? Only you can answer those questions based on your personal goals, but this little exercise serves as a gentle nudge and perhaps a course correction if needed.

<u>Step Five</u> — Practice makes perfect.

"Finally!"

Before we got to Step Five, I had to cover the other steps to a positive attitude because you might not see the power behind this simple statement: "Fake it 'Til You Make it!"

Some of you have a problem accepting the "first" step of these five steps to a positive attitude because you don't know if you have enough desire to change or are merely "dissatisfied with who you are becoming." If that's you... then Winning Way #3 is for you.

Quick Story: One Sunday, after teaching a particularly difficult gospel doctrine lesson to a class in adult Sunday School, I was approached by one of the attendees who asked, with sincerity: "Have you always been so happy? You seem to always have a smile on your face." I sobered at the question, instantly reflecting upon the "slime story" I just related to you.

"Not at all," I answered truthfully. "In fact, for many years, I allowed personal trial to define my actions, but once I had had enough of slinging slime on others, my road to recovery started by "faking it." I "pretended" to be happy whenever I was around other people, and over time it became more and more natural to feel that way."

I could not tell this person just when it happened, but it did happen just the way I am teaching you now. For me, I just got tired of being the "slimmer." I didn't necessarily see "The Five Steps to Developing a Positive Attitude" as the foundation for winning. I just started by pretending I was happy.

Certain personality temperaments discussed in this book will find this step particularly challenging, but you can still appear happy "by the words you use" when someone engages you in conversation. I started using the word "marvelous" when someone asked me how I was doing, no matter if green slime dripped down from the corners of my mouth. To this day, the first word that comes out of my mouth when asked that question is: "Marvelous!" And the green slime is gone.

If you will try this exercise for a while, I promise you will soon start to feel something different. It will likely be subtle at first, hardly noticeable, but I promise you will begin to "feel" a change before others "see" it. You were born to win–but sometimes it takes talking the talk to get your inner self to believe you can walk the walk.

Have you noticed how often negative feelings course through your body when "change is suggested?" It might be a sign that your defensive mechanism is working fine on call to ward off the presence of danger. Or, you may just be resistant to change, feeling quite comfortable the way things are, thank you–in what, you don't know. In any case, negative feelings often arise during periods of change and must be dealt with, or they will assume control and often derail your progression.

Respond to every negative feeling with a positive affirmation, and you will experience an amazing power beginning to grow within you. This "power" is positive energy. It comes as we begin to "assume responsibility for our actions" (remember Step Two?) by choosing to feed our minds with offsetting positive thoughts, which eventually lead to positive actions.

Have you ever received notice of a bill you had missed paying? What was your reaction? If you are like me, there is never a good time for such surprises, and I would often let it ruin my day. I would sulk and pout and put on a front that said: "I am hurting! I dare you to ask me what's wrong!" And I carried that sign on my face and persona for days after.

If you relate to such responses, try reacting by repeating a positive affirmation, such as: "I can handle this! I am not losing my attitude over this silly bill!" Repeat the affirmation every time you feel the negative energy start to coarse through your body before it has a chance to lay eggs in your brain. I mean, is that not a great visual when you begin to feel negative thoughts–big, white (colored or with stripes?) eggs being laid in the cavity of your brain? That is precisely what happens when you "allow" *the* negative to control your thoughts and emotions, taking control of your actions.

You cannot always control what happens to you, but you can determine how you will respond. When negative thoughts begin to lay eggs in your brain, retaliate with positive affirmations until the eggs disappear. Do not let them hatch!

Filling your mind with positive affirmations also creates a time delay so that you are not led by your negative energy to do or say something you might very well regret later. Sending a hastily written email response or Facebook post to the cause of your negative energy might prove the worst course of action. Sometimes, "thanking" an employer for terminating you is more effective than going to social media or sending a nasty letter of retribution, given that you are gone anyway. And no one can criticize your behavior for taking a positive approach to trial.

Life in the "positive zone" isn't always positive because we are mortals, after all, and subject to the natural man (if it feels good, do it) within us. Negative thoughts will still coarse through your mind, but in time, you will learn how to handle those thoughts like a piece of junk mail–they are not worth opening.

<u>If you want to make this book more than just a good read, then take a few moments and write down those conditions in your life that put</u>

you in the negative zone.

QUESTION: What was the first thing that came to your mind when you searched your mind for what is negative in your life right now? Is it something within your ability to change? If so, write a solution next to the negative condition or attitude–take responsibility and write down "how" you will change it.

If you cannot think of a solution right now to your most pressing negative situation, then begin opening your mind to receive such answers by writing a positive affirmation such as, "I am in control of my life. My mind is open to solutions. I repel negative thoughts the moment they enter my brain. I absorb positive energy. My heart walks with God daily. I cannot tolerate negative energy, so I replace it with positive thoughts and affirmations. I look for opportunities to become better (not bitter) when negative enters my life…" and so on, "repeating at least ten times per session, three times per day."

With today's access to online information, you only need to Google "positive affirmation" to help you "personalize" positive programming–to help you move closer to defeating negative energy–by replacing it with a generally positive attitude equipped with a plan to keep you between the lines.

While ministering to the inmates incarcerated in Arizona prisons, I learned a very valuable lesson: Our very nature can change. Mostly, I am referring to the hardcore criminal types–but so can the neighbor next door change, our kids can change, and even you and I can change, given the right motivation and desire.

Our personal nature can change–to become better *or* to be-

come bitter.

One of the guiding goals of writing "Winning Thru Trial" was to provide you with more than inspiration and encouragement, with a few captivating stories thrown in to keep your interest. I wanted to equip you with proven ideas and practices you could implement immediately, even before reaching the last page of this book. I hope you have found that to be true thus far in your reading. In that same spirit, I offer these suggested "attitude" books as having been very helpful in my own recovery from "negative-itess:"

Recommended Books to Influence Positive Thinking:
- "How to Win Friends and Influence People" — Dale Carnegie
- "The Power of Positive Thinking" — Dr. Norman Vincent Peale
- "How to Have Confidence and Power…" — Les Giblin
- Og Mandino books (I think my favorite is "The Choice.")
- "Attitude is Everything" — Vicki Hitzges (Franklin-Covey)
- "Think and Grow Rich" — Napoleon Hill

Positive affirmation author:
- Shad Helmstetter

YOU'VE GOT STYLE!

As we close out this chapter on attitude, let me point out again that changing our nature from negative to positive takes a lot of work, patience, forgiveness, and time. In the process of winning–we fail over and over again. It's like a dance, two steps to the right and one to the left, and what we often don't realize is a combination of these dance steps that develops our "style." As our attitude begins to change, so does our behavior, which is reflected in our personality. This combination of attitude, behavior, and personality is what I call "style," which we are constantly in a state of "developing/becoming" throughout our entire life and beyond.

Style is what makes us interesting. Our individual style will be our trademark as we go through life... changing, adjusting, improving, developing, and becoming. It is what will endear us to those we love. It is what will be reflected upon at our funeral and remembered as our legacy. It is what makes us different. It is what makes us "great!"

Our beloved John Wayne (RIP) played a character known as Rooster Cogburn in the movie *True Grit*. He was anything but perfect, this rugged man of the Wild West, but he had style.

Throughout the movie, the character of Rueben (Rooster) Cogburn is portrayed as cold, rude, and insensitive to love. His reputation as a U.S. Deputy Marshall brought him much acclaim, enhanced by fear that the stories of his quick hand on the gun and cold nature were true.

Sporting a patch over one eye, which hid its loss from a gunfight, added to his character. But his unique walk, eye patch, and giant frame, with an occasional hint of softness, endeared us to his "style."

I shall never forget the most intense action scene towards the end of *True Grit*, where Marshall Cogburn rode out to face an outlaw band of desperados... totally outnumbered, and with the horse reins in his teeth and twin revolvers in each hand, he rode straight at them with both guns blazing. I remember thinking, "That is how I want to go out, living life to the fullest, guns a-blazing, reins in my teeth, and charging hard to meet the next trial head-on." Now that's style. That's also "choice."

Style brings "interest" to a personality. A person's style often radiates their habits, tastes, actions, moral standards, even economic level... and of course, the subject of this chapter – "Attitude!"

A person's attitude is reflected in so many ways within a person's style: how they walk, talk, dress, drive, act, treat others, treat themselves, perform tasks, etc. I suppose style in terms of attitude could also be detrimental to achieving success in life if society does not consider our actions and choices to be acceptable. But maybe a person's undesirable style might prove to be more successful [for a time] within the illegal framework of society. Or even prove to be a benefit while incarcerated in a confined institution. A person who joins the military soon finds out that their former "style" will need to adapt to the military's rigid interpretation of style and is not open to civilian "styles."

I like to think of myself as having "style" as I experienced life... as a high school athlete, musician, drummer, Eagle Scout, Boys State Rep, religious pioneer, church missionary, student of higher learning, romantic, husband, father, college graduate, breadwinner, entrepreneur, home builder, failure, direct marketing achiever, landlord, Realtor© 53+ yrs, public speaker, franchisee, builder/developer, failure, church activist, prison minister, grandfather, temple sealer, stake patriarch, married 57 years, writer/author, and Podcaster.

As you follow the various steps of life I have encountered, as written above, you will see "steps," and then you will also see landing platforms, even steps that descended, but "all" steps & platforms combined to form my "style." Back then, I didn't see myself as a winner after my first failure. I didn't see my losses as an "opportunity for growth" and to develop "hidden talents and spiritual gifts," as discussed in Chapter Five of this book; nonetheless, each step and platform contributed to developing my style.

I invite you to take a few moments before moving into Chapter Four (*Choice Defines Character*) and create your own "steps of life" timeline, knowing that if you are reading this book, you are still creating yours, and it is still within your power to change, to develop the type of style you want to be known for, "no matter your age."

"You can't help getting older, but you don't have to get old."
– George Burns

According to "Ranker.com" and stage and screen actor George Burns... you can still accomplish incredible things after you turn 50.

- Gladys Burrill earned the Guinness Book of World Records record as the oldest female to complete a marathon. At age 92, she finished the race, which took place in Honolulu, in nine hours, 53 minutes and 16 seconds.

- In 1987, Teiichi Igarashi, a former lumberjack who had been climbing Mt. Fuji every year since he was 89 years old, became the first centenarian to climb Japan's tallest mountain. Igarashi attributed his accomplishment to eating raw eggs and all the encouragement he received from his supporters.

- In 2013, on her fifth attempt and at age 64, Diana Nyad became the first person confirmed to swim from Cuba to Florida without the aid of a shark cage. The journey was 110 miles long and took her 53 hours straight.

- Grandma Moses, the spry, indomitable "genuine American primitive" who became one of the country's most famous artists, turned out her first painting at the age of 76. She took up painting because arthritis had crippled her hands so she could no longer embroider. Later, her art was hanging at the Museum of Modern Art in New York.

- Colonel Sanders was 65 years old when he received his first Social Security check. It was then that he decided that he needed to change his life. With his chicken recipe, he took action and traveled the nation until someone took a chance on him, and Kentucky Fried Chicken was born.

- Peter Roget began keeping lists of words as a young man but didn't publish "his" first thesaurus until he was 73. His collection of synonyms and antonyms was not the first to appear, but his was far better organized than others' previous efforts.

- Nelson Mandela was elected president of South Africa in 1993, serving one term in office. He was the first non-white head of state in South Africa's history and the first to take office following the dismantling of apartheid and the introduction of multiracial democracy. He was also the oldest head of state in South Africa's history, taking office at the age of 75.

Even if your birth years might indicate you are "over the hill" and unable to contribute successfully to society, you can still accomplish incredible things. "You still got style!" And you still have time to "add" to your style. So, let's do this... Let's choose to wake up tomorrow morning with a fresh "attitude" that says: "I got style!" Choose to make a difference. Choose to continue "becoming!" Choose to look at trial as your ally, your trainer, your coach–your link to having an intimate relationship with your God–a key to unlocking the greatness within you.

Let's hear it... **"I got style!"**

Chapter Four

Choice Defines Character

"Life is 10% what happens to you and 90% how you react to it" — **Charles R. Swindoll**

One night, while George (not his real name) waited in the shadows behind a regular distribution point near his apartment, excitement from the promise of a big sale caused his stomach to turn flips... and blinded his awareness that the buy was staged. The minute George handed over the white package hidden in his coat and reached for the envelope extended to him, steel cuffs were snapped over his wrists before George could get away. George was subsequently sentenced to ten years in prison for dealing drugs to minors. The judge was sending a message to others like George that selling drugs to minors would not be tolerated.

When I first met George, he was a guest of a fellow inmate at one of our Sunday church services sponsored by the Church of Jesus Christ of Latter-day Saints in one of the Arizona State Prison complex units. His fellow bunkie, a regular attendee, whispered before introducing George: "He really needs God in his life right now. His wife just served him with divorce papers, with no chance of seeing his kid while in prison or after."

After speaking to George briefly before the service began, I became aware that this man was mad at the world, as are the many inmates who considered themselves "innocent" of the crime they were charged with, which brought them to prison. But George did not blame others for his confinement, nor did he shift responsibility for his actions. He blamed himself entirely and refused to forgive himself as well. Because of that attitude, George considered himself a "loser" and therefore just waited out his time before being returned to society a free man with possibly less than ten years (for good behavior) taken from his life–yet the only trade he possessed was how to deal drugs, and would likely end up right back in prison, like so many in similar circumstances. The recidivism rate for released felons is very high–mostly over sixty percent. And those are the ones that are caught.

Our Arizona prison system seems content with incarceration rather than rehabilitation, so there is little chance that a felon who has been incarcerated for years will make it on his own, outside, without family support. There is something to be said for two good meals a day and a form of acceptance amongst like offenders–and many released felons find out that "freedom" is neither free nor comfortable. Being dropped off at a street curb in downtown Phoenix, with no place to stay, no phone, no money to buy more than a day or two of existence–no job, no car. How many of us would survive after being removed from the invention of current technology for years and be expected to survive from day one?

Okay, off my soap box and back to my experience with George. I understand that there are many factors at play in prison administration, and because I do not have all the answers, I will avoid calling out those tasked with caring for the incarcerated. But that does not remove the frustration many volunteers feel as we try to bring change to the lost and forgotten, only to be checkmated by the "system."

Something inside me connected with George. Deep down, he was a good man, a child of God like me, but for his choices and circumstances, our paths may never have crossed. I reached out to George, one man to another, but there was no connection… yet!

Over the subsequent weeks and months, I saw a change come over George, which startled me. Because I didn't see him regularly when I visited the prison, I didn't see the subtle changes coming as George was taught "why" to make correct choices. He first had to "want" to change–and the rock that encased his heart didn't break loose easily. But the trial of losing his wife and son and the frustration of being locked up miles away and unable to do anything about it finally made George want to change.

The first hint of subtle change came one Thursday night during scripture study class with a smaller group who typically attended on Sundays. George would sit and stare during the readings and discussion. We were careful not to push any inmate into a corner with a direct question that would embarrass him in front of the other inmates. Still, our scripture study classes were smaller, allowing us to involve the attendees directly.

It was a question to another brother that caused his hand to rise. It was not an enthusiastic raise of the hand, more like a Harley Davidson rider might wave at another cycle brother when passing on the road–subtle and very "subdued," but it was a signal that he had a question.

"How do I change?"

Before I could ask George to clarify his question, he said, "How do I recover from my mistakes?" Then another question–"How do I become happy?"

"Wow!" I thought as my co-teacher, and I looked at one another in surprise.

"You just decide that today you are going to take control and stop letting circumstances ruin your day," came a soft reply from the brother sitting next to George.

"Happiness is a choice, George," I added, casting a confirming smile at George's seatmate. "It is more about putting yourself into a happy state of mind than how you feel when you wake up each morning. You start with being grateful for what God has given you, however small and insignificant that may be." Before proceeding, I let that sink in a moment since he still had his eyes open. I was hoping that signaled that his mind was also willing to listen.

"You must forgive yourself for failing yesterday and look forward to today without carrying the burden with you. God sent his Son into the world to relieve us of the burden of failure. If we would but repent and cast our burden aside, looking forward to a brighter day, we can one day come to taste the 'sweetness' of our trials," I concluded before moving on to another question by one of the other inmates, leaving George to ponder over what I had said. Without realizing it, George had given me a huge spiritual boost, as the spirit confirmed that he was finally opening his heart to change.

George, and many like him, have let the Light of Christ dim over the years from making choices that led them further away from God than towards Him. For those who may be unfamiliar with this term, the Light of Christ is one of Heavenly Father's gifts to all humanity (John 1:9). Some may refer to this Light as our "conscience," a compass of sorts to warn us when we cross the line leading away from the source of the light–our Heavenly Father.

While all born into this earthly life and receive a body of flesh and bones are equipped with this Light..the principle of "agency" allows us to either enhance this Light or shut it off altogether. George, by his "choices," had rationalized his way into a life of illegal activity, which led to his incarceration. But the great news of the atonement is that Heavenly Father's eternal flame of hope embedded in each of us–a honing device of sorts, albeit dimmed over time to appear dark and forgotten, can be restored.

George's newly acquired desire to change was somehow ignited to express the pent-up frustrations that had buried themselves for years, digging deeper and deeper into his soul until the flame of hope had been extinguished. Deep down, George had a good heart–someone had once loved him, and time in prison had given him plenty of time to think. His invitation to attend a prison church service held by The Church of Jesus Christ of Latter-day Saints would nurture that once-upon-a-time feeling of being loved, and by his own "choices," George would begin the road back to spiritual nourishment, led by the Light.

My prior belief that human nature can change was enhanced by my front-row seat to the blessings of the atonement in action, even in the dark and dank confines of a worldly prison. God sees through our façade–those emotional blockades set in place to keep the Light from reminding, from offering... tugging at our remembrances–and He is relentless in His pursuit to bring each of His children safely home. "And this is my work and my glory to bring to pass the immortality and eternal nature of man." (Moses 1:9). Yet He would not deny us the choice of exercising agency in deciding how we would react to trial.

The principle of choice was instituted into mortality at the beginning of time. Adam and Eve were given a choice whether to eat of the forbidden fruit or not. Their choices defined their future–and ours.

Like Adam and Eve, George's choices–reaction to trial–defined his future. And now, years later, this same principle allowed George to begin the process of repentance... and forgiveness.

The subsequent months after George's choice to open his heart to change brought a gradual restoration of the Light and revealed pronounced changes to his hardened core. Change is constant in prison life for many reasons. Eventually, George was transferred to another area within the vast confines of the Arizona State Prison, placing him in a smaller confinement of fellow inmates and a much smaller gathering of Thursday and Sunday worshippers. But he still continued to attend.

It had been several weeks since I had seen George due to his change of residency to another section of the prison, and my heart leaped for joy when I spotted his small frame encased in an orange jumpsuit stride through the classroom door as if he owned the place. There was an air of confidence about him I had not seen before but was definitely present now. George had made friends with fellow Christian inmates who had similar issues and concerns, and he was visibly feeling better about himself.

I learned that George was faithful in writing positive affirmations regularly and then mailed them to his wife... or x-wife, as he assumed. However, she must have noticed the change in George from those affirmations because she held up the divorce proceedings and waited to see what was going on with George. And she was not disappointed, apparently. And neither was I.

During services on the first Sunday of each month, the inmate attendees were encouraged to share their feelings by bearing a testimony. Each brother would stand before the others present and tell of his feelings. I generally needed more than one tissue to capture the falling tears springing from my emotions during those special times. One would read a poem he had either received or written. Another would tell of a recent visit from his church mentor / ministering brother, or in George's case, express gratitude for the atonement and life-restoring forgiveness he had felt through the process of repentance.

George had begun to taste the "sweetness" of Christ's atonement in his own life, which showed in his face and step. His circumstances had not changed, but his choices of how he would respond had now taken on a different persona, with a lighter heart–and hope for a relationship with his family.

George's story was still being written when my prison service ended after five years and being honored by the State of Arizona as Volunteer of the Year, a distinction I never coveted nor sought. Still, I could not express in words my surprise at receiving it since the selection came from the prison administration and not the men themselves. But the award received paled compared to the satisfaction I felt from assisting men like George through their trial–and their becoming better because of it.

I have thought often about what choices made earlier in George's life led him to make the choice that led him to incarceration. When the Light of Christ dims within us, it affects our ability to make correct choices. The Light of Christ assists in absorbing correct principles in our life, which guides our choices–in becoming who we are.

Without this guiding "Light" of Christ burning brightly within us, we are more susceptible to what is called in scripture the "natural man" (1 Cor. 2:14, see Mosiah 1-3) within us, no matter our gender. I call this the "if it feels good, do it" part of humanity or giving in to the "carnal desires of the heart."

This carnal condition is a result of the fall of Adam and Eve, choosing to eat from the Tree of Good and Evil while in the Garden of Eden. Were it not for their choices, Adam and Eve would never have had children (here comes the "joy and pain" part) to gain the experience necessary to fulfill the purposes of God.

The Book of 2 Nephi teaches in verse 25 that "Adam fell that man might be, and men are that they might have joy." The type of "joy" referred to in this scripture is the kind that leads to everlasting happiness and comes from choosing to feed our spiritual growth (lasting joy) over satisfying our carnal appetites (temporary pleasure).

As we make choices to feed our spiritual light, it makes it harder for Satan to deceive us, for we now see clearer. Our conscience burns a little "hotter," and we are warned of impending danger. George's choices, however, were more about satisfying his carnal joy and less and less about seeking what brought spiritual growth... until his mind was opened through trial.

It sounds a little complex–but simply speaking, our choices define our character–and our character influences our choices.

We are put in a position daily to make decisions at every turn:

- Do I go to bed early enough to give my body sufficient time to recover?
- Do I get up early and accomplish things I would not usually get done?
- Do I brush my teeth twice a day as the ADA recommends?
- Do I lean into the gas pedal when I see a yellow light?
- Does it matter that I am habitually late for appointments?
- Do I read scriptures today? Do I ponder over what I read?
- Do I stand when a woman enters the room?
- Do I play with matches?
- Do I wear a seatbelt? Sometimes? All times?
- Do I exercise today or pass?

- Today, did I say, "I am sorry" or "I love you" to someone who matters?
- Did I think about helping someone other than me today?
- Did I feed my spiritual self "more" than my carnal self today?

I could go on, but you get the point. Each choice–simple by itself, when combined with another and another, becomes absorbed into forming our nature–and very well may lead us to Heaven or Hell.

Sometimes, we make wrong choices, no matter the strength of character within us. Life is not about making correct choices "every time!" It is about making choices and learning from them, doing our best but recovering from choices that do not turn out as expected.

As a guest speaker, I once shared with a group that I had learned more from poor choices than my correct ones. Boy, did that honest admission cause more than a few lifted eyebrows! Knowing I may be responsible for a stampede of lemmings headed over a cliff, I had to do some quick clarification.

"Before you all decide to run out of here and rob a bank or something, let me explain," I responded quickly. And before you, the reader, misinterpret my bold "learning" declaration, let me clarify.

When bad choices are made, it often opens the door to more bad decisions, such as in George's case, leading him to prison. This in itself is not the stimulus of learning–not yet. The learning comes when sufficient "pain" is inflicted, a state of humility is attained, and the acknowledgment of error is felt.

The Holy Bible contains numerous accounts of how God strengthened those He loves (all of us). He sent tribulation through wars, famines, plagues, and other attention-getting devices and conditions. Some may interpret these acts as punishment rather than a "show" of love, but our Heavenly Father knows our nature better than we do, and He knows without fire, there is no purification. Without fire, we never reach our true potential. And without pain, there is no need for self-examination.

Unless we look inside at who we are becoming due to our choices, we may only see clearly enough after it is too late. Individual Pain, discomfort, inconvenience, and loss are common denominators in becoming all we can be.

I often jest with the Lord (yes, He has a sense of humor) that it would be okay to bless me with wealth because I can handle it (LOL). If you are into scripture reading, you caught my little tongue-in-cheek comment. Worldly wealth is often the cause of pride among Father's earthly children–and pride often comes before the fall, as recorded repeatedly in Holy Scripture.

I can attest that it has been my financial failures and not during periods of plenty that have filled the barn with spiritual growth and nourishment–but sometimes not until "after" I had rebelled, showed pride, and fallen lower before I reached a point in my life where I was humble enough to ask with sincere humility for God to open a few doors for me to walk through, leading me back to safety.

I believe the key to making good choices lies in how we train ourselves to respond to bad choices, which doesn't usually present itself until we experience pain and suffering. Those conditions offer up another set of choices on how we will react–do we become bitter or better? Proud or humble? Do we sit down on the curb, or do we finish the race?

Winning Way #4 — Opportunity, look for it!

Recognizing the opportunity in trial sounds more challenging than it is. More often than not, you have likely experienced opportunity in former trials, but they were disguised as something other than opportunity at the time. But when looking back, without your vision distorted by the emotions of the trial, you tend to see more clearly. What if we could "learn" to see more clearly during the trial?

I certainly did not see the opportunity on my fourth "failed" attempt at producing a retirement income. I had carried forward the emotional scars from previous failed attempts at becoming a financial hero to my family, and I was about to be blindsided once again.

My last construction project ended in 2008, amidst the turmoil of the real estate meltdown, assisted by the deregulation of the financial industry and resulting in widespread foreclosures and plunging our national economy into the abyss of the Great Recession.

As I mentioned in the Preface of this book, I was somewhat sheltered by what was going on around me while finishing up my out-of-town construction project, other than I knew house prices were rising so fast that my wife and I quickly sold our almost new "move-down" home for a much "larger" older one in a neighborhood we had wanted to live in for quite some time. Our rationale was that if prices kept rising, our larger (and older) home would soon be worth "much" more than we had paid for it.

Also, I had entered into an agreement with a business associate to form a partnership owning and managing a longtime dream of mine–Self Storage. I would receive a monthly fee for putting everything together and managing the asset, plus 49% of the business. Things were finally looking up for the MaloneZone!

Six months later...

It was a bright and beautiful morning as I found a parking spot in front of the Pinal County Building Department. "Yes! This is going to be a great day," I remember celebrating with a big smile on my face. I reached for the cashier's check lying on the dashboard of my Silverado pickup to pay for the building permit, which would begin the process of constructing the first of at least three self-storage facilities, but stopped abruptly when my cell phone rang. I still remember that call and my reaction to it even today.

The voice on the other end of the call was that of my financial partner, asking if I had already paid for the building permit. A feeling of dread began to creep up my throat and practically cut off my breath as I tried to push out a response to his question. It came out more like a squeak than a man's voice, but my shaky answer of "no" drew a relieved reaction from the other end of the conversation.

"Please turn around and come back to the office," he instructed, with more emotion than he had probably intended. "The bank has withdrawn their support, and we cannot fund the project," he completed, with solemnity replacing the emotion in his voice. My partner, years later, took his own life.

When trial strikes, the pull of the natural man within each of us will try to bring us down if left unchecked. Having survived years of depression from failed attempts at success, I was immediately assaulted with a dredging of former negative voices. I can't remember how long I sat in my truck before gaining the strength to insert the key to return home, but I do remember the numbness wearing off before I turned the key and my pleading prayer to my Heavenly Father to guide me safely home to my waiting family.

I had one hour–sixty minutes of "distance run" to prepare myself emotionally before arriving home in the middle of the day to let my wife know that our funding was pulled. Our future was once again in jeopardy.

Instead of criticizing myself, second-guessing what I could have done differently, or "allowing" myself to dwell on the parade of passing negative thoughts and implications–"I 'chose' to express my gratitude for what I did have," in the form of positive prayer and affirmations. I knew I needed to keep my mind from shutting down, so after offering a humble prayer to God, I repeated out loud these learned positive affirmations to combat the negative natural man assault:

- I know this, too, will pass.

- I know how to provide for my family.

- God will be at my side, guiding me through this.

- I can do this.

- I will not give in to negative thoughts.

- I have God's strength to embrace me.

- I will learn from this experience and become better because of it.

- With God's help, I can do hard things.

- My mind is open to solutions.

- I love opposition, for it makes me think and grow. Bring it on! (I think I was pounding the steering wheel with this one.)

You get the point. By the time I reached home, I was in a much better frame of mind to address this situation with my wife, as I calmly explained what had happened and to please shut down any unnecessary expenditure(s) until I could come up with a solution. I wanted to shout and scream and beat myself over the head as my beautiful wife just shook her head in agreement. Her only question was: "What would you like for dinner?" She had been through this same scenario so many times before, and she knew we would survive–but the tiredness of it all showed through her façade as she walked to the panty and began preparation for dinner, shoulders squared as she stood and just stared, expressionless.

Please remember this positive affirmation... and blend it into your soul if you can: "When one door closes, another opens." Although I do not remember repeating that affirmation at the time of the trial related above, I have used it many times since, and it has become a strength and source of hope for me. It embodies Winning Way #4–to expect solutions, to be alert for impressions and doors to open that were not there before. As my mother would say, "Listen to your body, Charles."

When trial strikes, step back for a nanosecond and do a quick check of what is "right" in your life before following the natural man instinct of putting your fist through the wall and having to pay a drywall tech to fix it. I was usually quick to do the latter, but in this case, I was "once again" shocked over having the "brass ring" snatched from my grasp. And I was once again unemployed.

My wife and I would be okay for the time being, and although I was not overly concerned with the loss of monthly income as part of my financial arrangement with my partner, I was devastated over the loss of opportunity to secure a retirement vehicle for my wife and me. Our five children had each grown into self-supporting adults and left the nest to create their legacy, leaving us (now) empty nesters in a very large home we had recently purchased… and wondering, "What were we thinking?"

I began my chosen profession in the real estate industry in 1971 in the rural setting of Mesa and Gilbert, Arizona, and considered myself well-connected and highly experienced in just about every facet of real estate. My resume looked like a cat with nine lives; I had been blessed with many opportunities over the years, each adding another layer of experience and perspective. And I had also added age.

Ah, the elephant in the closet–age! Of course, I knew it was there, but I was counting on my experience in many facets of real estate to keep others from noticing it. "Once word was out I was available, the phone would start ringing," I assured myself during times of self-talk.

(Note: I had not yet developed an automatic response for keeping my mind positive during trial and soon became easy prey for Mr. Negative once my expectations were not realized.)

Life does not hide from you just because you have trial.

As weeks of job searching turned into months without even one interview, my resolve to stay positive began to wane. During this dark period, our married daughter with five children developed breast cancer. As you read this, you are probably wondering, "Where is the opportunity in this?" And I would have responded at the time, "Great question!"

This might be the time to explain once again the definition of "opportunity" as intended within the pages of this book. Webster's Dictionary defines opportunity as: "A favorable juncture of circumstances; a good chance for advancement or progress." But I think I like this one best, leaving room to script your own situation: "A set of circumstances that makes it possible to do something." Isn't that an excellent, inventive definition? It still leaves you "choice" to decide what "something" will be!

Now, in case you have forgotten that the title of this chapter is about "choice," I want you to consider choosing to always look at the positive side of trial rather than the negative side. If you want to make a meaningful impact in this world of negative thinkers, which is a very noble goal, then choose to think positively and look for the opportunity to advance or progress "in something important to you."

When my wife and I learned of our daughter's health challenges, exacerbated by no insurance and no job while finishing law school, the big home we had purchased for the two of us and had questioned our actions for a year afterward–now became home to five young, and very active children. The upstairs primary bedroom was as large as an average apartment, so my wife and I turned the rest of the home over to our daughter's family for the next two and a half years while we successfully battled for her life, together.

C A N C E R. There may not be a more feared word in the English language–but when it turns personal, there isn't a word strong enough to describe it. All concerns about our own financial condition took a backseat to our daughter's health and well-being once this dreaded word was uttered as a diagnosis. We geared up for the biggest battle of our lives.

Remember my challenge to "think positive" when trial strikes? While the effects of this challenge may be debated as having little or no effect toward preventing or curing serious diseases, it can profoundly affect "how you live" during such trial. When we are in a negative state of mind, we tend to lose ambition, energy, and hope, often missing the "opportunity" to change and grow from our trial–even if the eventual outcome is life-ending. Please remember that trial is not just about you and me, the recipient(s) of trial, but trial also impacts those closest to you and even those who know you and are watching from afar. Our positive energy can give hope to others when trial knocks on their door.

I hesitated to bring health conditions into this section of the book because for the American Medical Association (AMA) or the American Cancer Society (ACS) to endorse such mental therapy as positive thinking and self-affirmations, their case studies would have to show results without question–which they do not.

The ACS offers this advice: "People with cancer and their families may sometimes feel guilty about their emotional response to illness. They may feel pressure to keep a "good attitude" at all times, which is unrealistic. This feeling of pressure can come from within themselves, from other people, or both. Sadness, depression, guilt, fear, and anxiety are all normal parts of grieving and learning to cope with major life changes. Trying to ignore these feelings or not talking with others about them can make the person with cancer feel lonely. It can also make the emotional pain worse. And some people feel guilty or blame themselves when they can't "stay positive," which only adds to their emotional burden." -American Cancer Society Website

While I do not necessarily "disagree" with a generic statement from a nationwide entity charged with eradicating this terrible disease from the earth, I applaud those who "choose to remain positive" while in the eye of the storm, looking for opportunity rather than dwelling on the normal parts of grieving sufficiently to take them down. Still, I understand and support the right to choose by those who do not, and by no means intend anything written in this book to point fingers or intentionally make someone feel less than encouraged, no matter their choices in life. We are each on the same side when trial strikes, and each has agency to choose how best to react.

I, too, have felt the "emotional burden" from trial as a natural effect of grieving, in the form of sadness, depression, guilt, fear, and anxiety–as I am a mortal man, a sinner falling way below Christ's challenge to "Be ye therefore perfect..." (Matthew 5:48).

But I also believe that perfection is a process that will continue beyond the grave, and this "second estate" of mortality (earth life) is to "experience" those emotions associated with opposition and trial so that we might better learn how to grow from them.

Growth, in my world, is "Failing Forward." Remaining positive through trial is a goal–a sought-for-attitude to keep you from succumbing to the pull to "stay down," and should help you feel en-couraged rather than dis-couraged.

Writing about trials of any kind is a sensitive topic, easily ignited when differing opinions are expressed, which is why I support choice as a means of defining one's legacy. Whether you use none or many of the Winning Ways I have included in this writing, it is your choice as a human being entitled to agency. I do not claim to have scientific "proof" of the effectiveness of positive over negative thinking to affect the outcome of all health issues, such as those described above. However, there are strong proponents of both. I do, however, defer to a higher law contained within revealed scripture as the word of God to all humanity, citing "faith" as a curing agent against our natural instinct to always require proof of all things before believing.

The Bible's definition of faith is found in Hebrews 11:1: "Now faith is the substance of things hoped for, the evidence of things not seen." <u>Faith is the prayer before the answer. Prayer unlocks the door to change–Faith is our escort when we choose to walk through that door.</u> It all begins as hope, but acquired faith can move mountains (Matthew 17:20) or draw upon the powers of Heaven to heal (Matthew 9:27-30), as Jesus Christ taught in this stirring scripture of two blind men asking to be healed. Jesus asked them if they "believed" (faith) He could do this, and they both responded, "Yes, Lord." Then His message to all humanity followed– "According to your faith, let it be to you." And their eyes were opened!

Winning Way #4 only asks that you "open your eyes to opportunity," as these two blind men were blessed to have their sight restored–through faith.

It was prayer, expressing my cry for help to recover from severe depression stemming from the loss of our first business, which led to opportunity presenting itself one morning in Lake Tahoe in the form of a Doctor golfing partner specializing in depression, which put me on the road to recovery. It was faith, ignited by hope, which led me to follow my Doctor's unique prescribed instructions for replacing the negative energy that had coursed throughout my body and mind for years.

It is my choice to believe that faith is critical in recognizing opportunity in trial.

Our eyes are most often blinded to opportunity when in the eye of a trial. According to scripture, earth life was not designed to be a walk in the park at all times–that was life in Eden. Mother Eve's declaration to Father Adam after choosing to partake of the forbidden fruit of the tree was that "sorrow was necessary to distinguish between good and evil." It takes faith to believe in something which cannot be seen but is true. And it is often not until the storm has passed that our eyes are opened to see what was disguised as opportunity. Wouldn't it be great to gain an attitude of– "opportunity, look for it"–when trial strikes rather than after? Mother Eve seemed to understand this concept in her wise persuasion of Adam to partake (opportunity) and learn.

Failure is merely the key to the door of opportunity toward becoming.

"FROM CHICKEN COUP TO COUNTRY MANSION – An American True Love Story."

Don and Wendy had both tasted the sorrow of early life's choices and yet found one another to experience joy. Life's choices for one created opportunity for the other, and Don saw the opportunity.

They were a young married couple with big dreams and an immediate family of four small boys aged four and under. "We felt like we could accomplish anything," recalls Wendy, after experiencing the joy of finding one another. And they set out to prove that feeling of invincibility by starting their own business. And they lived happily ever after–except that they didn't.

Wouldn't it be wonderful if life always worked out the way we planned? I admit to being hooked on Hallmark TV Movies (Yes, I have grown to become a 'chic-flick' fan). I think I am drawn to these movies because they are safe. Now, don't get me wrong here–I also love drama and strategy and hero-type movies with a good dose of mystery thrown in. But Hallmark producers have developed a winning recipe with such ingredients as romance, a simple storyline, conflict and drama, and happy endings. It is the safe, happy ending to which I am drawn. However, it is but a few minutes of escape before I am thrown right back into the ring of life to continue becoming–tasting both sorrow and joy.

Don and Wendy would fail at their first attempt as business owners. It sounded too good to be true, and it was.

They were a little smarter during the next venture, but the results were the same non-Hallmark movie ending–the next two attempts at building their own business as entrepreneurs also failed.

Please let me clarify the word failure as I choose to define it. It is such a negative word and sends a message of finality, yet it is anything but final. Final is when you depart from your second estate (aka earthly experience), leaving behind that mortal body to return to dust, having served you for whatever time was allowed.

If we choose to have faith that all experience is for our good, meaning that we always take something with us after the trial has passed, having tasted both joy and sorrow and having gained perspective, conditioning, knowledge, and wisdom–even change of nature, perhaps. Is that failure? It has taken me years of experience to develop the faith to believe that failure is the key to the door of opportunity toward becoming.

Realizing they were both still alive, Don and Wendy put their faith to the test once again and decided to try their hand at building a home in anticipation of selling it for a profit. Although many stories of success exist in building and selling "spec" houses, including several of my own... times and seasons in Grove, Oklahoma, were not conducive to speculative ventures by young and naïve entrepreneurs like our stars in this non-Hallmark story.

With everything riding upon their success, this young family found themselves homeless, without the resources to care for themselves and their children because they refused to declare bankruptcy and lost all they had in an attempt at righting the ship.

With no money and now deeper in debt than ever, Don, Wendy, and the four children packed up their beater truck and drove to Monett, Missouri, where Wendy's sister and her husband owned and operated a dairy business. Not calling before their arrival, the little family sat crammed inside the truck for what seemed an eternity while the parents considered how they would ask for help.

Finally opening the driver's side door, Don set his eyes on a small, frame-cladded building a few hundred feet from the main house and began walking to it while Wendy and the travel-weary boys climbed out of the truck one by one. All heads turned toward the little building as clucking sounds of chickens being chased out of their house began to break the chill of the early morning air, followed by Don sporting a most satisfied grin. He had just discovered a housing opportunity.

"We needed the shelter more than the chickens did," remembers Don, as he began right then to turn this little shed into a home for his family while Wendy and the boys walked to the farmhouse to break the news to her sister that they were homeless and needed a place to stay.

After shoveling seven wheelbarrows of chicken manure out of the building, Don hit pay-dirt in the form of a concrete floor. "We scoured what was to be the floor of our new home with bleach and then evicted the small–and large rodents who had previously made themselves a home there," Don remembers proudly.

The small, two-room structure had been built in the early 1900s, as evidenced by the dates of old newspapers wrapped around oak studs, acting as a form of insulation underneath the old lap siding, which was nailed to the studs, serving as the only barrier between the little family and the outside elements.

An old pot belly stove was located in one of the two rooms, connected somewhat to a rickety and incredibly old chimney–illuminated by a single light bulb hanging from the ceiling. With some skill and lots of farmer ingenuity from Wendy's brother-in-law, a loft was added above the stove, which was only four feet tall at its apex, leaving room for a few small mattresses as the boys' sleeping quarters and stern instructions against any horseplay that may bring down the new bedroom.

The fact that this home did not have running water, bathroom facilities, laundry room, plumbing, electricity other than one single light bulb, and heat from a pot-bellied stove did not dampen the spirits of the family one bit. That is until one night, they discovered a chimney fire in the little home in time to rescue the boys from what could have been a severe accident. With only minor smoke damage to the ceiling and walls and a newly cleaned chimney, the family settled in again to make this little coop a home.

"Happiness begins on the inside," I once heard a friend declare. Although I might beg to differ that in my case, it began by faking it on the outside, Don chose to embrace their trial as an opportunity for growth and, as Wendy remembers with much concern at the time, continued praying for obstacles to make them grow, in between offering thanks and rejoicing over what they did have.

"Don, do you think it would be okay to stop praying for problems now, just for a little while?" Wendy remembers asking as tough times settled in like thick fog over San Francisco. She remembers Don's unwavering answer that it would actually be those problems that would ultimately be their rescuer from their current plight. "If we embrace opposition as our friend and not as our enemy," Don offered, "we will grow sufficient to figure out the solution to our problems, which will develop talents and abilities we would never had otherwise."

"Sacrifice brings forth the blessings of Heaven," Don loved to say, quoting a scripture found in the book, Doctrine and Covenants, Section 78, verse 19.

"And he who receiveth all things with thankfulness shall be made glorious; and the things of this earth shall be added unto him, even an hundred fold, yea, more." Don emphasizes "ALL THINGS," which includes things that are difficult or hard.

Over the next couple of years, Don added plumbing to the tiny kitchen area and one bathroom, which a neighboring snake liked to slither into from a crack in the cement floor. "We lived in that chicken coop with the snake for four years," Wendy explained. "And with such low overhead, we were able to start another business which actually began to produce some income, which opened the door to opportunity by moving to Kansas City to be closer to their client base. Today, that business has over 300 employees.

"Bringing what we had learned from our experiences in the chicken coop and keeping our overhead low, we moved into a very small split-level home with three bedrooms and two small "indoor" bathrooms," Wendy laughs– remembering the boys' excited reaction when they first walked into their new home. "Is this a mansion?" After pausing a moment, reflecting upon their journey, Wendy answered with emotion showing in her eyes, "Yes! Yes, it is!"

The story does not end here for this family, and although there would still be tough times ahead–embraced as opportunity, not punishment–Don and Wendy's business did continue to grow. There would be minor setbacks, but overall, they failed forward and were eventually blessed to build a true mansion of their dreams. People would always shake their heads in disbelief that this strong family once lived in a chicken coop.

When asked how they got through so many periods of failure to the point of being homeless and living in such dire circumstances, they usually look at each other and feel like they were given a beautiful gift. "It was easier to feel blessed because Don was so full of gratitude for everything!"

"I never felt poor because of his prayers, which were so full of gratitude. There were hard times as we would spend hours looking for loose change to buy groceries, wondering how we would eat, buy gas for the car my mother gave us, or pay for clothing for the kids, but we paid our tithing on every dime we found or earned, and the Lord never let us go hungry or without clothing," Wendy recounted.

Don was a believer in visualizing what you wanted out of life. He and Wendy spent time dreaming about what they wanted their future to look like. They maintained a positive outlook no matter the difficulty, never losing sight of where they had come from, looking behind them with fondness and appreciation. They would spend hours creating spreadsheets and drawing out plans for the expansion of their business, as well as their plans for their dream home.

Wendy became quite accomplished at putting to paper what began as a seed in her mind but appearing now on paper as every square inch of their visualized dream home was transformed into reality, complete with detailed drawings of tile design, cabinetry style, fireplace composition, beautiful staircases sweeping across the entrance inside the home–all were the result of seeds in the mind, and now lay visual upon detailed drawings which would one day become a reality. Wendy referred to this exercise that she and Don both embraced as "seeing with the eye of faith!" (Alma 33:40)

Finally, many years following their occupancy in the chicken coop, Don and Wendy would see their business grow to become successful on many levels. One of those successes was reflected in the construction of their beautiful dream home, complete with five levels of extraordinary architectural design and beauty, not the least of which was the stunning view overlooking Cedar Creek Lake, an outdoor kitchen, indoor basketball court, rock climbing wall, billiards, theatre room, and... did I mention the stunning view of Cedar Creek Lake?

I am so happy as an author to have been permitted to include this story in Winning Thru Trial... and as a brother-in-law to have witnessed their early struggles amid the pre-chicken coop days, as well as their development into the businessman and woman they are today, with great emphasis upon filling their new role as grandma and grandpa.

"Neither Don nor I would exchange our experiences [in trial] for all the Mansions in the world. We hold them near and dear to our hearts and are still grateful for our little chicken coop home to this day, and lessons learned along the way from Coop to Country Mansion." -Don and Wendy Morris (and their six children).

While you and I may not experience opportunity in the form of a business that ultimately produces mansion-building cash flow, we do possess within us the ability to learn success principles and apply them throughout our lives in pursuit of those dreams that are important to us. If Don and Wendy had "quit" after their first failed attempt at building a successful business, their story might have read differently.

Here is an essential mindset in achieving financial success: "You must be willing to sacrifice all that you have in the storehouse for the achievement of a dream." This separates so many of us from ever becoming ALL we can be because life is not without some risk.

Searching for what we do not know and being willing to fail until your dream is realized is schooling of the highest caliber. Its admittance tuition is "faith." One must develop faith sufficient to pay the price, even if that price leads to temporary setbacks. Don Morris used this quote to remind himself of this price when school turned exceedingly difficult: "Whether your education comes from a University or the School of Hard Knocks, both require tuition."

I sought permission to use Don and Wendy's story and insert it within this chapter dedicated to Choice and Opportunity because it is the story of a regular guy with dreams of success and a regular gal who grew up the youngest of seven siblings in a small Arizona town. They both tasted trial individually early in life, yet took a risk with one another. They dared to dream as a couple and followed that dream–willing to pay the price, no matter how long it took.

My son Trent reminded me of a family trip when we were touring church history sites in Ohio and Missouri, and we stopped in to visit Linda's two sisters at the dairy farm. Trent got to sleep in the loft that night with his cousins–in the chicken coop. Love filled that little coop, and no one thought living within one's means was anything but ordinary, even if it meant your home had once been home to a bunch of clucking chickens.

While pursuing the restaurant industry as an additional source of income for my own family many years ago, I remember reading about a young family who immigrated to America from Vietnam. Their previous life was once filled with prestige and status, but when the political climate grew unbearable, they gave it all up for a chance at freedom. They risked it all–for opportunity.

Upon arriving in America, without a roof over their heads and only the clothes they could carry, this industrious couple found a job with a cousin who owned a bakery.

Because they had no place to live, they slept in the back storage room of the bakery, free of charge, in exchange for rising at 3 am each day to prepare the ingredients for the day's baking. The little family could eat all the bakery products they wanted by helping bake the donuts and other pastries–and serve customers.

It took the couple only a short time to prove themselves of value, and their two small children began accepting responsibilities before and after school. Soon, the little bakery had begun to generate additional income, generously shared with the Vietnamese family. But instead of using the funds to buy groceries and other essential lifestyle accommodations, the little family put aside every penny they made from working at the bakery and continued sleeping in the storage room and eating free bakery products for over two years.

Opportunity — Look for it!

It was sometime during the third year that the Bakery owner announced his plans to retire at the end of the year and would be selling the store. Because the little family had put every cent earned into savings, they agreed on a price for the store in addition to terms after a sizable down payment.

Two years after they assumed ownership of the now prosperous bakery, the remainder of the purchase price for the store had been paid and was now owned free and clear. With the increased income, the family renovated the store to provide adequate living quarters for themselves and their two children. However, they still needed to buy a car and adjust to the lifestyle their income would have provided. Buying a car would only add expense, they reasoned. Doing without now so they could have whatever they wanted later guided their spending for another three years. Their spending went toward investing in another bakery location. And then another. Soon, they developed a brand that drew investors' interest, which led to offering the brand as a franchise, producing significant, recurring income.

I am not going to finish the story because it is still being written, but I will tell you that this Vietnamese family went on to develop a line of food products sold internationally through multi-level marketing channels, and although their business was severely challenged by the Federal government, among other trials, setbacks, and opposition, their business prospered.

The story of Don and Wendy Morris is not unlike that of the immigrant family, and you could probably add a story just like it about someone you know. It is a story of winning against the odds, except that both families found a way to balance the odds–they put themselves in a condition to seize opportunity when it came while battling what the "world view" might consider failure. Remember my comment about failure not being final? Just because you have fallen on hard times does not define who you are or mean that your current situation is absolute. But so many of us have bought into the mindset of the moral majority who seem to think that if you don't wear a particular brand of clothes, live in a certain neighborhood, or vacation where the beautiful people vacation, you have failed. But think again!

Life has become so complicated–driven by emotion and status, that most of us would never live in a chicken coop. No, let me say it another way–The majority of us would never risk the here and now for a shot at a country mansion "if" losing it meant [temporarily] living on the street, in a cardboard box, or a chicken coop–bakery storage room. <u>As a society, I believe we have become so afraid of failure that we have become content with never taking a risk to find out who we really are or who we could become.</u>

I have noticed that even in our schools, the early formative years of a child's life are often geared to protect the children against the reality of failure. No one "loses" is what many schools teach now. It's not about winning–it's about "not losing." And when trial strikes, it's not about looking for opportunity; it's about protecting the status quo or assessing blame.

During the real estate meltdown of 2007-2010, and a few years before and after, many Americans lost their dream of homeownership because residential real estate values plummeted so far under the mortgage against the property that those who "had" to sell at that time couldn't–and those who didn't have to sell became frightened that their home investment would tank even further and so they joined the chorus of "The sky is falling! The sky is falling!" And indeed it was.

I, too, was affected by this phenomenon, having purchased a large home at almost the peak "before" the meltdown began and watched my potential million-dollar home shrink by two-thirds in value. Even a seasoned real estate professional like me was drawn into the promises of rich rewards, only to experience a substantial loss of equity. But as I shared earlier, having a home for our daughter's family while battling cancer was a "priceless" return on our investment.

Now, this is the interesting thing about how our mindset was affected through this trial. Nothing had changed the "utility" of our home. It was still the beautiful home we purchased, intending to make improvements through our own sweat equity. But something had changed in our perception of the house due to its loss of value "when compared to other homes" at the time. Although we continued making payments on our home, many didn't–or couldn't because of the loss of jobs or reduced income from the national recession, which was concurrently plaguing our nation. These were difficult times. The Great Recession, as it would become known, was the worst economic condition, second only to The Great Depression. There was no opportunity, only preservation–or was there?

According to Quora.com: "economic recessions produce huge opportunities to take life into your own hands and create the life of your dreams."

It is a fact that some of the largest and most successful companies worldwide were created during a recessionary period, including Microsoft, Fed-X, Lexis Nexis, CNN, Hyatt, GE, and many others, who recognized a need and were able to fill it successfully.

Quora.com makes the point that as in the four seasons of the year (in most areas of the country): winter, spring, summer, and fall, there are also different financial seasons, such as recessions, economic booms, and depressions.

"Economic downturns are the times in which you should be planting your financial seeds in preparation for the spring of the next economic boom." – Quora.com

According to Len Clement of MarketWave Inc., a recession causes people to open their minds to other sources of income because they come to realize their secure "job" is no longer secure, and they would like to find a different way to take hold of their future, looking for that perfect storm of opportunity.

Early in our marriage, my wife and I had a dream of owning our home free and clear of a mortgage. We got the idea of building our own home rather than pay a general contractor to build it and pocket the savings. We figured if we could build and occupy the house for two years and roll the profits forward again and again, we would not be risking our primary income from my first job out of college, and eventually, we would be able to build our dream home without a mortgage.

Opportunity - look for it!

We found a vacant piece of dirt at the end of the street behind the house we had purchased after graduating from the university. The lot was owned by a local family, and I remember driving to their home late one night and seeing them at the dinner table eating. As I walked up the driveway, my stomach began to tighten, sending my prepared sales pitch away with a flutter of butterflies, removing any idea of what I was going to say. I began by knocking on the door and took a deep breath as the wife approached the front door, turned on the front porch light, and after introducing myself, she invited me in to meet her husband.

As it turned out, the family had been contemplating the sale of the property for a while but hadn't got around to listing it. I explained my idea of building our family home and how the lot would be paid out of the first draw so the lender would own the lot until a permanent loan was established. The owner agreed, and we shook hands on it.

Our next challenge was to obtain financing–both for the construction and permanent loan. Because of my vast real estate experience (part-time over a couple of years), I was able to arrange construction financing while I still had stable employment (a job) and obtained a financing commitment letter as evidence we were going to build a house. I would learn later in life how difficult it is for self-employed people to obtain home financing. Loan approval criteria are heavily weighted in favor of salaried individuals over us flakey commission-only types. We do get loans, but not without pledging our firstborn.

Sorry, I digress!

Two weeks later, I had a letter from the bank acknowledging their commitment to provide construction funds to build the house, and then I drafted a simple contract with the lot owner.

With a signed purchase contract in hand, I went to the Town of Mesa, AZ Building Dept. and showed them my purchase contract and loan commitment letter, along with a legal description of the lot I was going to buy. This meeting with the Building Dept. proved to be my first "home run."

The lot I wanted to purchase was located at the end of a street. The information received from Mesa Building Dept. disclosed their need to extend the street "through" our lot, connecting on the other side, effectively creating "two" lots. We were able to lower the cost of our lot by selling one of the lots and building on the other.

We ordered a set of house plans from a catalog, and when the plans arrived, I took them to the City Building Department to apply for a construction permit to build our first home. I rolled the plans open for the inspector to see, and after a few minutes of review, he just laughed. "Where did you get these plans?" he questioned, "They have 'crawl spaces' under the house. We don't build houses in the desert with crawl spaces," he continued and laughed again, which drew the attention of the other plans examiner, and he too, couldn't hold back a chuckle.

We had come so far toward accomplishing our dream of building our own home, only to be squashed like a bug into the windshield of an oncoming car. Times like this define you when you have a choice to either be the bug–or to become the windshield. We chose the latter!

It was difficult admitting we had blundered by ordering our house plans through mail order. I mean, back in the day, brides were ordered from mail order, weren't they?

Didn't you ever see the movie Seven Brides for Seven Brothers? So, how difficult could it be to find a great-looking elevation and well-designed floor plan the same way? Apparently, it is "quite" difficult!

After giving it some thought, we followed Winning Way #1 and called upon God for direction. Although we didn't know how to build a house, God did, and we prayed for His help in finding a way to keep moving forward. The answer came in the form of a carpenter named Ron.

Solutions to life's problems are rarely handed to us. The caterpillar does not become a beautiful butterfly because God designed its cocoon with a zipper. And we do not learn how to drive a car from sitting in the passenger seat. We did not want to hire an architect to redraw the plans for our home, costing us more time and money, so we started calling various sub-contracting firms and making appointments after work to show our plans. Mostly, we got the same reaction as we did from the Plan Inspector, and always with an extremely high price associated with the bid, but we kept at it. My wife got rather good at tracking down busy subs, putting our eastern plans in their hands, and explaining what we wanted.

One day, about dinner time, the house phone rang. It was a carpenter named Ron. He had a slow drawl about him and mentioned his connection to the White Mountains, where my wife and I had family ties. We arranged a time to meet, and Ron, the carpenter, became our treasured advisor and trainer throughout the construction process of our very first home. This is not to say the process was easy or always fun. In fact, my marriage was tested more than once during the subsequent months of construction.

It was carpenter Ron who got us out of a massive conflict between the plumber and the block layer when both bathroom windows ended up in one bathroom and none in the other. I learned early on the value of a creative framer. You see, you can gain experience from trial.

My wife and I went on to build another home a couple of years later in a subdivision across from Mesa High School and over a period of fifteen years or so, built and lived in another seven homes right in the same subdivision until we finally built our dream home–a "Victorian Splendor," self-designed with four levels–basement, up four feet to the family room, up another four feet to the main level, and up nine feet to a loft which overlooked the kitchen, living room, dining room, and level-two family room.

We had traveled to San Francisco several times to select colors and elevation. The result was so different from the standard desert home of the time that on any given Sunday, a line of cars would form at the front of our house, cameras clicking, and even daring attempts at scraping off a shard of color from the house. Our kids were the envy of their school friends as the ones living in the "Cinderella" house, probably because we had a real Pepsi machine in our garage, almost always full of delicious beverages, which our children enjoyed inviting their friends over to partake of after school, courtesy of my dad who was the manager of a Pepsi-Cola Bottling Company, in Tucson, Arizona.

The most exciting part of building this dream home was the fact that there was no mortgage.

During this period of economic growth, I became a partner in a new start-up home-building company and later served as its president. Our partners borrowed money from a relative's pension fund to get started. I also brought cash from my real estate business, which had doubled our income over my salaried job, and we built our first subdivision near downtown Gilbert, Arizona.

In a few short years, we grew into a real estate powerhouse of over fifty sales associates, three thriving subdivisions, and a leader in creative housing concepts in response to rising prices and decreasing affordability. But we had built a well-tuned machine over the ten years of operation, which demanded more land to develop, yielding more homes to build. Life was certainly "coming up roses."

Any well-tuned machine requires all moving parts to function in harmony. If but one of those parts fails to carry its share of the load, the machine begins to falter. In a home builder's case, the engine that drives production is sales.

Just think of the multiple obstacles to buying a home to which you, the reader, have been exposed, assuming you have owned more than one home. Or if you have dreamed of owning a home, only to experience the bug on the windshield example used earlier, you also know firsthand the obstacles of achieving homeownership.

During every period of economic growth, history has shown an offsetting period of economic recession to some degree; just how deep depends on too many factors to be addressed here, but rising home mortgage interest rates are almost always involved in slowing sales.

Economic conditions during the late 70's and early to mid-80s were significantly affected by rising mortgage interest rates–reaching twenty percent. Yes, you read this correctly–twenty (20%) percent.

Our home-building business took ten years to put the machine in full gear and only one year to unravel. When you see ten years of blood, sweat, and tears go down the drain, it does strange things to your brain. And for me, I wanted out. I had developed early stages of depression as I watched my financial security quickly erode before my eyes, leaving me feeling selfish and self-centered. I would eventually cut and run.

Less than three months later, I was a regular on the golf range with my two young sons under the care of a golf professional. Life was good. My buyout from selling my company shares of ownership included twenty apartment units I had built and managed personally to become future retirement assets. I thought I had finally proved myself as a capable breadwinner to my family, a shrewd negotiator, and a hero to my children. I was overjoyed!

Although I had done my best to protect my family from the outside world's exposure to the calamities caused by such extreme interest rates affecting our livelihood, I soon learned that even doing one's best is sometimes not enough.

The world is full of 'successful failures.'

A good friend sent me a quote that fits into this chapter about choice and opportunity so well: "Everything we want is found on the other side of hard."

Wanting to do a little research about this quote, I found that the

Phoenix Sun's basketball coach (at the time), Monty Williams, also used this quote to express perhaps some frustration over the team's progress, or lack thereof, as quoted on Facebook. I believe I like this full quote a little better, for what it teaches us about the purpose of "hard."

"Everything we want is found on the other side of hard. This is our hard, and we are going to find out who we are." - Phoenix Sun's Head Coach Monty Williams.

My take on this expression by Coach Williams is that "hard" is necessary to reveal our true potential." Most of us when faced with "hard" consider that condition as "opposition," or trial [if it hurts]. And it is by overcoming "hard" that we learn most about ourselves. This is where "choice" comes in.

When the trial first hits, it comes as a thief during the night, unexpected and swift. We are often confused and lost, unable to find a bearing that will give us hope. –"The Sweetness of Trial"

This paragraph above was taken from my first book to describe my feelings after being broadsided by trial. It came in the form of a phone call. I felt the world cave in beneath me as I learned that my former company was on the brink of bankruptcy, threatening to take down with it many faithful sub-contractors who had benefited from our growth over the years, were patient with our slow pay as conditions worsened, and would now follow us to the courts of the land to protect themselves from personal ruin.

Although one might rationalize away the responsibility to provide any form of assistance to those who were now living by their own business decisions, I had made mine and had counted myself a blessed man for doing so ahead of the tidal wave that was now engulfing my former industry. But something didn't feel right as I learned of the damage that would occur without an infusion of cash to pay sub-contractors who had acted in good faith–the repercussions of bankruptcy would ruin lives.

I am a simple man in many areas yet complex in others; I am not particularly gifted in any one area, especially not financial analysis. I can't describe with any amount of detail or rationale why I agreed to do what I did, but I agreed to mortgage every free and clear apartment unit I had received as my buy-out to provide the cash lifeline to my former company to settle with sub-contractors and lenders.

However, the cash infusion from the apartment mortgages was insufficient to cover the delinquencies on their own, so in addition to mortgaging the apartments, I added our personal home to the bailout, creating a cloud of despair and disappointment at home. After ten long years of sacrifice and planning, we were right back where we started, albeit a little worse.

But what about the assets–the apartments themselves? Didn't they grow in equity and eventually pay off? I know it is difficult to imagine, but there was a time in our real estate investment history when such mortgaged-investment real estate like apartments were more of a liability burden than a positive asset–this period of my life being one of those times. I gave away the mortgaged apartments for $1,000 each just to remove the burden.

I believe the term "second-guessing" to be one of Satan's greatest tools in bringing unhappiness and misery to the human race (Galatians 5:1, 2 Nephi 2:26-27). The term essentially has "little" positive vibe in it and serves primarily to undermine our faith. In other words, it is of no value to us–so "stop doing it!"

Second-guessing our prior actions implies we have control of the past, and if we beat ourselves up enough, the results of previous choices and actions will magically change. We both know that is not going to happen. But we can use past decisions and actions to change the "future"–by striving to make different choices and actions.

I use the word "striving" because of its power to explain why we, as mortals, continue to make mistakes without achieving complete perfection in this life. Striving gives us hope to win "next time." It implies the game is not over until God says it is over and I am called home, unless by my own carelessness or that of others exercising agency upon me.

In my case, however, I did not strive to forgive myself over the financial plight I had put myself and my family into. Instead, I did what I explained most people do when making decisions and choices that lead to unfavorable circumstances–I beat myself up by second-guessing my actions. Instead of looking for opportunity, now that I was out of work as a real estate marketing professional/former company president, I sulked, withdrew from my family, and allowed the tentacles of depression to envelop my being. I was a real mess.

You don't "catch" depression!

According to the World Health Organization (WHO), more than 350 million people worldwide suffer from depression. It is a leading cause of disability. It hinders ambition. It destroys relationships. It opens the door to both physical and mental health diseases. Yet, you do not "catch" depression–you must let it in, feed it, even nourish it to keep it growing–from "feeling blue," which we all experience at times in our lives, to a full-fledged grey-blanket depressive state where all color has left your vision except for hopeless grey.

Although there doesn't seem to be a consensus on the exact cause of depression, numerous contributors tend to extinguish the fire in our soul–if we let them. <u>If just one of my Winning Ways in overcoming trial helps just one reader fight depression and win, then this writing endeavor will have been worth it.</u>

And yes, I am aware that family genetics can increase the risk of depression, but just because a family member succumbs to a depressive state of mind does not mean you cannot control your choice not to follow suit or become more informed on how to avoid that dastardly pit.

Certain personality types are probably more prone to experience depression than others. One who is generally a worrier, critical of others, and never satisfied with themselves will experience bouts of depression just because it fits with their personality. But even an unhappy person can "fake it til' you make it" and maintain a cheery exterior while a battle is raging inside.

From my experience with depression over several years, I admit to feeding my depressive state with more negative than positive affirmations, contributing to a more chronic depression than merely feeling the "blues." I needed to learn how to replace negative with positive brain food.

"Learn to talk positive to yourself rather than listen to negative about yourself."

Many years ago, I happened to focus my attention on a photo of my wife and I standing in front of a partially completed Church of Jesus Christ of Latter-day Saints "Temple" in Gilbert, Arizona, my eyes not focusing on the beautiful person next to me or the holy edifice under construction behind us, but instead I "chose" to see the over-weight person with my face, and immediately assumed an attitude of disgust over the extra weight I had "allowed" myself to carry, choosing to purchase larger sizes rather than correcting the problem, which in my case was not medical, but rather choice of what and how often I fed my body.

I tried "cutting back" on the food I usually ate, but nothing changed other than I felt hungry more often. It was only when I changed my eating habits altogether, reinforced by goal setting, that I lost the desired weight. I put myself under the care of a professional weight loss clinic, replacing my old habits with new ones "designed to reprogram my brain to look at food differently." The results were amazing, both in how I looked and in how I felt.

However, the most challenging part of changing behavior is "after" the celebration of reaching a goal. Unless one achieved goal is replaced with another yet-to-be-achieved goal, you will likely return to your old habits.

I am living proof of what I just said–as time marched on, my daily self-affirmations and meal-planning efforts used to change behavior to meet the "goal" were subtly put aside because of my new "I got this now" attitude. I admit to feeling so "deprived" of eating convenience foods I had eaten for so long before losing weight that my "here and now" celebration of reaching my slim goal became a distant memory, absorbed into a busy life, travel vacations, and eating out. It was not long before old habits started creeping in again, and yes, in time, I started pulling out the larger-sized jeans, rationalizing that my body was "unique" and could handle a little more padding.

Someone forgot to tell the "natural man" within me that the food "he" likes would never be eaten again.

Without a goal in place to "stay" slim, the foods I once used for comfort and reward began to replace the low-calorie, nutrient-rich foods I had eaten to reach my weight goal. I had allowed the "purpose" of why I wanted to lose weight months earlier to dim in my memory, which led to weakened resolve, and without constant "remembering," I was soon back on the road to weight gain.

Trial is often a masterful excuse to change eating habits. Without a plan, trial can feed the natural man instincts with fear and loss of control, leading us to abandon our goals of better eating. It also can affect how we think, treat others, and even our moral compass, and before long, we find ourselves drifting as a ship without a rudder, tossed upon the waves of life, unprepared for what lies ahead.

If we do not maintain conscious control over what we eat, read, and listen to, we are easy prey to external influences that have the potential to define us without our say in the matter but manifest in our attitude and actions.

Have you noticed there is "self-talk" going on inside your inner thoughts most of your waking day? And what about at night, just before closing your eyes, finally able to unplug from the demands of the day placed upon you? Have you ever noticed that moment of clarity when you take a deep cleansing breath, slowly exhaling the stress of the day? For me, this is when my self-talk appears to be the most vulnerable–the last thoughts of the day, to hibernate as seeds of influence toward my becoming; a subtle reminder of that which I feed the brain, conscious or not, is revealed in my attitude and actions starting as early as the very next day.

Please try this little exercise the next time you prepare for sleep:

Before assuming your most comfortable sleep position–beating the pillow into submission, or whatever you do to hopefully fall into blissful unconsciousness–hold firm to your conscious self and take an intentional deep cleansing breath, holding for a second or two to collect all the stored stresses of the day, then exhale slowly, visualizing the expulsion of tiny dark bubbles–each carrying a negative influence. The first few times, you might find yourself falling asleep before starting on the second stage of inserting the positive... but stay with it.

The second stage of preparing your mind for pre-sleep positive self-talk could be the most dramatic and beneficial change to your life ever experienced. You can thank me later (smile). Remember the five P's–Proper Preparation Prevents Poor Performance? You need to prepare your mind food ahead of bedtime feeding time.

While recovering from chronic depression, I sat at my bedside each night for weeks with a yellow pad of paper and a pencil (Ballpoint pens hadn't been invented yet –J.K.) and scripted positive affirmations into my brain. After I had worn out the cassette tape recordings my Doctor had given me to get started, I purchased others and kept them playing in the car and on my portable player while around the house.

Negative brain food programming is not static. In other words, if you don't input more "positive brain food" than the ongoing negative food selections, your dramatic change will take longer and yield not-so-dramatic results... but "any" positive affirmations recited and internalized "on a regular basis" will make a difference, even if not noticeable at first. You may not see or feel the difference within the first few weeks, but others will–so ask them!

With your mind free of whatever it was that burdened you that day and in your most vulnerable and accessible state just prior to sleep, you are now ready for your first **Controlled Positive Affirmation Exercise**, or "CPAE," as I have just named it.

Choose a positive affirmation that describes a desired outcome or character trait. Build into your affirmation's words like "I am" and "I do," so the brain doesn't have to decide "if" a particular outcome is your target.

You must affirm as if you are already there, having "already achieved" the desired outcome or character trait for your affirmations to result in more than "feel good" exercises.

Since most household stress revolves around financial matters, let's build a CPAE around taking control of your financial needs:

I am excellent at meeting the financial needs of my family.

I am always open to opportunity that leads to a firmer financial foundation.

I resist adding lifestyle to my financial overhead.

I am in complete control of my finances and spend only on necessary things.

I look for opportunities in my trial to benefit others.

I am generous with my financial means.

I tithe my financial earnings to help others.

I study my finances regularly and make correct decisions on my spending habits.

I provide a wonderful life for my family by using my talents to _____ (you fill in the blank)

I feel joy when my bills are paid on time.

I think you get the idea!

For me, because of the grey blanket of depression wrapped so tightly around my heart, I often felt smothered, unable to breathe or think. I found no trace of joy in life–even going home each day to face my family became a burden. I longed to be free from this emotional prison. I chose these affirmations to feed my brain at night just before sleep overtook me–I wanted them to be the last thoughts entering my mind so it had plenty of room to work:

I am a child of a loving Father of my spirit who loves me and wants me to succeed.

I am ready for greatness.

I am hungry for greatness.

I am great in the sight of God, and He sent me here to win.

I feel the sun shining in my heart.

I love to laugh.

People love to be around me because of my sense of humor.

I laugh all the time.

I find humor all around me.

I choose not to feel depressed.

My family loves it when I come home.

I feel the wet blanket being removed from my heart.

I look for opportunities in my trial.

I always look at the bright side of things.

Whenever someone asks me how I am doing, I always say 'marvelous'–and I mean it.

The key to the effectiveness of each CPAE is consistency. Although once a day at bedtime is good, three times a day is even better. You want to choose two or three self-affirmations you can memorize and recite aloud throughout the day. Use "shower talk" each morning to get in some verbal recitation. Be passionate in your recitations to gain more impact on yourself. Let the neighbors hear you – the more passionate, the better.

Try memorizing verbal self-talk instead of phone talk while driving. Don't bother wondering if the driver stopped next to you at the traffic light is looking at you–they are, so pour it on!

Positive self-talk can be enhanced by listening to positive input throughout the day avoiding certain music and radio stations that do not fit into your preparation. This preparation to rid yourself of depression (or whatever your goal is to become) offsets the subconscious negative programming we are "all" subject to as we drive around the city, use the Internet, wait for the red light to change at an intersection, or exercise at the gym. It seems that "everyone" has a message to sell. Your subconscious mind is so wonderful in "remembering," so you don't have to keep "re-learning" the basics of life every day (auto-pilot). It is also a sponge to whatever the eye can see, the ear can hear, the lips can taste, and the nose can smell. So, unless we have a plan in place (5 P's) on how to become _____ (you fill in the blank), then the natural man, the carnal man, the worldly man(or woman), within us will reign.

You might listen to a Brian Buffini podcast about how to succeed in real estate and take what you hear and learn to the next level by putting into "practice" those shared "secrets of success" by changing your daily habits to align more with those found consistent with others who have reached similar successes. You cannot expect to become without moving into the next level of practice. You reinforce the goal by putting into real-life "practice" the principles necessary to learn and understand how to achieve whatever measure of success you hope to achieve.

Brian Buffini recently shared in a podcast the following narrative: "You want to become as successful in your financial life as I am? You want to do what I do? Then pack your bag tonight and meet me at the airport to fly to my next event, missing "your" daughter's recital. Staying in motel after motel, night after night, weekend after weekend! No success in this life comes without 'sacrifice' in one form or another."

If you want to lose weight, learn to write books, or become the next American Idol performer, you must "prepare" to win! And you must "keep on, keepin' on," to use a familiar mantra if you expect to "stay" on top.

I want to relate my recent experience to drive home the point of how attitude affects behavior. As a full-time real estate professional for the past 53 years, I am not immune to the natural man's "negative self-talk." I had been listening to a new real estate podcast discussing the impact of what is called the iBuyer Disruption to the "traditional" way we bought and sold real estate, and frankly, I let my fears and prior experience with "age discrimination" get the best of me, and when I awoke the next morning, I felt moody and impatient. As the day progressed, I sunk deeper and deeper after my attempts to understand a new social media app failed, and the two iPads I use for writing (one at the gym and one at home) now failed to sync. I tried a new free storage app and ended up filling it up with duplicate media stored in another app and spent two hours deleting it, only to have my daughter show me how to do it in seconds.

By the time the sun was finally setting on this miserable day, I had had it! I was mad, discouraged, afraid, and ready to quit and join the army (LOL). I had convinced myself that I was too old to adapt to new technology and that the changes in our industry would soon have no place for an "old guy" like me, based on the drop in business since COVID-19 and the current changes to our economy.

I had "allowed" negative thoughts to dominate my mind, and oh, how quickly it took control.

And did I mention how I "spewed" negative all over those closest to me during this takeover by Mr. Negative? It brought back scary feelings of times past when these thoughts and actions had built a home within me. And it frightened me!

As the day ended, I finally gave up the ghost and spent the time until bed sulking and grumbling over everything that irritated me, until my wonderful wife of 56 years boldly said, not looking up from her handiwork project: "Why don't you practice a few concepts taught in your book, dear?"

This entire book is an entirely transparent look into my soul... why would I begin now and not disclose my human frailties even as I write this chapter? In fact, I "did" take my wife's counsel to feed my attitude with some positive affirmations. But mostly, I just opened my heart to my Savior, Jesus Christ... and allowed His atonement to heal my troubled mind and spirit.

When I awoke the next morning, those feelings of dread and frustration were gone. I solved the issue of linking my two iPads, and I overcame the negative self-talk by finding a new app that could add text and fun graphics to my videos to make them more interesting... and posted a new video–all before noon. And just so you know, I was the #1 producer at my company that year.

So, what changed? How did I work out of such a bad mood the day before? That is the answer... I did "work" my way out of it. My first call was to God! With the assurance that all was going to be ok, I began to feed my mind with positive affirmations in the form of self-talk, positive talks and podcasts, and a bit of extra sleep. I think my short night before the lousy day may have contributed to my stinkin' thinkin.'

For those of us who have experienced a deeper set depressed attitude, the most effective time for a CPAE is just before bedtime as you script in handwriting those chosen self-affirmations you want securely embedded in your brain. And the next morning... after morning prayer and before shower talk–recite those same affirmations; how long depends upon you and the time available. The more often and longer will generally yield better results. CPAE is like changing your diet from bad to healthy food–if you stop eating healthy food long enough, you will find yourself right back where you were before changing your habits, trust me.

For me, the only way a change of diet as a way of life will work "long term" is if I "convince the natural man within," through self-affirmations, that this new lifestyle includes "him too!" And "when" the occasional clouds of doubt gather overhead, thick enough to affect your behavior, you now have the skills necessary to work out of it.

My "fake it 'til I make it" persona may still be working in some areas of my life, but without the support of CPAE, it would be just a matter of time before I fall back into my old eating habits and once again fall prey to the natural man within me.

I have NOT offered the preceding discussion and controlled positive affirmation exercises (CPAE) in any way to be intended as medical advice or to suggest CPAE as a substitute for seeking professional counsel or treatment for medical or psychological symptoms (my disclaimer). These are my personal experiences meant only as encouragement and a means of providing a self-help skill to overcome negative-thinking habits, which you may or may not have.

Obviously, any principle of truth, or perceived truth, if used over-excessively, has the potential to do harm. Use common sense, please. And by all means, do your own research into positive affirmation and self-talk. Don't google the acronym CPAE just yet because it doesn't exist except in this book, as relating to controlled positive affirmation exercise(s). However, there is sufficient data and studies online to more than support the general acceptance and benefits of self-talk. Check out www.learnmindpower.com.

My first experience with positive self-talk was with Shad Helmstetter, but there are now libraries full of such information you can check out for the price of a library card.

During my research at Arizona State University for my psychology classes, I internalized the relationship between mind and the physical body operating on two separate plains, backed by such greats as Plato, who, in 387 BC–"suggested that the brain is the seat of mental processes. Plato's view of the "soul" [self] is that the body exists to serve the soul: God created the soul before the body and gave it precedence both in time and value and made it the dominating and controlling partner."

From Timaeus, as quoted in Wikipedia ("Timeline of Psychology"). I interpret this historical information as the soul (aligned with the brain) and the body (aligned with the natural man within us) were formed to create "Man," subject to agency and opposition as designed by God to prove us–to test us–to develop us into becoming.

Winning Way #4, titled: "Opportunity–Look for it," blends well with the chapter devoted to "choice." Depression is a symptom, not a character choice–but it affects character if you choose to do nothing about it. I have attempted to equip you with methods and information to use, but it is your choice to do so.

When the brain runs on negative programming, it shuns opportunity. When trial strikes, you need a clear mind–but rarely do you have time to prepare. Today is the time to prepare your mind and heart to face trial when it comes–and it will come.

To conclude this chapter on "Choice Begets Character" and "Winning Way #4," which teaches us to look for opportunity in trial, I can think of no better story that exemplifies both principles of successful navigation through trial than that of the Old Testament account of Joseph, the eleventh son of Jacob the Israelite, grandson of Isaac and Rachel, and great-grandson of Abraham.

You would think that such a righteous man as Jacob, blessed with lineage from Abraham and posterity in the form of twelve sons, two of which would one day grow up to lead the twelve tribes of Israel, would be given a bye (rest day) from trial, but the unthinkable happened anyway–his youngest son at the time (Benjamin had not been born yet) was apprehended by his jealous brothers and sold into slavery far away into Egypt, using a torn and blood-soaked cloak of many colors–young Joseph's coat–to explain the favored son's disappearance.

To lose a son or daughter to death or irreparable separation hardly makes any difference. The pain and suffering had to be unimaginable for Jacob and Rachel. The pain our Heavenly Father must have felt when one-third of his spirit children whom He loved left their heavenly home out of discord to follow Satan had to be mind-numbing, even for a God. My wife and I experienced just a small taste of that and would never be the same again, and our child was alive.

Joseph was an average child in many ways, working hard with his brothers as shepherds in the land of Canaan. But Father Jacob favored Joseph as the "birthright son" of his wife Rachel because Reuben, the oldest son, had forfeited his right as the firstborn because of his immoral actions, which spurred a growing rage of jealousy among Joseph's older brothers. And then there was that beautiful cloak, woven with many bright colors to remind them again and again of their father's love for their younger brother.

It didn't help that young Joseph, maybe seventeen years of age at the time, began sharing particulars of dreams he had been having of becoming a very important person one day. In fact, he liked to tell of one dream in particular, where even the sun, moon, and eleven stars would one day bow before him.

I suppose there is some value in parenting skills learned in this story of Joseph, of the importance of loving and treating all children you are blessed to have under your care–birth or adopted–with unconditional love. While a higher form of love must develop in the parent to attain this level of parenting, it is attainable not as "perfection" during this earthly life but as "striving for" throughout the eternities. Nonetheless, making mistakes in parenting often yields an opportunity to learn... and to change.

Although I knew my parents loved my older sister and me, I never remember her being disciplined the way I was, probably because I was too busy looking for the next way to get into trouble (look for the next book titled That's Charlie!). According to what I later learned from scripture, my parents loved "me" more because I was chastened more (Hebrews 12:6).

Well, back to our story of Joseph, who by now was well on his way to being sold to serve some wealthy Egyptian. But as "fate" would have it (God's way of remaining anonymous), young Joseph was bought by an officer and head of Pharaoh's kitchen (Potiphar), who took a liking to Joseph and made him his personal assistant. In time, Joseph assumed responsibility for Potiphar's entire household.

Again, I must pause this story to emphasize Winning Way #4–"Opportunity, Look for it!" The boy Joseph was taken from his parents and forced into bondage–now that is trial. But how we react to trial is "choice," and Joseph is about to be tried and tested and given a "choice" on how he would react when tempted. That is the presence of agency, even when in bondage.

You know the story from here–how Potiphar's wife was attracted to young, [probably] well-built and easy on the eyes, Joseph, and repeatedly tried to seduce him? She was also jealous of Joseph's relationship with her husband and sought to bring Joseph down from his position of trust and authority. But Joseph knew who he was, and for him, the choice was "to run."

Temptations are a daily occurrence in today's immoral climate, and families are destroyed daily because of poor choices. Oh, if we all could use our agency to make "correct" choices and follow young Joseph's example.

Joseph escapes from Potiphar's wife's grasp, but this time without his coat, which she uses to spin a tale accusing Joseph of impropriety, which leads to Joseph's imprisonment with the Pharaoh's butler and baker, who were also on the wrong side of the law. While in prison, Joseph befriends the chief jailer and gains his trust, leading to another opportunity for leadership and responsibility over all the other inmates. I can tell you this was a big thing, and it gave Joseph an opportunity to interact with the other captives and tell parts and pieces of dreams he had, which is also probably why when the Pharaoh's butler and baker started having unusual and disturbing dreams themselves, they went to Joseph.

Opportunity once again presented itself before Joseph, who interpreted the butler's dream to mean he would soon be released from prison and return to his former station. As Joseph had said, the Butler was released and reinstated three days later. During the Butler's release proceedings, Joseph asked him to remember him to the Pharaoh and put in a good word, which went totally ignored until one day about two years later when the Pharaoh started having strange and disturbing dreams himself–and the door of opportunity once again opened for Joseph, as the butler did recall the amazing talent he possessed at interpreting dreams and relayed this information to his boss who immediately summoned Joseph to his court.

Opportunity in trial does not usually present itself as one big, brightly wrapped package labeled "OPPORTUNITY!" Nor does it come when we expect or need it. Often, we don't recognize the opportunity in trial until long after the wounds have healed. Then, looking back, we see with clearer vision how our pain and suffering opened doors to our becoming, to character development, to bring forth the development of spiritual gifts and talents, even hidden treasures discovered within the confines of our broken hearts.

The God of Abraham, Isaac, and Jacob used trial to prepare the Children of Israel to arrive in the Promised Land. You would think that after 150 years of Egyptian captivity and the incredible miracle God created to free them, that would have been sufficient to motivate them to change enough to inherit the Promised Land, but it wasn't. They still lacked the faith to see beyond the intimidation of a fortified city and believe in the strength of the God who freed them from captivity. They were still not ready.

Has it ever occurred to you that God has placed us in our life circumstances so that we, too, might prove our faith in Him and attain greatness? Is it possible that even "you," my reader friend, have undiscovered talents and spiritual gifts within you that only a desert journey (trial) would cause to be born?

Let's continue with our story of Joseph and his trial...

Joseph had aged during his confinement and was now around thirty years of age, but who's counting? Perhaps Joseph had to season a bit more before his once-in-a-lifetime debut with the Pharaoh. Perhaps if Joseph had been younger, without the experience gained from his responsibility over those incarcerated with him, he might not have been as confident in his interpretation of Pharaoh's dreams—nor the confidence to offer advice. Can you imagine that scene before Pharaoh? "King Pharaoh, sir, uh—what I'm reading from this dream you keep having is seven great years of plenty (cheers from Pharaoh's court), followed by seven disastrous years of famine (boos from Pharaoh's court)."

"And if I may be so bold sir–I would recommend appointing a "wise man" to be responsible for the gathering and storing of food in anticipation of the famine to come." (gasp! from Pharaoh's court).

I really don't know if my insertion of melodrama from Pharaoh's court actually happened, but I do know from recorded scripture that Pharaoh was impressed with Joseph's recommendation so much that he appointed Joseph to be that wise man, second in command, and charged with filling the storehouses with grain and other food sources for the famine that Pharaoh wisely believed was coming (aka Opportunity)

In revisiting Joseph's story once again, I came to understand even deeper my belief that trial–yours and mine, has the power of influence. I call this "opportunity!"

In today's world, it may not be noticed by others as a noble gesture to take our eyes off our own pain and cast them toward others, but our "reaction" to trial can profoundly affect others, as did Joseph's. Joseph may have been a spoiled little boy at one point in his life, but he became a man through trial and influenced the highest ruling power in all the land for good.

Joseph was about to be placed in a position where he could make a difference. He was exposed to trial in order to carve from him talents, which may have lain dormant as a sheep herder. He was given temptations so that he might come to know who he was and what he stood for.

Joseph's story does not end here, nor does his opportunity to influence others, but for our purposes, I think the examples shared about Joseph's life do very well in describing the power of Winning Way #4: "Opportunity–Look for It."

Some time ago, while serving a client in the sale of their home as a real estate broker, I arranged to meet an appraiser assigned to place a lending value on my client's home I had just sold. She (the appraiser) was already in job mode when I arrived but still greeted me professionally before returning to her fact-gathering process.

I tagged along quietly, not wanting to get in the way but also wanting to make her job more manageable. At one point, I asked her a question I ask all appraisers who carry the power to make or break a deal: "Are you familiar with this area?" And "When was the last time you appraised here?" Much to my relief, I learned that she conducted her appraisal business from her home, which was not far from the subject property, and she was quite familiar with the area.

One question led to another as she robotically took measurements of every inch of the home and still responded to my sincere questions to get to know her. As our time together ended, I extended my hand of appreciation for her efficiency and asked if there was anything I could do for her. Her response surprised me: "Do you know of any homes to rent?"

She explained that her twenty-six-year-old son had been living with her but recently died from pneumonia. As she said that, her eyes welled up, and tears began to threaten a breach of their confinement, as did mine. "I wrote a book just for you," I blurted. And I had–and for everyone else who does not understand the purpose of trial. I carry a couple of copies of my first published book, "The Sweetness of Trial," in my car for such opportunities to be a blessing to a child of God, who, like me, was sent here to earth to learn and grow, and sometimes we just get overwhelmed with that eternal purpose.

As I handed my new friend a copy to read, I pointed to the cover. "This is my grandson, Mighty Jake. He was born autistic but later developed a terminal disease affecting the mitochondria power cells in his body. There is no cure, and the disease is brutal and totally unforgiving. With a quivering chin, I mentioned that one of the best chapters is "Why Bad Things Happen to Good People." My friend cautiously responded tongue-in-cheek, "Can I read that chapter first?" But quickly followed with a more sober request, "Can I give this to my friend? Her son is also dying."

I suppose every writer who has authored a book goes through periods of doubt and frustration as to why they spent so much late-night/early-morning time trying to put into words this ever-present urge to write, only to discover the world isn't beating a pathway to their door to read it. A publisher warned me that there is no money in books, and she was correct–I have given away more books than I have sold. But it is times like this experience with my new friend that brings to mind the "real" reason I write books–it is my way of making a difference, if only for one.

If people are too busy to read, they are most definitely too busy to post a review on social media or the bookseller's website, although I am thankful for those who have taken that brave step. But those who sent an email or actually picked up a phone and called… keep me failing "forward." It was the turnout of friends and family supporting my first book signing event. It is one-on-one experiences like that just described that help to pick me up and dust myself off and head back to the gym the following day with iPad in hand and fresh enthusiasm to mount my favorite stair-stepper or treadmill, and shout (to myself), "Let the thumbs begin!"

So, when trial strikes, remember Winning Way #4 – "Opportunity! Look for it!"

Chapter Five

Seek the Best Gifts - Look for the Miracle.

I must relate a spiritual experience to how hard this chapter was to write. I had all but finished this book, satisfied that five (5) chapters would adequately portray and teach principles of success in winning through trial–until one morning, while in my daily talk with my Heavenly Father, a thought so clear came into my mind: "You forgot to include 'gifts of the spirit!' This impression led me to spend the next hour on my iPad, writing thoughts about how trial and opposition are often catalysts in discovering our spiritual gifts and hidden talents and offering a palate for claiming the presence of miracles in our lives.

It was during this pondering exercise, thinking through the impression I had received that morning to include "spiritual gifts" in this book–that Chapter 5 was born, revealing how, throughout my life, I have experienced firsthand how trial has uncovered hidden talents, revealed spiritual gifts, and provided miracles–all contributing to who I am today... and trial *may* also be your key to success.

Why did I choose to italicize the word *may* in the paragraph above instead of "promising" that trial would bring you gifts, talents, and miracles? I thought you would like to know... <u>because I believe that none of these blessings from God will come with Satan turning your crank.</u> In a more modern phrase, If your reaction to trial, no matter the intensity, results in continued anger, resentment, or refusal to put into action Winning Way #1 taught herein (Call upon God), there is little chance you would recognize such spiritual gifts, hidden talents, or miracles if they were securely placed upon your lap. Trial is intended to "bring" you to Christ, not separate you from His embrace and outstretched arms, which beckon you. But it is your choice of how you will react.

If I may borrow the counsel of Alma (the Nephite prophet who helped establish the church of Jesus Christ in the Americas in approximately 145BC – Wikipedia) to his young son, Helaman: "...*for I do know that whosoever shall put trust in God shall be supported in their trials, and their troubles, and their afflictions, and shall be lifted up at the last day.*"

What I get from this scripture is to "trust in the Lord with all thine heart; and lean not unto thine own understanding" (Proverbs 3:5). I've just given you the key to unlocking the power to discover your spiritual gifts, develop hidden talents, and experience miracles–Trust in God! No matter the outcome!

Do you think you can do that? Do you think you could learn to trust God "in all your afflictions with a little more encouragement and understanding?"

Now let me throw you a curve ball–it takes more than "trust in

God." It takes action on your part to put yourself in a position to trust. It takes "seeking!" Seeking to find light in adversity, seeking to discover something about yourself that is unique in overcoming opposition, choosing to see God's hand lifting you up to become all you can be, and yes, choosing to believe even if you cannot see a visible reason to.

Let's begin our journey toward understanding together. You need to know that the challenge I faced while writing this chapter is that it is the most spiritual and most transparent look into my inner core–and that is what frightens me because it took a very long time, trial after trial, to learn what I am going to share. And depending upon where you are in your spiritual development from trial, you may brush over this chapter to get to the next and totally miss the most amazing message contained herein–that we win "thru" trial by discovering and developing hidden talents, then sharing our spiritual gifts with others, and becoming the miracle of transformation into a disciple of Jesus Christ. It's all about "becoming" as we learn to trust in Him while moving "thru" our trials.

It is often deep within our most fiery trial that we may see God's loving hands shaping and molding us to become like His only begotten Son.

It is also during trial that we are often found to become discouraged... and quit!

Again, the word "choice" appears in this book about trial and winning. If we choose to "allow" ourselves to become discouraged, we will likely not discover hidden talents, develop spiritual gifts, or experience miracles in our lives–those extraordinary experiences most often appear when we push through and keep fighting to become.

I grew up in a little Community Methodist Church listening to stories of the Bible taught by a very devout Sunday School teacher, Mrs. Hilbert. I remember her stories like it was yesterday, teasing my imagination to produce the most vivid images of God's heroes and villains as they fought for good and evil. She would pause, look over her small, wire-rimmed glasses directly at me, as if to say, "You had better not interrupt me before I finish my story, young Mr. Malone," and then continue her lesson, satisfied she had put me in my place even before I could think about raising my hand to ask a question, or more likely to practice my stand-up comedy.

Mrs. Hilbert's lesson, on a beautiful Sunday morning in the early 1950s, was about standing up for what you believe, even if it costs your life. To drive home her message of faith in God, she told the story of Shadrach, Meshach, and Abednego, the famous three Hebrew boys thrown into a fiery furnace for standing up for their beliefs. I didn't dare breathe as the king ordered his servants to prepare the furnace seven times hotter than ever before and throw those disobedient Hebrews into the fire as a lesson to all who might disobey his rule.

The servants did as they were told, but as they pushed the three Hebrews into the flames, they, instead, were consumed with fire and perished. Further, the king observed, to his dismay, "four" figures within the flames of the fire, walking around, apparently unharmed–the fourth figure "being in the image of the Son of God," the scripture account reveals.

At this point in the story of the three Hebrew boys, you might be thinking that if Jesus, or someone in the image of God, such as an angel, is in our trials, why didn't He just put out the fire in the first place? Why did our Hebrew heroes have to walk into the fire if Jesus or one of Heavenly Father's other messengers was planning to rescue them anyway? The answer might just be one of the keys to understanding trial.

While you are giving that last question some thought, let me throw you another hint–a story you are most likely familiar with because it centers on our three heroes' fellow-countryman, Daniel.

After Nebuchadnezzar, king of Babylon, besieged Jerusalem in 589 B.C., he chose noblemen from Israel's royal household who were handsome and showed an aptitude for learning to be trained in the ways of the Babylonians. Daniel and his three Hebrew countrymen from Judaea were among those so trained. You already know the story of Shadrach, Meshach, and Abednego, refusing to worship the king's image, but did you know that Daniel was also placed into a sure-death trial because he, too, would not conform to standards he knew to be against his beliefs?

Daniel was being trained to become a future leader because of his exceptional qualities, which made many "wanna-be" leaders very mad. To sabotage Daniels's chances at leading the entire kingdom, King Darius was tricked into signing a new law prohibiting anyone from praying for the next thirty days except to him, or they would be thrown into the lion's den. Are you seeing where this is going?

Daniel 6:10 - Now when Daniel knew that the writing was signed, he went into his house; and his windows being open in his chamber toward Jerusalem, he kneeled upon his knees three times a day, and prayed, and gave thanks before his God, as he did aforetime.

Even though Daniel knew of this new law, his faith in his living God was not altered, nor was his belief that he would be protected, be it his God's will. Daniel continued praying vocally three times a day as he had done before the new law, making himself vulnerable to those who would see him destroyed.

When it was observed by those who plotted against Daniel that he continued praying to his God, in violation of the new law prohibiting prayer other than to King Darius, they brought this information to the King. Now the King loved Daniel and saw such possibilities of great leadership in him, and although he was bound by this law he himself had decreed, albeit through deceptive means, he called for Daniel to be brought before him and with great displeasure with himself for signing this new law which could not be revoked, he sentenced Daniel to the lion's den, but with this personal message: "Thy God whom thou servest continually, he will deliver thee."

Well, you no doubt know how this story goes–Daniel was thrown into the lion's den, secured by a stone rolled across the den opening, not to be removed until the next morning.

The king spent a sleepless night, fasting and without "instruments of musick," to then rise early the next morning and move with haste to the lion's den, and most likely with great emotion, called out to Daniel from the other side of the stone which blocked the entry: "O Daniel, servant of the living God, is thy God, whom thou servest continually, able to deliver thee from the lions?"

Daniel answered in the affirmative that God had sent an angel to shut the mouths of the lions so they could not harm this innocent and brave young man who would live to accomplish many great things in service to his God and king.

Mrs. Hilbert taught our class that the point of both stories is–Jesus Christ is always with us, even when we are in the middle of a fiery furnace of trial… we may not perceive He is there during an unspeakable tragedy, but Satan certainly sees Him by our side and will do everything in his power to cloud our minds from discovering who we really are–who we can really become.

I believe that is why so many marriages, family discord, and spiritual breakdowns happen when we are hit with trial; Satan wants to confuse us so that our first call (Winning Way #1) "isn't" to God. He wants us to be edgy, discouraged, afraid, selfish, and unable to remember that Jesus Christ is here for us, waiting with open arms to offer succor when needed most when we are about to quit "after all we can do." As we learn to trust Him, we discover He is always here to offer strength, solutions, development of spiritual gifts, discovery of hidden talents, and even provide a miracle to help us win.

Thus, the title of Chapter 5 was born.

So, what say ye? Did the retelling of these inspiring stories instill in you a desire to jump into a den of lions or a fiery furnace to see if your Heavenly Father would send an angel to bail you out? Hopefully, it inspired you to consider how strong your personal faith is in the face of trial. Would you have praised the person responsible for your dire situation as Daniel did after the stone was rolled back and then greeted by the king? I'm sure the attitude of the king toward Daniel in finding him safe had a lot to do with the greeting between these two men, but the point I want to make is in each trial we face, there is always *choice* when we come out on the other side, as to how we will react, what we will learn, how we will change, and who we will bless with what we have learned while in the midst of the fiery furnace or a den full of hungry lions.

In this Chapter on Gifts, Talents, and Miracles, I hope to successfully show you why trial is so necessary to our purposes in coming to earth in the first place.

While these two stories we just read of faith and courage are fresh in your mind, let's try to understand why they (the trials) were necessary in the first place. If God is so powerful and can see the beginning and end of all things, why didn't He just blow out the fire Shadrach, Meshach, and Abednego were thrown into so the King's servants didn't have to die? And why did Daniel have to endure a night of trial with lions all about if God was going to send an angel to restrain the lions anyway? Why did the king have to endure a sleepless night of second-guessing himself over the fate of Daniel because he allowed himself to be tricked?

The answers to these questions and many others regarding the purposes of trial lie within what we know of the early beginnings of Adam and Eve while living in the Garden of Eden. They were not there by accident or by some freak of nature. They were born into this earth, which was created for a grand and glorious purpose–to give humanity *experience* by which they may learn and grow to overcome the natural man within them and, therefore, become like God in preparation to live eternally with Him.

Trial and/or opposition is the required ingredient necessary when mixed with endurance to lead us "out" of the fire and onto the road to success, or (aka) becoming!

God may rescue us from the fire, but He will not necessarily prevent the fire. It is often our walk through the fire that we are humbled sufficiently to dig so deep within that we find our true selves.

Think about Psalm 23. In verse 4, the Psalmist says, "Yea, though I walk through the valley of the shadow of death, I will fear no evil: for thou art with me; thy rod and thy staff they comfort me." -KJV

As a boy, I remember hearing my grandmother, Ethyl (Memaw) Malone, read Psalms from the Holy Bible. The 23rd Psalm was one she recited often. It offered her comfort when she experienced affliction. It provided her strength when she felt incapable of rising above her trials. She knew affliction, but she often told me she did not belong in God's kingdom without first having to walk through her trials. It took me many years before I came to personally understand what my Memaw meant. She had accepted trial in her life to " purify" her in preparation to enter God's kingdom. She felt *comfort* in her trial because she trusted "*her Jesus*" (as she was fond of saying) to protect her (the reference to the rod and staff of the Good Shepherd) when in trouble, but also to guide her when life became dark and dreary. She was a great person of faith.

Memaw believed she had to not only *endure* the purifying process but she had to learn from it and become closer to God throughout her trial so she could be molded and shaped to become like "her Jesus."

David the Psalmist taught in his 23rd Psalm that life is going to be full of valleys and hills with all sorts of dangers lurking about, *but fear not, little flock; [for I am with you] for it is your Father's good pleasure to give you the kingdom!"*

What a marvelous blessing for *winning!*

The prophet Isaiah describes the Good Shepherd in such a beautiful manner as well, fitting very nicely with David's Psalm about caring for "the flock:"

Isaiah 40:11 – "He shall feed his flock like a shepherd: he shall gather the lambs with his arm, and carry them in his bosom, and shall gently lead those that are with young."

The next time trial knocks at your door, and you start to feel alone and forgotten, I want you to remember this most tender visual of the Savior, "your Savior," looking out over the field (earth) at His lambs (you and I), and with rod and staff (protector and guide), He keeps a sure count of each of us, caring for and protecting us, feeding us, guiding and watching over us, gathering the young lambs (those with growing testimonies perhaps? Maybe we sinners who feel unable to be forgiven?) into His bosom (what a marvelous feeling to know He desires to draw you close to Him) and what could be more tender than a parent with child, to be gently led (He does not force) and taught in the ways of parenting? Taught how to love unconditionally? I hope you can learn to picture this scene and remember the prophet Isaiah's beautiful words when things get tough. I know I will.

Okay, one final biblical example before we move on to the actual Winning Ways of Chapter 5. The subject setting is taken from Mark 4:

36-41 and focuses on the story of the Savior and His disciples crossing the Sea of Galilee, when Jesus "rebuked the wind, and said unto the sea, Peace, be still.' You remember that story, don't you? Like most, you probably focused on the miracle of Jesus calming the raging sea rather than the tender rebuke given by Jesus to His disciples.

Jesus suggested to his followers that they move to the other side of the sea as nightfall was almost upon them. Partway across the waterway, a storm arose, causing those in the boat with Him to cry out to Jesus, who was asleep on a pillow in the hinder part of the vessel, to save them. "Master," they cried... "carest thou not that we perish?'

And he said unto them, "Why are ye so fearful? How is it that ye have no faith?"

I have thought about this experience with Jesus and His Disciples and wonder how I would have reacted if I was one of those in the boat carrying the Son of God. Of course, those in the boat with Him at the time were just beginning to experience His miracles and understand His teachings. Could they be expected to possess faith sufficient to wait as the tempest filled the boat without at least crying out to Jesus to save them?

I wonder what the purpose of that tempest was in the first place. Maybe to get His disciples' attention so He could build them into the great leaders they would need to become after He was crucified? His rebuke was simple, but two words are more significant than the others when considering our reaction to trial: Fear and Faith! Do we really think that Jesus didn't know the boat's condition as water from the storm began to fill the hull? It doesn't say what these experienced fishermen did to protect themselves and their craft "before" they cried out in fear," Master, save us!" But I think they missed an excellent opportunity to learn from their trial when they chose to appeal their plight to a sleeping Jesus instead of "calling upon Heavenly Father" first.

Yes, the miracle maker "Yeshua" was right there in the boat with them, and He surely could produce a miracle to calm the sea... but I wonder, what if we all could be so strong in faith and void of fear when trial strikes as a thief in the night, as to condition ourselves to first seek help from God in finding a solution. But perhaps another equally important purpose of trial is to help us become teachable until we can grow in sufficient faith to "look for opportunity?"

Let me see if I can recap what we have learned so far in this Chapter:

-There is purpose in trial.

-There is opportunity in trial.

-Trial and opposition provide an opportunity to connect with Jesus Christ amidst the storm.

-We can learn from our trials.

-Without struggle, we can never truly experience victory.

-Jesus Christ will always be by our side, even during our most difficult trials.

-Often, the lesson in trial is not learned until we have passed through it–until our faith has been tried.

-Trial can open our minds and hearts to change.

... and others you will surely find hidden just for you to discover!

Heavenly Father has not left you without

Spiritual Gifts, Hidden Talents, and Miracles to help you through your trials.

I want to go back to the scripture example of The Good Shepherd in Psalms 23 and call upon your imagination to have you visualize a familiar painting by artist Simon Dewey of Jesus Christ as The Good Shepherd, titled "Dear to the Heart of the Shepherd," as He sits comfortably upon the side of a grassy hill, Rod and Staff at His side, his familiar red robe draped over His shoulder, overlooking a beautiful green pasture–the sun setting slowly, casting a warm glow about Him and the baby lamb sitting peacefully on His lap–the Savior's hand resting gently upon the lamb. This scene reinforces the tenderness of our Savior's love for each of His lambs (you and I) while watching tirelessly over all His remaining flock.

What I hope you take from this visual is what the Rod and Staff of the Shepherd have to do with Spiritual Gifts, Hidden Talents, and Miracles. Shepherds generally use the staff to gently guide, direct, and teach the sheep under their care; the rod protects and supports. Thus, with the aid of these implements, the shepherd can see His sheep fulfill the measure of their creation as a blessing in so many ways to the survival and comfort of humanity.

Likewise, "our" Good Shepherd–yours and mine, has given His 'all' that we might live to fulfill the measure of "our" creation–"*For behold, this is my work and my glory—to bring to pass the immortality and eternal life of man."* (Book of Moses 1:39). God's purpose in creating this earth was to provide a place of learning and experience where we could receive a physical body as clothing for our spirit and learn how to utilize both the spiritual-self and natural man within each of us to become all God intended us to be, and then return to His presence when our earthly trial is completed.

God started teaching and preparing us (His children, His sheep) from the very beginning, even in the Garden of Eden, where Adam and Eve were commanded to "dress" their garden and enjoy the fruits thereof, but also commanded our first parents to not partake of the fruit from *that* tree – or else they would "surely" die.

Much of our earthly experience would come from exercising "agency," as Adam and Eve discovered by choosing to experience eventual death over life forever in a state of... contentment. But in choosing eventual death, they also chose life. They were now free to experience true joy because they would also experience pain. And because of battle and opposition, they would also experience winning. Without Goliath, there would have been no David the Conqueror. All experience was to be for the good and education of man (and woman), even those unthinkable experiences you would not wish upon an advancing enemy.

As humanity progressed in their learning and earthly education, the Son of God was sent to earth to provide a loving atonement for all sins–retroactive to the beginning and extending to the end. This gift of freedom from 'spiritual' death opened a portal to eternal possibilities of who we could become. We could learn, as Adam and Eve did, and *fail forward,* as Adam and Eve did, and through the gift of repentance, as Adam and Eve did, we can now become clean from the stain of those sins because of our Good Shepherd's atoning sacrifice for us.

To further guide us into becoming, Jesus once said in His dialogue with a lawyer, a Pharisee:

"Thou shalt love the Lord thy God with all thy heart, and with all thy soul, and with all thy mind.

"This is the first and great commandment.

"And the second is like unto it, Thou shalt love thy neighbour as thyself.

"On these two commandments hang all the law and the prophets" (Matt. 22:37–40; Gal. 5:14).

In our preparation of *becoming*, our Good Shepherd has made it quite simple to understand how we are to assess our priorities in life: Loving God with our whole self leads us and opens the door to a portal containing unlimited access to spiritual gifts, hidden gifts, and miracles to assist us in becoming like God.

It is the *second* great commandment, however, that validates the acquisition and power of these gifts, talents, and miracles by using them to bless the lives of our neighbors. And who are our neighbors Jesus referenced in His counsel to the Pharisees? Every man, woman, and child within our sphere of influence.

You see, we acquire gifts, talents, and miracles as we learn to love God with all our heart, mind, and soul. But to truly "fulfill" the measure of our creation, we need to learn to love and serve our neighbor as ourselves, as we would hope to be loved and served. This is truly the essence of *becoming*.

Winning Way #5 – Trust in God

Doesn't this simple statement of Winning Way #5, a declaration of incredible magnitude, accurately reflect the Good Shepherd's role in our lives and that of our Heavenly Father? Trust embodies the purest form of love. Who can deny a young child's pure love and trust for her parent or loved one when she voluntarily falls backward, knowing capable hands will be there to catch her? Boy or girl, we have all had that experience in our life, in some form, haven't we? Wasn't it exhilarating?

But it's likely quite different now as an adult to maintain that same innocent trust you possessed as a child. But my friend, that is precisely the point of Winning Way #5. You can… no, you *'must'* recapture that feeling in order to *win thru trial.*

I know what you might be thinking right now, and no, you are not expected to run into a blazing inferno to show your trust in God (unless you are trained and equipped as one of our hero "first responders") or jump into the lion's cage at the zoo… unless it is empty.

But I think our 3rd story (Jesus asleep in the boat) might be a great example of where trust starts, even if Jesus rebuked His disciples a little for their apparent lack of faith. The way I see it, the disciples at least knew who to wake up to calm the sea. They didn't abandon the ship, leaving Jesus to fare for Himself. Of course, their trust would grow as they received the power of the Holy Ghost and began to discover their gifts and talents and develop faith strong enough to perform miracles. They were on the road to *becoming,* and even this challenge of their trust and faith did help them to *fail forward.*

There will be times in your life when your faith, love, and/or trust in God will be tested, maybe severely. Winning Way #5 is a reminder that

He will always be there for you, His hand reaching out to you... but you must develop sufficient trust in your Savior to "take His hand," for He is that same begotten Son of your Heavenly Father who walked through the valley of the shadow of death to claim each of us. In His role as The Good Shepherd, Jesus Christ can be trusted to teach, guide, and protect us, even when we think we have failed Him. He is quick to forgive and forget our shortcomings and stands at the ready, with outstretched arms, to welcome us back, as the parable of the prodigal son teaches us in the Book of Luke.

Without complete trust in the Lord, we are unlikely to develop spiritual gifts to the extent they were designed to be a blessing by our Heavenly Father.

However, we may find ourselves walking away from a door that just closed behind us to one that is open, only to discover and develop new talents in the process–maybe even enjoy financial gain from doing so. This is the right and blessing of agency. But, to do so and not bring Jesus Christ into the picture is to walk a very fragile road... in my opinion.

I am not trying to convert you to my way of thinking here, but would you really trade temporary earthly fame, power, and riches for an eternity of happiness without end? Just keep your mind open a little longer, and I promise you will see a clearer picture of who you are and who you can become.

What are Spiritual Gifts, and how are they different from Natural and Learned Talent?

"Everybody has talent, it's just a matter of moving around until you've

discovered what it is." -George Lucas

Paul the Apostle taught that gifts of the spirit are "given to every man." 1 Corinthians 12:7.

The quick answer to the bold question above is that spiritual gifts are given, and natural talent is inherited. And learned skills are... learned! This may arouse some discussion among you, my readers, but just for the record, let's agree that spiritual gifts and natural or learned talent and skills all flow from the same source – our Creator.

For one to receive spiritual gifts, one must be a believer, or else how will such gifts be recognized as the source from which they are received? Natural talent is often hereditary and environmentally based, available to believers or non-believers alike, and further developed by hard work and desire. Now for the big difference: <u>spiritual gifts grow and are magnified as they are used to bless and serve others</u>. Natural and learned talents generally serve only those possessing them, although others may benefit from observing or associating with such talent.

With such personal attributes as character traits and personality temperament often playing a role in developing both gift and talent, it is sometimes extremely hard to clearly define one over the other. But let us be clear: they are definitely different.

In my case, I developed (learned) a talent to play the trumpet. I could not read music before I started taking private lessons in my youth–but over time, I developed my musical talent and used that skill to earn a full-ride music scholarship to University.

Would I say that I was gifted in music? Nope, not one bit. But I would keep practicing until I got it right. The students with a natural ability for music (some would argue they were gifted) were already out into the night while I was still burning the candle in the practice studio, trying to learn the day's assignments. I watched them, the ones who just "got it!" They seemed so far ahead of me when it came to writing music and playing by instinct. One of my heroes at University was a legend as a jazz musician. When his eyes began to close, I knew he was about to leave the written page and enter his world of runs and melodies that somehow kept in sync with the orchestra as he once again landed successfully–to the crowd's applause.

My attempts at departing from the printed page were most often a disaster, which is why I never did succeed in jazz class. Oh, I could play the notes, but I didn't make the notes fly off the page in free formation like my music colleague.

I also had a passion for guitar, but not enough to work at it every day. I taught myself guitar chords, which was sufficient to feed my desire to play and sing before small crowds. When at University, I joined the choral group and was asked to entertain the crowd with a few songs and jokes out front while the other choir members were taking a break. I loved the sound of acceptance and worked hard to be good enough, but I didn't push harder. I made embarrassing mistakes, but I kept trying.

Earlier in this book, I mentioned that I worked in a music store during summer break. A fellow came in one day and asked the owner if he knew anyone who could play the drums. Without thinking, I lied right in front of the store owner, who also happened to be my high school music teacher, and I told the man "I" was a drummer! We agreed he would audition me when he returned in a few weeks. When the door closed, I immediately turned to my boss and asked if I could please check out a set of drums.

I banged on those drums every day for weeks, driving my poor mother crazy. But when the fellow returned to audition me, I was hired to play for a dance up in the White Mountains. This was my first "gig!"

Learning how to bang on drums and keep a beat helped nurse me financially through two years of University. Talented? I wouldn't say so. Gifted? Naw, for sure on that one. But I learned something about myself that would carry me through 53 years (and counting) in one of the most volatile industries–real estate. As a real estate broker, I will do whatever it takes to serve my client. Maybe I developed that character trait while learning trumpet, guitar, drums, and piano. It did not come easy, but I just persevered, nonetheless. Hmm! Maybe my spiritual gift is "perseverance."

Did you know that "you" possess some form of innate talent? Like me, you may not think that you are exceptionally talented–but if you take a moment to look at yourself, I bet you will discover "something" you possess in more abundance than others. While you are at it, please write a few of your talents in the margin of this book. Go ahead, and don't judge yourself based on your knowledge of someone you know who is better than you at your particular talent. Being better or worse is not the point. Believe me, there will *always* be someone better or worse than you. The fact that you are capable at *something* is worth writing down as a talent.

You may have a skill at video games that shows off your quick mind and reflex dexterity. That's a talent. Maybe you enjoy cooking and receive pleasure from serving a great meal. Believe me, that's a talent. Perhaps you have a characteristic that causes you to volunteer for things when no one else is stepping up. What a marvelous talent. Now, keep at it until you have listed at least five talents you possess. Maybe you enjoy being the one to clean up after dinner because it gives you a sense of satisfaction… and you just like to do it. Maybe that is a gift, or maybe we had the same Mama who insisted we clean up. But if you keep at it, I think it is a gift to share.

I would love to see you dig even deeper for talents you don't think would even register a one on the Richter scale and write those down also–<u>because one day, when trial comes-a-calling, you may find that hidden talent exposed for what it is–a life preserver.</u>

But how do you know if this particular ability you're considering is a "natural talent" or a "spiritual gift"? Well, maybe we should start by looking at what the Bible says about spiritual gifts. The apostle Paul taught the saints at Corinth: "Concerning spiritual gifts, brethren, I would not have you ignorant." 1 Corinthians 12:7-11

We learn in the 12th Chapter of Corinthians that "…there are diversities of gifts, but the same spirit. And that "…it is the same God which worketh all in all."

Before we lose sight of "why" I am dragging you through this minefield of "Oops, that's a gift!" Or "Nope, mine is a natural talent, not a gift!" Or, "Hey, I had to really work hard to get where I am today. Nobody gave me nutten!"–let me explain the connection.

We were not placed here on earth as defenseless lambs, to become the easy prey of ravaging wolves, without being armed with spiritual defenses, guides, and support in the form of–spiritual gifts, hidden talents, and yes, even a miracle or two. The intent of Chapter 5 is to assist you, the reader, in discovering these laden gifts and talents throughout your life.

The next time you are confronted with trial and opposition, genuinely humbled to seek protection, guidance, and a healing embrace from The Good Shepherd, remember to open your mind to the discovery of hidden talents and pray to understand which spiritual gifts you possess that can be used to bless His other sheep.

"The gifts of the Spirit can guide and enrich our lives. They can strengthen us spiritually and temporally. They can help us bless the lives of others. Most important, they can bring us comfort in times of trial. They can help us magnify our callings. They can help guide us in our relationships. They can help us avoid being deceived." (Robert D. Hales, August 1, 1993 • BYU Devotional).

The subject of "spiritual gifts" in a book about trial might be a stretch for many to understand, which is why, I suppose, I was impressed to include it in this chapter with Hidden Talents and Miracles. It could be a chapter of its own, for most of us have little idea of the greatness that lies inside us, waiting dormant until the right trial of our life ignites our eternal flame of *becoming* and a new spiritual gift (AKA: talent or character trait) is born.

What are these "gifts," one might ask? How do I know if I have one? How and why does one "seek the best gifts?

All good questions!

Let's start with the basics and another question: Have you ever observed a flower garden at the beginning of springtime? Likely, these beautiful flowers were planted from a packet of seeds, yet each flower is distinctive–no two flowers from the same package of seeds are exactly the same. Each is uniquely beautiful, although when observing them as a garden cluster, row, or field of flowers, they appear similar–almost as one.

We are like those flowers, created spiritually from the same heavenly parents and possessing physical and spiritual characteristics that are similar to them (Genesis 1:27, Wisdom of Solomon 2:23). Yet, we are uniquely different from one another in so many ways.

First, a caution: do not be misled by the word "gifts."

Unlike receiving a Christmas or Birthday gift that is adorned with colorful wrappings and bows which are discarded to reveal a worldly representative of one's feelings for another, often discarded for another seemingly more attractive gift that plays, flies, rides, or any other action deemed more to the recipient's liking–the gifts we will be learning about in this book are not tangible objects, but instead gifts of the spirit to enable us to better navigate our path through this mortal life into the next. These gifts of the spirit are meant to enhance our personal joy in life and to aid in our character development as we strive to become more like God, our Creator, and His only Begotten Son, our Good Shepherd.

But unlike the tangible gifts referenced above, meant for personal pleasure and gain, the gifts I am speaking of are intended to be shared with others, the body of Christ, of which we are all members–both believer and non-believer, Jew and Gentile, as referred to by the apostle

Paul in 1 Corinthians 12, which is an excellent resource for better understanding the *diversities* of gifts available to all.

By sharing our gifts and talents with others, we magnify them. It's like spreading the seeds from one packet all over the flower bed to grow and fulfill their purpose in life, adding much joy and satisfaction to both the gardener and observer.

If God, our Heavenly Father, placed us here on earth to be tried and tested for a time, then it is that same God who lovingly placed within us the power to not only survive (endure) trial but to learn and grow from it. Yes, we were born into this world naked, in terms of visible clothing, but <u>each of us came armed with "one important and very distinctive gift" - *the Light of Christ,* to act as a spiritual compass to help us find our way through this maze called earth.</u> This light, a true gift from God, is also referred to as a conscience, an inner light not to be confused with the Holy Ghost, but acts in tandem as an inner-influence available to grow or diminish with the use of agency to choose good or evil (John 1:9; Ephesians 5:14; Doctrine and Covenants 84:46; 93:2). *Notable writers on the concept of the light of Christ include Ephrem the Syrian in the fourth century, Severus of Antioch in the sixth century,[3] and the Quaker William Penn. [4] -Wikipedia.

There is a constant war going on inside ourselves between two forces–good and evil. As explained earlier in this writing, this inner "tug-o-war" was permitted by God to prepare His children for spiritual greatness in the world to come. This inner light referenced herein is deemed a true "gift" to each one of us as a means to find our way back to Him who created us. This light grows or diminishes as a reflection of our actions. It dims when we make choices (agency) that lead us away from God, and it burns brighter as we strive (the act of becoming) to become more like Him–doing our best, then occasionally falling, getting back up through repentance, and doing our best to become better–inch by inch we grow, with the Light of Christ ever burning, ever lighting the way, internally encouraging us to do better, be better, at living God's commandments.

However marvelous this gift of conscience is in lighting the way toward becoming, it is not in itself sufficient in fulfilling the great purpose of our being. Our Heavenly Father's mission statement for each of His children as we were sent on our earthly mission is found in the Book of Moses, Chapter 1:39 *"For behold, this is my work and my glory—to bring to pass the immortality and eternal life of man."* He clearly wants each of His children to return to His presence and has provided this earthly experience as a second estate from our pre-mortal life to learn and develop our nature(s) to become *like* Him–with a magnificent earthly body designed to house our eternal spirit, and "gifts of the spirit" to aid our development in preparation for when the waves of opposition and trial descend upon us. "We don't want to learn how to swim when the boat is already sinking," Elder Robert D. Hales said in his devotional to BYU students in 1993.

In addition to the Light of Christ, which we all possess in some degree of brightness, a thorough examination of recorded scripture reveals that the Apostle Paul taught that <u>every single man or woman ever born also has at least one 'unique' spiritual gift</u>, a talent or ability to call their own, unique in every way:

11 For all have not every gift given unto them; for there are many gifts, and to every man is given a gift by the Spirit of God.

12 To some is given one, and to some is given another, that all may be profited thereby. (See Doctrine and Covenants 46:11-12;1 Cor 7:7; 12:7; Ephesians 4:7; 1 Peter 4:10; and Romans 12:6).

We are free to enlarge upon or hide this spiritual gift, but it is there, nonetheless, waiting for us to discover and use as part of our earthly school of becoming.

The relevance of receiving "at least one gift" is that each contains a characteristic of our Lord and Savior, Jesus Christ. It is fitting that we, recipients of our Savior's atonement, carry within us a part of our Savior's nature to do with as we will. It is through the identifying and enhancing of spiritual and physical gifts that enable us to discover our seeds of greatness and use that experience to grow in our faith to become more like Jesus Christ as a defense against the one (Satan) set free on earth to try to weaken our faith through trial. This book and its many references were written as Winning Ways to help us not only endure Satan's attempts at putting us down through personal fiery darts of trial (AKA: ravaging wolves) but to act as a guide in using the pain inflicted as a catalyst for unleashing the God-given power within us to become spiritually MIGHTY. Without battle, there is no win! Without experiencing pain, we are less likely to become our greatest selves.

As I shared in Chapter Four, I have learned firsthand that the pain of trial often opens the door to personal discouragement and self-criticism. It is not uncommon to find ourselves being rather harsh toward the image in the mirror after sustaining a loss from trial. Blame leads to self-analyzing ourselves as incompetent, incapable, and lacking in many ways, giving in to Satan's attempts at bringing us down to his level, convinced that we have no gifts, and helpless to recover.

But somehow, at some point, this inner light finds a crack in the grey cloud encasing our hearts and begins to shine through again, helping us feel the love and protection of the Good Shepard for us, His flock.

There is much written about spiritual gifts in scripture, and the door is open for interpretation. But if you will bear with me, I would like to focus on how the righteous, well-intentioned use of personal and spiritual gifts can become a blessing in times of trial. Remember Winning Way #4 – Opportunity, look for it. Then consider this challenge of finding opportunity: "When trial hits, look for gifts, talents, interests, or desires to expand."

It often only takes a shift in the routine of daily life to open one's mind to personal change. As my mother used to tell me: "listen to your body!" You have choice when it comes to your reaction to trial, remember? Then, choose to identify a gift that may have been lying dormant and activate it. This is a time of opportunity that doesn't come around very often, so let's use it to the fullest–and rather than mope around the house feeling sorry for yourself about something you most likely cannot change at this point (trial), why not take a good look within and take a survey of your interests or ask someone you trust emotionally to help you see what is good about yourself, seen by others but perhaps not by you.

Our gifts are meant to be enhanced, magnified, and shared,

not hidden and undeveloped.

Perhaps you have a talent you used for a while but, like me, got too busy to develop it, and like any talent or gift that is shelved for any length of time, it becomes covered with dust, hidden from view, destined to live as a memory, only; or maybe there was this 'interest' you never got around to exploring. Maybe there is someone going through their own trial who could benefit from your gift. The sure way to enhance or magnify your gift(s) is to use them to bless others.

Ok, it must be time for another personal experience: Early in my business career, I made a choice to leave what some might have considered a "safe" position of employment for a very risky attempt at becoming an independent business owner in the field of real estate, captaining my own ship, experiencing freedom of choice, and reaping the rewards of free enterprise. And yes, it was one of the best decisions I would ever make because it quickly revealed areas of my professional development that were weak and others that were surprisingly strong.

This entrepreneurial experience opened the door for expanding what I considered weak talents that needed professional guidance, so I studied and attended seminars, enrolled in real estate professional certification courses, and slowly but surely began to see improvement. I was excited about my growth, which showed in my speech, giving me the confidence and power to build a successful business from scratch.

Over my 53 years (and counting) in the real estate industry, I have used my gifts and developed talents to bless not only my immediate and extended family but hundreds of other families who needed the help of a professional to navigate through the ever-changing, ever-challenging process of buying or selling real estate.

However, an earlier chapter of my life found me wallowing in self-pity after my 10-year run at home building came to an end during the era of high inflation and 21% mortgage interest rates in the 1980s.

I started over in another business, which took little capital but required lots of time at nights and weekends to build a team of like-minded entrepreneurs who wanted to create another source of income from their day job and possibly one day experience what it felt like to live "debt free."

Having built an income-producing machine in my home building and real estate companies, I saw the "opportunity in trial" and started over, only to once again become keenly aware of my lack of skill and talents in certain areas necessary in communicating with others, such as public speaking and voice strength.

I had never thought of public speaking as a gift, but I soon learned that I had a talent for self-expression within me. I had done very well as a sales rep for a General Electric distributor of kitchen appliances right out of college, learning how to communicate a product's benefits to a retail outlet's owner or appliance manager, and then again as a self-employed real estate agent. But when this new business took hold, I found myself in front of groups of people, in living rooms and coffee shop back rooms... and then on auditorium stages. It was then that I started to develop this talent... or gift–I really didn't know what it was at that time–by taking voice lessons.

Although I had begun to develop a talent for singing while at the University, I hadn't followed through with developing it any further, and it became weak through my trial of self-pity and depression.

When I joined the City of Mesa Toastmasters Club (I was the only non-employee in the club), I enhanced my gift of self-expression by learning how to think on my feet when giving a talk, how to use voice inflections of tone to draw interest, and how to tell stories that would bring others to their feet.

I also learned how to strengthen my ability of self-expression with study and hard work. Was it really a gift, or was it merely a bit of talent mixed with lots of hard work? Perhaps we shall only know for certain the individual answer to that question once we once again meet our Maker and have the opportunity to report on how well we did with our time (developing gifts and talents) on earth. But from my experience with trial, I genuinely believe that our gifts are meant to be enhanced, magnified, and shared, not hidden and undeveloped. You may want to conduct your own study of gifts; there are plenty of scriptural references if you just look for them, no matter your chosen faith to associate with.

Take for instance, the Parable of the Talents, taught by Jesus Christ and recorded in the Book of Matthew 25:14–29. Although the parable uses a unit of money to represent a "talent," one could just as easily use "spiritual gifts" that the Lord of all shares with us, His servants, with the intent that we are to develop and magnify what we are given.

In verse Twenty-one of the 25th chapter of Matthew, the man (representing the Lord) returns after a time to see how well his servants have done with the talents they were given. The amount of growth didn't seem to matter to the Lord, for he gave the same praise to both men who received different amounts of talents and had magnified what they were given: 21 His lord said unto him, Well done, thou good and faithful servant: thou hast been faithful over a few things, I will make thee ruler over many things: enter thou into the joy of thy lord. But to the servant who hid his talent because he was afraid and did not enlarge upon that which he had been given, these words were spoken: 29 For unto every one that hath shall be given, and he shall have abundance: but from him that hath not shall be taken away even that which he hath.

The Lord - our God, expects us, His servants, His disciples, His believers, His children, to do our best to enlarge upon that which we have been given by sharing our gifts with others, by being His hands to bless those who are in need, by being His feet to walk with those who mourn, by being His voice to those who stand in need of encouragement and love. <u>We can become His rod and staff</u>.

The Apostle Paul reinforces this understanding in the Book of Galatians 6:7-10, often referred to as the law of the harvest. Perhaps you will recall parts of this recorded scripture without knowing its origin: "…for whatsoever a man Soweth, that shall he also reap." (Galatians 6:7)

Paul goes on to teach: 9 "And let us not be weary in well doing: for in due season we shall reap, if we faint not.

10 "As we have therefore opportunity, let us do good unto all men, especially unto them who are of the household of faith."

This teaching of one of the Lord's early apostles seems to reinforce the teaching of the Savior in the Parable of the Talents, that if we share our talents and gifts with others and focus on using these gifts for the well-being of others, we too, shall receive.

Now, there is one additional piece of news for you. We are expected to also "seek ye the best gifts." (Doctrine and Covenants 46:28-33) "But earnestly desire the best gifts." (1 Corinthians 12:3; 14:1)

Just *possessing* certain spiritual gifts and talents does not appear to be sufficient. We are expected to "seek" such attributes–even the best, which may help to perfect our insufficiencies.

George Q. Cannon, a territorial delegate to the United States Congress (1873-1882), and editor, publisher, businessman, educator, and a faithful member of the Church of Jesus Christ of Latter-day Saints, was quoted as having taught the following about the why of seeking the best gifts:

"How many of you ... are seeking for these gifts that God has promised to bestow? How many of you, when you bow before your Heavenly Father in your family circle or in your secret places contend for these gifts to be bestowed upon you? How many of you ask the Father, in the name of Jesus, to manifest Himself to you through these powers and these gifts? Or do you go along day by day like a door turning on its hinges, without having any feeling upon the subject, without exercising any faith whatever..."

"... If any of us are imperfect, it is our duty to pray for the gift that will make us perfect. Have I imperfections? I am full of them. What is my duty? To pray to God to give me the gifts that will correct these imperfections. If I am an angry man, it is my duty to pray for charity, which suffereth long and is kind. Am I an envious man? It is my duty to seek for charity, which envieth not. So with all the gifts of the Gospel.

They are intended for this purpose. No man ought to say, 'Oh, I cannot help this; it is my nature.' He is not justified in it, because God has promised to give strength to correct these things and give gifts that will eradicate them. If a man lack wisdom, it is his duty to ask God for wisdom..." (In Millennial Star, Apr. 1894, pp. 260–61.)

This chapter is not intended to cover every possible interpretation or application of gifts and talents, but before we move on to the subject of "miracles," I did want to stimulate your thinking about the kind of gifts and talents you might possess now and not recognize them.

Because I have used the epistles of Paul so much in this chapter, let's continue with his teachings on the subject of spiritual gifts that a believer might possess, found in 1 Corinthians 12:4-10:

4 Now there are diversities of gifts, but the same Spirit.

5 And there are differences of administrations, but the same Lord.

6 And there are diversities of operations, but it is the same God which worketh all in all.

7 But the manifestation of the Spirit is given to every man to profit withal.

8 For to one is given by the Spirit the word of wisdom; to another the word of knowledge by the same Spirit;

9 To another faith by the same Spirit; to another the gifts of healing by the same Spirit;

10 To another the working of miracles; to another prophecy; to another discerning of spirits; to another divers kinds of tongues; to another the interpretation of tongues:

If you are not familiar with the writings and teaching of Paul, the great convert to Christianity, I invite you to partake of his insight by studying his epistles to the saints of the early Church of Jesus Christ. He is such a great example of a man who had long before extinguished the Light of Christ within him as a persecutor of those who believed. It took a miracle of sorts, on the road to Damascus, to gain his attention and loss of sight that he might see.

Other spiritual gifts you might recognize in yourself or others are:

- the gift of asking
- the gift of listening
- the gift of hearing and using the still, small voice
- the gift of being able to weep
- the gift of avoiding contention
- the gift of being agreeable
- the gift of avoiding vain repetition
- the gift of seeking that which is righteous
- the gift of not passing judgment
- the gift of looking to God for guidance
- the gift of being a disciple
- the gift of caring for others

- the gift of being able to ponder
- the gift of offering prayer
- the gift of bearing a mighty testimony
- and the gift of receiving the Holy Ghost.

What about these gifts:
- the gift of healing
- the gift of being healed
- the gift of receiving revelation
- the gift of interpretation
- the gift of patience
- the gift of leadership
- the gift of testimony
- the gift of teaching
- the gift of music
- the gift of understanding numbers
- the gift of art
- the gift of expression

- the gift of appreciation
- the gift of wisdom
- the gift of love for parents
- the gift of casting out spirits
- the gift to discern evil spirits and, in contrast discern the pure spirit of others
- the gift of faith
- the gift of understanding the scriptures
- the gift of connection with the Holy Spirit
- the gift of a light heart
- the gift of self-mastery
- the gift of working with your hands
- the gift of a positive attitude
- the gift to nurture others
- the gift of charity
- the gift of intuition
- the gift of virtue

- the gift to ponder
- the gift to bring beauty and color into your home
- the gift of courage and strength to defend and protect your children against evil influences
- the gift to love
- the gift to be loved
- the gift to express love
- the gift to strengthen others
- the gift of mental clarity
- the gift of being agreeable
- the gift of not passing judgment
- the gift to create family ties and relationships
- the gift of a joyful nature
- the gift of hope
- and the gift of gratitude

Do you know someone who has a gift or talent to:
- make others laugh

- stay calm in the face of danger

- speak reason and instill confidence

- dance

- cook

- make things with their hands

- repair broken parts

- analyze complex data

- memorize or recall facts once known

- stay in touch with friends and family

- feel compassion

- decorate

- change

- work

- know when it's time to play

I could go on and on... but I think I made the point very clear: if you don't see a talent or gift that is listed, then "ask" God to help you attain one and then another, but be aware that receiving spiritual gifts come with the support and blessing of God to help you accomplish miracles in your life "and in the lives of others," <u>for to magnify our spiritual gifts can come about "only" when used in the service of others.</u>

I thought the day of miracles ceased with the final book of the Bible.

What comes to mind when you hear the word miracle spoken? Likely, you think of some extraordinary happening that cannot be explained or documented. But why include the subject of miracles in a chapter about gifts and talents? In a book about trial? Because God uses our gifts and talents to perform daily miracles in people's lives. And He often uses trial as a backdrop to His miracles.

But I thought the day of miracles ceased with the final book of the Bible. Or maybe it was when the apostle Peter was killed? Doesn't the Bible say something about miracles being discontinued? How come we don't hear about miracles occurring today?

The answer to these questions and many others is contained in the world's definition of a miracle. When Charlton Heston, aka Moses, raised his staff and commanded the Red Sea to open so the fleeing Israelites could pass through to the other side, and then again commanded the waters to close down upon the Egyptian army chasing them... now that was a miracle! Uh, "two" miracles!

And reported miracles "do" happen in our day! I'm sure you will remember this one: In 2009, a US Airways Airbus 320 carrying 155 passengers and crew lost both its engines seconds after takeoff, less than 3,000 feet in the air. Now disabled in the air the big plane would not have time to land safely on any runway close by, but in less than four minutes of losing its engines, flight 1549 cut through New York City and successfully landed on the Hudson River, saving the lives of all aboard.

The news headlines described the incident as the "Miracle on the Hudson," calling airline captain Chesley "Sully" Sullenberger a hero, courageous, and "phenomenal" in his ability to make an impossible landing. It was indeed a miracle!

But as impressive as these two miracles and others like them are, I would like to revisit with you the scripture account of when King Nebuchadnezzar demanded that Shadrach, Meshach, and Abed-nego worship the golden image he set up as a god, threatening, "If ye worship not, ye shall be cast ... into the midst of a burning fiery furnace." Then he taunted them with, "Who is that God that shall deliver you out of my hands?"

You will remember how the three Hebrew boys were pushed into the fiery furnace but were unharmed. And yes, that would certainly qualify as a miracle, but what is easy to overlook in light of the apparent miracle recorded was the response uttered by the devout three to the King's taunts: "Of course our God is able to deliver us from death by fire," they responded, "... **but if not**, be it known unto thee, O king, that we will not serve thy Gods" (Daniel 3:18).

To me, the faith these young men had in their God to protect them was, in itself, a miracle. They are the miracle, not just their death-defying leap into the fiery furnace, but their remarkable faith to accept God's will in their trial. Can't you see the fantastic miracle in that? We often pray for miracles in our lives and then curse God because things turn out differently. Asking for a miracle without adding "but if not..."

seems to color our pleading request with a shade of selfishness. We want the miracle, and we want it "our way!"

I think to show further we are willing to accept God's will in our lives, we pledge to God–but if not... please show me how to use this [whatever it is] "outcome" to bless the lives of others and strengthen the body of Christ. Our Heavenly Father loves to hear us pray for guidance on helping and serving others, especially after [seemingly] we just got turned down on our request for a miracle.

Often, we describe a miracle as a person being healed without a clear explanation, even by using medical science. Then, another miracle is born from one avoiding imminent danger by heeding a "prompting" out of nowhere–both examples unexplained by using logic or scientific data.

Did you realize that even heeding's by the Holy Ghost, the third member of the Godhead, qualify as 'miracles' in our lives, and we rarely give them miracle status?

One such story involved my choice to drive exceptionally late at night across the state of New Mexico after a full day of business meetings to reach a hotel in Albuquerque, where I had a reservation. I admit to being directionally challenged from birth and never have grown out of it, and this night would prove no different. I got lost in the mountains somewhere east of Albuquerque after receiving directions from a friend intended to be a shortcut; instead, I was on top of a mountain at midnight and needed help figuring out how to get to where I was going. I followed Winning Way #1 and called upon God for directions. The answer was not what I had hoped for: "Turn around and go back the way you came."

Two or three hours later, I found the road to the freeway and settled into the satisfaction that I was at least finally on my way to a waiting bed, only three more hours away.

I set the cruise control to the speed limit of 65 and began the most challenging night of my life, trying to keep my eyes open. And I really thought I could make it when I saw the sign that said "Albuquerque–15 miles," but it must have been the sun's rays just starting to wake up ahead of me, bringing heavy eyelids slowly to a close, when I first heard the sound of something like a bicycle with a face card attached to the wheel spoke of the front tire with a clothes pin like I used to do when I was little, that caused my eyes to awaken to the scene before me–I was headed off the road into a concrete overpass. I think it was an impression in my head, or a calm and clear voice–that I actually heard, felt, or saw first... but I don't know which before my eyes opened enough to see the quickly approaching concrete wall before me.

"You have fallen asleep."

"You are off the road headed directly toward a wall of concrete."

"Turn your steering wheel 'slightly' to the left without applying your brake," came the directions into my brain at warp-lightning speed. I calmly did as instructed, guiding the piece of steel I was piloting back onto the freeway, seeing, without turning my head, the concrete grave marker with my name slowly disappearing from it.

When the shock of what happened began to wear off after driving a couple of miles down the road, I pulled over to the side, put my car in park, and cried like a baby. I had just become the subject of a mighty miracle. Somehow, God sent the Holy Ghost to breathe something into my brain to awaken my senses enough that in the instant it takes to awaken light from its slumber, I received a clear and distinct message communicated to me so purely that I immediately obeyed. I had dodged a huge bullet, the consequences of poor choices, yet I was spared.

This incident, this miracle, would never make it into the Daily News. It wouldn't likely even be retold amongst family members for more than a mere mention if that. But I know what I heard/felt... and it saved my life. How would I ever be the same knowing the Heavens had parted... for me?

Miracles happen in trial because our hearts are the most vulnerable to change.

Miracles happen not because someone is more special than another. But they happen because in God's plan for each of us, we are sometimes entrusted with encounters like this to prove our willingness to change. Maybe you already had a life-changing trial and know exactly what I mean. Trial opens the door to change, but what we choose to do once confronted with the open door–therein lies the test. It starts with faith–that our Heavenly Father would never send us a trial that we could not learn from and change from– for the good... even if you had prayed for a miracle to save a loved one and there was no voice of confirmation, no instruction to the doctor about how to save such a precious life. But that door... was there for you, beckoning you toward the depths of humility, to taste the "Sweetness" of repentance, forgiveness, and service, all of which will help in cleansing you/us in preparation to dwell with our Heavenly family. And it is your choice whether or not to walk through it.

Trial can provide valuable and eternal perspective and even bring to the forefront of our life, neglected priorities, which can influence us to make choices that qualify us for eternal life, the greatest of all the gifts of God. (See Mosiah 5:2)

Sometimes, in the routine of life, we might get comfortable, content, or pacified, or yes, even a bit lazy about moving forward in our chosen profession, until that day when our world gets turned upside down, and we are no longer employed. Without income, we generally panic first, throw out some blame to whoever, and then turn the finger internally with enough doubt and anger to put us into a state of depression, taking down those we love in the process. Sound familiar? Hopefully, you started at the beginning of this book and have at least adopted a few new "Winning Ways" to help you get through those difficult times as they cycle through your life.

In my readings, I came across a marvelous poem-prayer attributed to Sir Francis Drake, an English sea captain during the 1500s, that fits perfectly into this book about overcoming trial. I love Sir Drake's words of pleading to "disturb us, Lord," from becoming too worldly, too satisfied with ourselves, too content, and too safe because we chose to sail too close to the shore and never risked having Jesus Christ be our captain and lead us into fulfilling the measure of our creation of *becoming* all we were blessed to be:

Disturb us, Lord, when
We are too well pleased with ourselves,

When our dreams have come true

Because we have dreamed too little,

When we arrived safely

Because we sailed too close to the shore.

Disturb us, Lord, when

With the abundance of things we possess

We have lost our thirst

For the waters of life;

Having fallen in love with life,

We have ceased to dream of eternity

And in our efforts to build a new earth,

We have allowed our vision

Of the new Heaven to dim.

Disturb us, Lord, to dare more boldly,

To venture on wider seas

Where storms will show your mastery;

Where losing sight of land,

We shall find the stars.

We ask You to push back

The horizons of our hopes;

And to push into the future

In strength, courage, hope, and love.

This we ask in the name of our Captain,

Who is Jesus Christ."

(attributed to Sir Francis Drake - 1577)

I conclude this Chapter filled with the greatest of possibilities, with a prayer for you to follow the lead of Jesus Christ, the Captain of us all, in fulfilling your dreams of becoming by applying the truths shared in this book, which, if followed may change your life forever as you learn to identify hidden talents and spiritual gifts while under the influence of trial and magnify them in the service and support of others. May your heart be filled with belief in your potential to rise above your trials and learn to trust in the Lord.

May we all fulfill the measure of our creation.

Chapter Six

Without Battle, There is No Win!

L et's begin this chapter with a story.

Once upon a time, a man came upon the scene of a struggling butterfly trying to free itself from being trapped in a cocoon. The man, now intrigued, watched intently as the butterfly struggled for quite some time, exhausting itself, resting, and then beginning the process again, but remained trapped. It was then that the man noticed a small hole in the cocoon, too small for the trapped butterfly to exit. Drawn to aid this poor creature, the man took his pocketknife and carefully slit open the small hole large enough so the butterfly could escape.

Freed from the struggle, the trapped butterfly managed to exit the cocoon, only to fall onto the ground, unable to fly away–its wings were shriveled and weak instead of being strong and fully developed. Not at all as beautiful as its brother and sister butterflies were. Unable to move, the butterfly with so much potential eventually died, unable to fulfill the measure of its creation as God had designed.

What the well-meaning man didn't know or understand about the butterfly was that to develop and strengthen itself in preparation to fly, the butterfly needed the cocoon; it was not his enemy, as the man had thought. It was his ally in God's plan of becoming.

Trial is a necessary part of our earthly experience.

Without battle, opposition, loss, misery, pain, and suffering, there is no recognition of joy, happiness, winning, overcoming, growing, or becoming. There is no win if there is nothing to lose. It was designed that way from the very beginning, settled and agreed upon as a condition of coming to earth–we would be tested.

- *I may prove them, whether they will walk in my law, Ex. 16:4.*
- *God is come to prove you, Ex. 20:20.*
- *Through them I may prove Israel, Judg. 2:22.*
- *When he hath tried me, I shall come forth as gold, Job 23:10.*
- *Lord trieth the righteous, Ps. 11:5 (Jer. 20:12).*
- *[To] know my heart: try me, Ps. 139:23.*
- *We must through much tribulation enter into the kingdom, Acts 14:22.*
- *Fire shall try every man's work, 1 Cor. 3:13.*
- *By faith, Abraham, when he was tried, offered up Isaac, Heb. 11:17.*
- *Trying of your faith worketh patience, James 1:3.*

- *Fiery trial, which is to try you, 1 Pet. 4:12.*
- *That ye may be tried, Rev. 2:10.*
- *Receive no witness until after the trial of your faith, Ether 12:6*
- *I will prove you in all things, D&C 98:14.*
- *They must needs be chastened and tried, D&C 101:4.*
- *After much tribulation ... cometh the blessing, D&C 103:12.*
- *That you may prove yourselves unto me, D&C 124:55.*
- *Ye shall be proved, Gen. 42:15.*
- *God led thee ... in the wilderness ... to prove thee, Deut. 8:2.*
- *Prove them, whether they will walk in my law, Ex. 16:4.*
- *God proveth you, to know whether ye love the Lord, Deut. 13:3.*
- *Examine me, O Lord, and prove me, Ps. 26:2.*
- *Through them I may prove Israel, Judg. 2:22.*
- *I did it ... to prove you all, as I did Abraham, D&C 132:51.*
- *We will prove them herewith, to see if they will do all things, Abr. 3:25.*

(See also Matt. 13:21; John 15:2; 16:33; Alma 32:27–28; D&C 35:23;

54:10; 122:5)

I purposely went over the top to prove a point—well, two points:

1. The Lord has been quite clear about the necessity of trial in the lives of His children, as recorded in scripture.

2. We must prove ourselves worthy to stand at the right hand of God, to enter His presence once again after having departed this earthly life.

Since this book was written for ALL faiths (Trial is non-denominational), I tried to pick scripture relevant to understanding "why trial?" and why we must prove ourselves. If you study the Quran and Torah, you will find similar scripture quotes containing references to the necessity of trial in proving one's self-worth and loyalty to God.

Abraham was tested to prove he would not blame God for the sacrifice of his son. It was indeed a supreme trial to be asked to sacrifice one's son, but with the blessings of eternal posterity promised Abraham, God had to know if Abraham's faith was strong enough to weather any trial passed upon him. And it was!

You and I may not see ourselves capable of passing such a test of faith as Father Abraham at this exact moment, but our individual reactions to trial and opposition are no less important. Our legacy, yours and mine, recorded in the heavens of our time on Earth, shall stand as a witness to our reaction to trial, whatever it may be—whatever our choices were; did we choose to do more than endure trial, and meet the minimum expectations of our earthly walk, or did we rise above and choose to win and become all we were sent to earth to accomplish. Some will magnify their purpose and choose to rise above Heavenly expectations. More on this in the book's last chapter titled "Be Mighty."

Does it make you feel just a little better about failing when you know it is part of a loving attempt to give us experience so that we might become spiritually stronger through the process? Why did Jesus Christ have to suffer, bleed, and die for all humanity, for the atonement to have meaning to every soul who came or will come to planet Earth? Why did he experience every sin imaginable to save even the vilest sinner? Exactly!

Failure is acceptable–failing to "try" is not!

If I haven't made this "disclaimer" before, in this writing, I must do so now... and hope that you will understand the nature and perspective from which I promote failure as a necessary part of "becoming." In our evolving society, the word "failure" has different implications. To a scientist looking for a cure, the term failure may imply the elimination of one more test that didn't work but opened the door to other possibilities, a positive reaction leading to more tests and closer to finding the cure.

But...

Receiving an "F" on a report card certainly implies–there are no more "tries," Mr. Malone! You have "failed." Finito!

Have you ever been "fired" from a job or failed at a task assigned to you that was given to another who completed it in record time? Would you classify your state of mind afterward as a "failure?"

In my world of personal growth, the condition known as "failure" implied "a negative or unsuccessful end to an attempt at becoming." I didn't understand then, as I do now, that the word failure has other, less negative implications, reflected in my writings on trial as a "necessary" ingredient to becoming.

In my quest to share a more positive view of failure, I may unintentionally "imply" that failure in "every" life application is necessary to achieve our becoming. <u>Believe me, that is "not" the case.</u>

Although I do believe that "all experience is for our good," in that it serves to give us the "opportunity" to gain perspective and understanding, compassion, and perhaps empathy toward others, I am by no means suggesting a "one size fits all" application to failure.

For instance, I pray that you "never" have to experience failure in your marriage, leading to divorce. This book is about "winning," not suggesting you should "intentionally" keep failing at personal relationships until you find Mr. or Ms. Perfect! Or that you should stop trying to make your current relationship work to gain experience.

Marriage is about give and take, yes... but more "give" than take, please!

Find a spouse you can love... and spend eternity trying to perfect "yourself" into becoming.

However (and there are always exceptions), if divorce does happen... and it does–a goal of this book is to encourage you to learn from that experience and work toward becoming the person you wanted your spouse to be as you contemplate future relationships, no matter whose "fault" caused the relationship to fail.

Holding grudges, blaming others (even yourself), and carrying baggage forward to the next relationship only hamstrings you in trying to make the next relationship work.

Conditions of abusive behavior, infidelity, substance abuse, and other such conditions have no place within the loving bonds of holy matrimony. Please obtain professional help if you find yourself exposed to such conditions.

So, just to put an exclamation mark to this disclaimer... please do not use the theories, principles, stories, and examples taught herein as permission to fail at _____ (You fill in the blank). Yes, there "is" much to be learned from failure "<u>after all we can do to prevent it.</u>"

Let me restate this extremely important disclaimer even more boldly:

There is much to be learned from failure, "after all we can do to prevent it!"

M. Farouk Radwan (a true story about success and failure–see YouTube) did not launch his first Internet business idea with the intent of failure. In fact, he thought it was a brilliant idea and would produce instant income. But Farouk soon "learned" that www.respectmyright.com was poorly designed, the programming was substandard, and the site was an easy target for spammers.

Yes, Farouk Radwan's first Internet business attempt failed, as did his second, third, fourth, fifth, and sixth, but with each failure, he began to learn more and more about what it took for an Internet business to be successful.

Mr. Radwan's seventh Internet business, www.2learn-online.com, was a good site, but it entered an extremely competitive niche product and got little recognition. But #8 was a winner! What if he had "quit" after the lukewarm success of #7?

The website www.2knowmyself.com (#8) incorporated M. Farouk Radwan's sixteen years of studying psychology and human behavior into a website that offers unconventional but effective techniques, "guaranteed" to effect change in behavior. The growth in this site confirmed to Farouk that he had finally succeeded... and succeed he did.

2knowmyself.com grew from 100,000 hits per month to over 500,000 hits per month... and then 1,000,000 monthly hits. And the rest is history!

I find Mr. Radwan's transparency of his failures to be helpful and in concert with my own attempts at providing you, the reader, with examples of success achieved after failure–even after several failures.

On his website, Farouk offers encouragement to anyone struggling with failure. "The more you try, the luckier you become," Farouk says. "If you don't give up, you will make it!" And "failure is ok! In fact, in most cases, it's a must."

"Failure is a prerequisite for great success. If you want to succeed faster, double your rate of failure." -Brian Tracy

***Attention! I must interrupt this train of thought with a recent experience in my real estate practice.**

In the year 2020, when the COVID-19 virus pandemic changed our lives most dramatically, the ripple effect continues, even into 2023, causing a seismic shock in varying degrees to our personal lifestyle, beliefs, attitudes, etc. Stay-at-home orders from local authorities impacted the real estate industry in many ways in 2020, sending shock waves into 2021-22, disrupting the "supply chain" of materials worldwide, and adding even more weight to the decreasing inventory of single-family homes available for sale. Coupled with increasing demand from new buyers moving into my home state for various reasons, we are currently experiencing forty percent (40%+/-) less inventory to satisfy a growing twenty-five percent (25%+/-) more demand.

This "perfect storm" of supply and demand meeting head-on has created a severe dilemma for someone wanting to buy a home. There are not enough (affordable) homes to meet the demand! We are now experiencing a high rise in interest rates and inflation caused by government intervention and a lack of supply to meet the demand. This ripple effect is creating "challenge and trial" in so many ways for buyers (can't find a home), sellers (yes, I can sell my house in one day, but where do I go when I give up my home?), and their real estate agent (why spend hours showing the same houses every other Realtor in town is showing, writing contracts to see who can offer the most ridiculous offer, and still end up being rejected?).

Yes, I admit… I know what it is like to take on a "hopeless" feeling that is starting to affect my attitude. I feel anger building toward world conditions. I cringe when a buyer-client of mine calls me about a house she wants to see, and I check the status of the home that "just" came on the market not even 24 hours ago, and it already has "multiple offers!"

But thankfully, as I have begun internalizing my own advice as I format this manuscript for publication, my attitude has changed. I am reminded that while I cannot control how many homes are for sale, "I can control my attitude!" I can control "not" giving up! That is what I needed to be reminded of this morning as I prepare for an entire Saturday of showing houses to my clients, which are the same houses being shown by other Realtors, and at the end of the day, only "one" of us will go home with a signed contract.

The only way you fail is to give up trying!

And I must tell you that out of twenty offers and a strong cash offer from another agent, it was "my" buyer who won!

This book is more about "winning" than it is about "failure," but because they are so inner connected, it may seem to the reader that I have spent more time trying to convince you that success without failure is more unlikely than I have spent spotlighting the "winning ways" to success. But you see, those winning ways are effective "because" you now understand that trial and failure have purpose.

Chapter Six is dedicated to "the battle" because it is so important that your attitude and personal preparation habits align with God's intention of your "becoming" and not fall prey to Lucifer's attempts to "drag you down to the miseries of hell."

If you find that all the focus on overcoming failure mentioned in this chapter about the battle (trials & opposition) produces a negative feeling within you instead of feelings of "hope," then you may want to pause a moment and consider the "Winning Ways" taught in the previous chapters in this book:

<u>Chapter One</u> – **Winning Way #1** teaches us to "make our first call to God" when trial strikes... and to adopt a "first call" attitude even when we win!

Chapter Two – **Winning Way #2** teaches us that "Proper Preparation Prevents Poor Performance" (aka Five P's). Learning how to "defend" yourself against the pull of the world shows "personal accountability" in preparing your reaction to trial (positive and proactive) and not just going with the flow of the natural man within us (if it feels good, do it).

Chapter Three – **Winning Way #3** teaches that attitude drives behavior. As an extension to the "Five P's" discussed in the preceding chapter, taking a proactive approach to feeding our brain "good food" unlocks the door to unlimited potential for success in every aspect of our lives.

Chapter Four – **Winning Way #4** teaches us how to create a positive mindset about trial–to open our eyes, heart, and soul to "Opportunity" when trial strikes. This chapter is dedicated to helping "open your eyes" to the golden opportunity of change when trial strikes. You are taught how to "choose" to see trial as a means of becoming–a natural consequence (and opportunity) of earth life's eternal principle of agency.

Chapter Five – **Winning Way #5** teaches us to trust in God to develop greater faith in becoming [the person God sees us becoming].

If success comes with a price, then how important is it to be willing to pay it, no matter how long it takes?

I am so grateful to have found the prayer-poem, shared at the end of Chapter Five, attributed to a risk-taking sea captain who appears to have captured in words the embodiment of the Parable of the Talents, the Law of the Harvest, and other affirmations of *becoming* taught throughout this book–that we should never let the 'fear' of failure keep us from discovering who we really are and who we can become. This excerpt is so applicable to this chapter (Six) as well:

Disturb us, Lord, to dare more boldly,
To venture on wider seas
Where storms will show your mastery;
Where losing sight of land,
We shall find the stars.
We ask You to push back
The horizons of our hopes;
And to push into the future
In strength, courage, hope, and love.
(attributed to Sir Francis Drake - 1577)

Don't you just love the phrase, "Disturb us, Lord?" I love it so much that it inspired me to write my own take on this inspiring plea:

Wake me up, Lord, so that I can realize the greatness within me. Get my attention, Lord, so I can focus on things that matter.

Shake me, Lord, from blazing my own path of life so that I may learn of God's plan for me instead. And to shake me out of my comfort zone to gain a broader view of life.

Remove my fear, oh Lord, from meeting the storms of life head-on... because doing so will give me power to develop my mastery in the form of gifts and talents that have not yet shed the cocoon enveloping them.

Allow me, Lord, to build my faith as I "dare" to fail, leaving behind the security of the known for the opportunity to expand and evolve in the unknown.

Push me, Lord, by expanding my belief of how far I can go in life with You as my Co-pilot. Help me see hope, even where others see none. Show me the path where angels walk, that I might find my way back to Thee.

Encourage me, Lord, to develop those spiritual gifts I have within me, of showing strength while in the storms of trial, having courage to rise again after failure, having a vision of hope to see the win after the storm, and a heart full of love for the journey.

And finally, **Disturb me**, Lord, if I am found to dwell upon the persuasions of others to settle for anything less than my best at becoming all I have been sent here to become. Amen and Amen!

I titled this chapter "Without Battle, there is no Win" to call attention to the importance of opposition in our life and to introduce another "attitude short" as our Winning Way #6. You will also read several stories of famous and not-so-famous people who failed "often" but chose to get up again and again. And I will share with you "the unpardonable sin of tempting trial." Got your interest, now? Enjoy!

Winning Way #6 – Choose to Fail Forward

Winning Way #6—*Choose to Fail Forward* (also an Attitude Short) embodies my intent in writing this book. It implies that it is okay to fail, and it is a "choice"–which by now, after spending quality time in this book, you should know is true; but it is not the act alone of failing which opens the door to greatness, but our "reaction" to failing–also covered previously in this book as choice.

Failure is the learning laboratory for attaining eventual success, IF we learn from each failure the "why" we failed and apply those principles inwardly towards our becoming.

I hear a phrase used often by those who suffered trial and were asked how things were going now that the trial had moved on–answering, hesitantly... "Well, I landed on my feet," or "I'm still alive!" While these answers may be appropriate in surviving or enduring trial, which is certainly a better answer than, "I crashed and burned," or "I quit!" It is not the embodiment of this book.

Then let's start at the beginning–or "in the beginning God created the heaven and the earth." (Genesis 1: 1 KJV). No, I'm not going to recite the entire Book of Genesis to you, but I do believe humanity's first earthly parents, Father Adam and Mother Eve, are perfect examples of failing forward (See Genesis 1: 26-28 KJV).

Warning! Curve ahead!

Once there was man–alone. God knew man wouldn't be Abel to raise Cain without a woman, so he created Eve (poor attempt at a pun, I know). In my case, God created "my" woman because He knew how directionally challenged I was and would need someone who didn't get lost just going to the grocery store (I am having so much fun with this!).

But seriously, there was no trial in the Garden of Eden without choice to exercise agency, so through the wisdom of God and in line with the plan of salvation prepared before the world was, choice (agency) was offered to Adam and Eve in the form of a commandment to not partake of the fruit of that tree... "nevertheless, thou mayest choose for thyself, for it is given unto thee; but remember that I forbid it, for in the day thou eatest thereof thou shalt surely die" (Moses 3:16–17).

Eve was the first to partake of the forbidden fruit because Adam was offered choice and played it safe. Eve must have understood, perhaps more than Adam, that without having mortal blood running through her veins, she would never experience the joy and pain of birthing and raising children. She would never experience the satisfaction of defeating worldly urges and temptations without the choice to remain pure and righteous. She must have known somehow that by failing to obey a strict commandment to never, no never, never eat fruit from that tree–she would be obeying a higher law to multiply and replenish the earth so that all her other sibling spirits who chose to follow God's plan of happiness could come to Earth, gain a body, and "learn" from their experiences.

This is the spirit of *failing forward*.

"When everything seems to be going against you, remember that an airplane takes off against the wind, not with it." Henry Ford

Henry Ford is known as the man who brought the automobile public. Most people, however, do not know that Henry Ford "failed" in three prior attempts at building a company to build an automobile. Ford Motor Company was the fourth company Henry started.

Although the first three companies Henry Ford started ended in failure, what Henry learned from those prior failures guided him to mass-produce an "affordable," quality automobile for the people.

There is a body of scripture within the Church of Jesus Christ of Latter-day Saints entitled "Doctrine and Covenants" (D&C) that contains revealed scripture about the nature (and extent) of trial in our lives, which I find extremely helpful to read when feeling a bit overwhelmed with "my" trial. Perhaps a little background will be beneficial in case you are not acquainted with this text.

The Church of Jesus Christ of Latter-day Saints was founded by Joseph Smith Jr. in the year 1830. Joseph was an unlearned young man who claimed to have seen God and Jesus Christ in answer to his prayer for wisdom.

The resulting vision seen by the young Smith was the beginning of a journey of trial and opposition to God's message Joseph was instructed to deliver, leading to the incarceration of the prophet and several of his friends in Liberty Jail, Missouri.

This unjustified imprisonment of Joseph Smith lasted five months, resulting in abuse, malnutrition, and separation from friends and loved ones. It was during this very bleak period of trial that Joseph learned of the terrible persecution being heaped upon members of the Church by the locals, forcing them out of their homes, unable to defend themselves.

In response to Joseph's pleadings with the Lord, the following revelation from God was received, as D&C 122:5-8:

5 "If thou art called to pass through tribulation; if thou art in perils among false brethren; if thou art in perils among robbers; if thou art in perils by land or by sea;

6 "If thou art accused with all manner of false accusations; if thine enemies fall upon thee; if they tear thee from the society of thy father

and mother and brethren and sisters; and if with a drawn sword thine enemies tear thee from the bosom of thy wife, and of thine offspring, and thine elder son, although but six years of age, shall cling to thy garments, and shall say, My father, my father, why can't you stay with us? O, my father, what are the men going to do with you? And if then he shall be thrust from thee by the sword, and thou be dragged to prison, and thine enemies prowl around thee like wolves for the blood of the lamb;

7 "And if thou shouldst be cast into the pit, or into the hands of murderers, and the sentence of death passed upon thee; if thou be cast into the deep; if the billowing surge conspire against thee; if fierce winds become thine enemy; if the heavens gather blackness, and all the elements combine to hedge up the way; and above all, if the very jaws of hell shall gape open the mouth wide after thee, <u>know thou, my son, that all these things shall give thee experience, and shall be for thy good.</u>

8 "The Son of Man hath descended below them all. Art thou greater than he?"

The Son of Man referred to in this scripture is Jesus Christ, born of Mary. He came to earth as a mortal–to experience mortality and gain an understanding of His supreme sacrifice for the sins of all humanity. He had to descend below the vilest of sinners to take that sinner's cross upon Himself. And we, in our journey through this life, add to His burden with our sins. Are we then greater than He if, through our walk on this Earth, we do not also experience pain and sorrow? If all trial, no matter the outcome, can be considered an experience for our good, how could one fail?

Many believers in a supreme being accept a general philosophical approach to sin and forgiveness. But what about trial and opposition? Why do you think we tend to treat opposition leading to trial as less experience for our good and more about punishment for our sins? The scriptures clearly show God loving those He chastens (See Hebrews 12:6). Why can't we see that? Likely because the world programs us to think when we make mistakes, intentional or not, there is an associated punishment. Had Jesus Christ not come into this world to pay for those mistakes, we would indeed be punished eternally for such deeds.

But He came, during a small window of opportunity, to teach, inspire, and set the record straight. Because of His atonement, we would not die in our sins and suffer eternal damnation but instead receive an opportunity to learn from our sins and misdeeds through the process of repentance. So, if sin can be forgiven and we can be washed clean through proper repentance, why can't we learn to accept trial as an opportunity to move forward in our life without adding the self-defeating negative self-talk, whose purpose only serves to feed the darker side of man?

Winning Way #6 reminds us that failing is not permanent, nor does it need to be self-destructing. *Choose to Fail Forward* is a powerful attitude short that teaches it is okay to take risks because there is a safety net–your attitude! My attitude! Our "attitude" determines our progression through life–through trial. As we learned in Chapter Four, attitude is a choice–either consciously (you are in control) or subconsciously (you take what life hands you), your attitude is being formed, followed by action.

Life in Eden was "heavenly"–another day in paradise for Adam and Eve, day after day of perfect weather and perfect sunsets. Have you ever given much thought to how Satan was allowed into this perfect picture? Or why was he allowed to exist there? The story of Adam and Eve, as revealed by God to–and written by Moses in Genesis 2 & 3, contains a portion of the answer. Satan was admitted into the Garden the moment (figuratively speaking) God gave Adam and Eve choice (agency). They could remain alone in the Garden forever or choose death over life eternal by partaking of the fruit of the tree of good and evil.

I often wonder what people living in Hawaii have to talk about, with the weather so perfect most of the time. Although this was meant to be a friendly dig toward our Hawaiian brothers and sisters, it was also meant as an extension of the preceding paragraph describing life in Eden. How would Adam and Eve know joy without feeling pain? You and I know that life in Hawaii is not the Garden of Eden, but when we leave our homes in Michigan or Northern Idaho, where twelve inches of new snow has just fallen upon the already white landscape, making the treacherous drive to the airport seem like a scene out of an adventure movie, but then only a few hours later to be sipping a cool drink while sitting on a beach dripping sun tan lotion somewhere over the rainbow, watching a magnificent ball of fire lazily drop into the ocean–is that not Eden?

Have you ever been found guilty of verbalizing the unpardonable sin of saying, "Life is so good right now; we haven't had a trial in years?" Yeah, me too. And what generally happens after you recite that phrase? Trial!–in pairs or triplets, usually. So, if things are going well for you right now, don't wake up the trial monster by sending him a personal challenge. He will awaken soon enough without tempting him prematurely. But then, would there have been a David without a Goliath?

One of my own attitude shorts is, "Without battle, there is no win!" I loved it so much that I made it the title of this chapter. I use this phrase quite often as a quick reminder every time one of my real estate transactions goes off-track, or an appraisal comes in lower than the sale price, or a home my buyer had their eye on accepts a contract before ours, that I need to shift back into low gear (younger readers may not understand this reference to a manual shift transmission, but shifting down to a lower gear is like slowing down to gain more traction and muscle to begin the steady climb over the obstacle. Whew!) and assess where we are, then resume position, facing forward. Just reciting this phrase has helped me clear my mind of the panic that often accompanies trial and opposition and, with practice, helps me see the obstacle as it really is–an opportunity to grow and win.

Failing Forward implies there is more to opposition than merely to keep us awake at night. When I was a paid motivational speaker traveling the independent business circuit teaching and inspiring fledgling entrepreneurs with success principles (Yep, you heard right–me the business failure teaching others how to succeed–remember the scripture I quoted a few pages back that ALL these things shall give us experience and shall be for our good?), and I often used a comparison between a buffalo and a cow to describe how to face life's storms.

When it senses a storm is brewing, the cow will begin to change direction away from the impending storm. Now, although that may sound like a wise thing to do, it actually puts the cow in harm's way because they end up headed in the same direction as the storm, which often catches up with them, and they end up running *in* the storm for miles, extending their exposure and potential harm for much longer than if they had followed the example of the buffalo.

On the other hand, the buffalo acts very differently than the cow when confronted by a storm. They do not try to outrun the storm; instead, they wait until it has just about reached its peak, positioning themselves toward the storm, and then begin running into it to minimize their exposure to it. The storm had the same intensity in both examples, but the buffalo chose to limit its time of exposure, meeting the storm head-on and running through it, while the cow ran from the storm, only to end up running alongside it and being exposed much longer.

What a great metaphor to use when trying to create a visual explanation of what we humans do when confronted with opposition and challenges in life, conditioning ourselves on how to react when the storms of actual trial descend upon us. We spend much of our lives trying to ignore the fact they even exist–even when we bring much of it upon ourselves because of our choices.

We may not be happy in a relationship but rather than address the problem head-on, we go to bed each night expecting things to be better in the morning. We may be in financial debt but choose to ignore the choices we make, which put us there and continue our spending ways of riding alongside debt. Some say the definition of stupidity is to keep doing what got you there, expecting different results (remember "treadmill mentality?"). I think I agree. The problem with this type of conditioning is that when trial strikes, your attitude is already in place on how *not* to deal with it–and opportunity is lost.

"When the trial first hits, it seems to come as a thief during the night, unexpected and swift. We are often confused and lost, unable to find a bearing that will give us hope..." (Sweetness of Trial).

I, too, had conditioned myself to run away from opposition, ignoring the symptoms until it was too late, and depression had set its dark fangs into my soul–I was the cow. I would have stayed in this comatose state the rest of my life, losing all that truly mattered, had I not somehow reached a point to desire to Fail Forward–strong enough to shed the characteristics of a cow and replace, bit by bit with that of a buffalo. I had enough!

A trait of achievers is that of action. They do not procrastinate. My mother was a great example of this–wise beyond her years, probably due to my daily assaults on her patience. As I aged into adulthood and realized just how wise she was, I would occasionally come to her for advice. She would not solve my problem but remind me that I was taught to think for myself. "Listen to your body," she would say. And I would often leave no closer to solving my problem than when I had arrived, until an idea or thought would enter my mind, causing me to reflect upon her counsel and driving me to respond to those thoughts–with action!

We each have characteristics of the buffalo inside us, waiting to be awakened. Generally, such awakenings come during or after trial strikes, pulling us to a level of humility that would otherwise not have been possible opening our minds to change. Choosing to fail forward is about action... taking control over what is put into your mind, and then listening–and acting upon those impressions. Procrastination will only work against us when we delay the inevitable of facing our trial head-on. We can either choose to run away from our trial, ignoring the impressions to do otherwise (Cow mentality), or we can stop procrastinating and dig our heels in, turn around, and (shift into a lower gear) face our trial through action (Buffalo mentality).

"Failure is unimportant. It takes courage to make a fool of yourself." -Charlie Chaplain

The mentality to fail forward requires a different attitude than our range cow example used earlier. Rather than "go with the flow, following public opinion, letting the natural man within us dictate our reaction to trial, <u>the failing forward mentality seeks to discover the "opportunity" in trial.</u> Those who possess it understand the purpose of failing and believe their losses do not define them but rather learn to use them to "win."

Charlie Spencer Chaplain, the most famous and successful star of "silent motion picture" fame, was born into poverty in London, England, in 1889. Abandoned by his father at age two, Charlie's mother did her best to provide for Charlie and his older brother, Sydney, by performing at a music hall until she damaged her voice during one of the shows. With a crowd to please and no one to take the ailing performer's place, the stage manager knew Charlie had a gift for singing and pushed him onto the stage with instructions to "sing, dance, or whatever you do!" Charlie stepped up and seized the opportunity by singing a few songs his mother had taught him. But what stood out was his comedy. Charlie cracked a few jokes about his mother losing her voice, and it took off from there.

Although Charlie's stage debut was successful, his Mother's career was through, as her voice never returned, sending the little family into instant poverty. Charlie's mother did what she could to keep the family off the streets by doing some housekeeping and occasional nursing, but at the age of seven, young Charlie and his brother found work in exchange for room and board in what was known as a "workhouse." One can only imagine the atmosphere amongst the United Kingdom's poor and destitute, working to stay alive barely. These times were even more demanding for Charlie's mom, who was later committed to a mental institution and eventually died there in 1928.

Charlie and Sydney's father was never in their lives, nor did he offer any financial support. He was an alcoholic and passed away sometime before his wife. Charlie and his brother eventually left the workhouse environment to live off the streets, sometimes without food for days. However, having inherited natural talents from their parents, the boys sought a chance to perform on stage to earn a meager living and perhaps begin a career. Charlie's opportunity came as a member of a juvenile group called "The Eight Lancashire Lads," featuring Charlie as an outstanding tap dancer.

Life, as we know it, may or may not be better—or worse, than the Chaplain brothers, but what remains a constant denomina-

tor between us **is our *reaction* to the life we are dealt.**

Although my research into the life of Charlie Chaplain did not reveal the exact specifics of when Charlie saw an opportunity in his trial, it was likely revealed at some point... because he did not quit! Perhaps he *listened to his body*–as my dear mother taught and continued developing talents that continued to impress others when he applied them despite having to stray into other lines of work. Charlie had become a toy maker, newsboy, and doctor's assistant, but he never lost sight of his dream of becoming a stage actor. Nevertheless, Charlie saw opportunity in stage plays and used his dancing ability, along with developing a comedy routine, to provide a meager living until an opportunity to move to Hollywood, California, presented itself.

Charlie was not openly welcomed in Hollywood; his style was considered too silly to sell. But Charlie continued anyway, believing in himself when others did not. Charlie's break came in a Sherlock Holmes film–as a paper boy. He went on to star in thirty-five films, bringing to the screen that *"too silly to sell"* action which made him famous.

We, too, have greatness within us, lying dormant until trial forces us to dig down into those protected areas of our brain and heart, breaking loose walls, fears, and untapped potential. Charlie Chaplain and others like him faced extreme odds against success but somehow continued failing forward, not giving in to public opinion or the natural man's instinct to quit.

What Charlie Chaplain didn't say in his quote about failure being "unimportant" is that without said failures in his life to "open up the door to opportunity," Charlie Chaplain may well have come and gone from this earth without really knowing who he was, and to what extent he had potential.

Failing forward is an attitude. It's an awareness that signals "choice ahead!" It is generally the battle that puts us in a position to defend or to attack. If everything went well every day, there would be nothing to claim–there would be no victory. There would never be loss without crossing the line and taking a risk. <u>Without a battle, there would be no win.</u>

A common misunderstanding among many people is that if we strive with all our might to live the Ten Commandments, nothing bad will happen to us. Or if we eat right and take vitamins, we will never get sick. But if you happen to read my first book, *The Sweetness of Trial*, and the chapter entitled "Why Bad Things Happen to Good People," you will learn the truth–that bad things may, and do, happen to the best of people.

The consequences of good and bad actions will come, but they do not always come immediately, nor are they always visible. And sometimes bad things happen to the best of people because it's needed to make good people even better.

I love these words written by Orson F. Whitney (1855-1931), demonstrating a clear understanding of the need for opposition in our lives: "No pain that we suffer, no trial that we experience is wasted. It ministers to our education, to the development of such qualities as patience, faith, fortitude, and humility. All that we suffer and all that we endure, especially when we endure it patiently, builds up our characters, purifies our hearts, expands our souls, and makes us more tender and charitable, more worthy of being called the children of God ... and it is through sorrow and suffering, toil and tribulation, that we gain the education that we come here to acquire." (*From a devotional address given at Brigham Young University—Idaho on October 30, 2007,* by Larry Richman)

The Lord Jehovah could have led the Children of Israel directly through the wilderness to the Promised Land, where milk and honey were plentiful–but He didn't. Instead, He "proved" them by withdrawing the daily comforts they had become used to, using Moses to comfort and lead them while they developed faith sufficient to become great. Yet despite the tyranny imposed by the Egyptian Pharaoh, they murmured!

The Israelites were a chosen people, and God needed them to be strong to fulfill their destiny–but like many of us, they looked at their trial as punishment and longed for things to return as they once were. They had forgotten just how bad things were under the rule of the Egyptian government when they could not see ahead. The blind eye of faith had not yet opened to see, and they murmured over their circumstances to the very one who had their best interests at heart–had parted the Red Sea right before their eyes and saved their lives. It took battle with the warring Amalakites to test their strength and resolve before entering the promised land. Those who remained after their test of faith were to be the Lord's chosen and inhabit the earth with posterity as numerous as the stars in the sky.

We, too, are a chosen people. We are God's offspring, inhabiting earth for the divine purpose of being proven, as so eloquently explained by Orson F. Whitney. Many Israelites chose to remain as they were without developing the faith necessary to move ahead in their lives and possess the promised land.

Similarly, many will turn the pages of this book without even putting the principles shared and taught to the test. As God invited the Israelites to *prove me* [see Exodus 16:4 & Exodus 20:20], I offer the same invitation to prove these principles are true–not to me, but to yourself. Become a willing student. Invite God into your life as your guide and tutor. He will never leave your side during battle nor famine, as He is always there during times of plenty and seasons of harvest–arms open in the gesture of invitation: "Come unto me, all ye that labour and are heavy laden, and I will give you rest" (Matthew 11:28). And John 6:37: "All that the Father gives me will come to me, and whoever comes to me I will never cast out..." And John 6:39: "... that I should lose nothing of all that he has given me, but raise it up on the last day."

Chapter Six is all about the *Battle,* planned and necessary for our progression to, and preparation for, that eventful day of graduation from this sphere to the next. I realize that many who read this book will not share the same belief as I do about the afterlife, but please know that it is not my intent to convert you to my way of thinking. I am but a mortal–a sinner, trying his best to figure things out, just like you. But I have done my best to share what I am learning on my journey to become "my" best self.

There is no one roadmap from which *all* humanity can agree on how to navigate earthly trial and opposition without *some* disagreement.

But I hope you will follow my Mother's sage wisdom and "listen to your body." Follow the impressions of your heart with an open mind, and you will capture the heartbeat of this chapter, as well as the intent of the entire book: (1) to help you understand the necessity of trial in your life and (2) to provide you with encouragement and Winning Ways to prepare for the next trial, and *Win!*

Choosing God as my co-pilot through life and trial has been the best decision I ever made, for He loves me more than anyone ever can–for He knows who I am and who I can become. And I choose to become *all* I can be, which is why I ended this book with the chapter entitled: "Be Mighty!"

Chapter Seven

BE MIGHTY! (The story of Mighty Jake)

"**A**lways do your best. What you plant now, you will harvest later." — Og Mandino

"His seed shall be mighty upon [the] earth..." — Psalm 112: 2

If you were to think of someone in your life who might fit the "be mighty" persona, who would they be? Mine would be Mighty Mouse, a cartoon *mouse* character created in the 1940s and found his way to the States during the mid-fifties when I was around eleven years of age. Every Saturday morning (before chores), I talked my mother into letting me watch Mighty Mouse cartoons, where the always–smiling, super mouse put his superpowers to work fighting evil or saving the beautiful Pearl Pureheart from certain death.

Mighty Mouse was considered a "superhero." His superpowers included the ability to fly, fantastic strength, and invincibility. I loved to see him swoop in just as the cat villain had the canary in his mouth and throw multiple super-punches under the cat's chin, freeing the bird to live another day. I loved to hear him sing as he flew down from somewhere in outer space: "Here I come to save the day!" Oh, how I dreamed that I, too, would "save the day!"

My father was mighty. Woodrow Wilson "Red" Malone was a red-headed Irishman raised in a very no-nonsense home environment by a father he never spoke of and a mother (MeMaw) who was as religious as Billy Graham himself. Yet he rose to the top of almost every service organization he joined, presiding over the worldwide Elks and USA Volunteer Fireman's Association–he was a leader.

My father was a businessman during the day and the local Volunteer Fire Department chief at night… or whenever a fire broke out. He had the keys to the fire station, and the minute the phone rang, pulsating out the steady rings announcing a fire, he was out the door to the fire station, starting up the water tanker fire truck while others arrived and donned their gear and fire fighting equipment as the big engine roared to life, siren screaming "get out of my way, I have work to do–I have come to save the day!"

I will never forget standing across the street from the local cleaners store as the black smoke and orange and red flames consumed the building in the middle of the block, with CLEANERS displayed over the front door, and seeing people scream and weep over the sight. There was my dad, clothed with a helmet and gloves and a white t-shirt, encased in the jaws of hell, but spraying water for all he was worth to keep the fire from spreading to the other buildings.

Unlike my favorite Saturday morning cartoons, Mighty Mouse did not swoosh down *to save the day,* but the heroes from the Holbrook Volunteer Fire Department did. Their heroic efforts against that fire-breathing beast saved most of the block containing other businesses vital to the community–the Greyhound Bus Depot being one of them. On this eventful day many years ago, the "Mighty" volunteers from Station 1 would indeed save the day, but not without incident. Among those injured in this battle between fire and water was Mighty Red, my father–his right arm the recipient of a scalding bucket of cleaning solution, leaving a burned mass of flesh and a huge patch of arm never to grow hair again.

My mother was also mighty!

Dorothy (Dot) Leopold Malone was home alone one late hot afternoon when a rapid succession of loud banging at her front door broke the silence of the end of an otherwise peaceful Saturday; both her husband and son were out of town. Dot was alone.

Before Dot could get to the door and greet whoever was on the other side, the door burst open, and Sue from next door pushed past my mother, looking as if she had seen a ghost, or worse, being chased by one. Before Dot could react to Sue's uncharacteristic arrival, another figure burst through the door–Sue's husband. He was carrying a shotgun.

Dot could not remember much after trying to restrain her attacker, grappling for the gun he held in his hands, but Dot was no match for the stocky Coca Cola® delivery man as he pushed her to the floor and, after a brief hesitation with the double-barreled shotgun aimed directly at her, lying on the kitchen floor, he stepped over her in pursuit of his wife.

The ear-ringing sound of the shotgun was all Dot heard before trying to stand, emotion overcoming her to the point of exhaustion. *I have to save Sue*, she thought to herself, legs shaking as she pulled herself upright, only to look again into the two round, dark eyes of her neighbor's double-barreled shotgun.

Dot heard pleading from somewhere in the kitchen. A voice, calm with reason, was speaking to this man, encouraging him to put the gun down and let her help Sue. It was Dot's own voice.

The neighbor never took his eyes off my mother... not until he placed the gun barrel under his chin and pulled the trigger. "It was instinctive," she would later explain her actions, never wanting to play the part of a failed hero but only reacting out of love.

This same love was demonstrated by my mother on my behalf growing up, time and time again–once fighting the surgeons of Phoenix Children's Hospital who wanted to amputate my right arm after being horribly crushed and sustaining a compound fracture from a horse-riding accident. I still have use of both original arms, using my two thumbs at this very minute to pound out another book while on a treadmill at the health club. Thank you so much, Mighty Dot!

It was also my mother who singlehandedly ended our high school hazing tradition, better known as "sports initiation." As a freshman, I had lettered varsity in football and was taken, along with a few others, out to a remote area and beaten, among other degrading exercises. When my mother examined the bruises and broken blood vessels all over my body, administered by several oak paddles, she stormed into the principal's office the next morning with fire in her eyes–and that was that!

This was the same woman who grabbed for the shotgun before the killer of her friend could complete his mission, trying desperately to talk reason into him. She had to get to Sue–and call an ambulance. But her efforts would fail again, resulting in the man pushing her to the floor again, with the gun pointing right at her head before turning it on himself and pulling the trigger. He would not be denied finishing the job.

My mother insisted on cleaning her kitchen of skull remains by herself. She wept for Sue, having lost her life in my parents' bedroom–but my mighty mother would not let someone's choices drive her from the home she loved–our home.

These were my parents. These are their stories. Yet, it was not these heroic trials alone that made them mighty. They were both flawed individuals, as I am–as you are. No, it was not their accomplishments that made them *mighty*, but rather their reaction to their imperfect nature when presented with trial, which earned them placement in the *Be Mighty* Hall of Fame. They often fell short but always got back up to try again.

My mother battled alcoholism, emphysema, throat cancer, depression, and larynx cancer. She felt betrayed and filled with self-doubt when her son joined another religious faith, and she felt deprived when she could not attend his wedding held in a Church of Jesus Christ of Latter-day Saints Temple, reserved for its members, such as the Masonic Temple mother belonged to. Yet she loved me enough to put aside her initial feelings of disappointment and disapproval to make way for future feelings of pride and support. I would say that makes her *Mighty*.

My father married my mother for better or for worse and took that promise literally. He was not a perfect man either, blemished by his father before him–his ways very much the same as his father's. But my father never deserted my mother during her worst days. He covered for her when her weakness often overcame her. I could hear them arguing way into the night, many nights. Life was, at times, difficult for them, but they hung on to one another instead of looking for a way out. He lost his job of twenty years when he was forty due to a change of ownership. He started over in a different town at forty-five and worked until he retired at seventy, finishing strong, more than appreciated–he was loved. I would say that makes him *Mighty*.

Although the word "Mighty," as used as a noun in scripture, infers "power" and "strength" (See Samuel 23: 8), it is also used to describe the capability of man to do good, such as "...he performed mighty deeds and mighty works."

In the case of my Grandson, Jacob Priestley, it meant all the above.

Life as you had imagined it may not have turned out. Such is the story of Mighty Jake.

Jacob Thomas Priestley (aka Mighty Jake) was born in Mesa, Arizona, on August 28, 2002. He was the first son of Thomas John Priestley and Britney Camille Malone (The author's youngest child).

"Jacob's entry into this life was pretty normal," remembers his grandmother, Linda Johnson Malone. But it wasn't until a few years later that Jacob's "energetic" behavior began drawing longer looks.

"We thought Jake was just following after his grandfather's early age antics of needing to be leashed anytime in public for fear he would run away or cause a disturbance with his overactive curiosity," his mother Britney chuckles.

Grandma Linda remembers. "But the way he ran drew our attention to the possibility that something wasn't right." Jake would run on his toes, almost like a ballerina, without the special shoes. As he aged, other actions also drew attention–Jake's inattention to learning activities becoming paramount.

Jake was officially diagnosed with Autism spectrum disorder (or ASD) when he was four. The 'A' word strikes terror into the hearts of loved ones–second only to the 'C' word, because there is such a wide range of health possibilities and is "distinguished by a wide variation of social, communication, and cyclical behaviors that are considered somewhat out of character for children." ("*14 Early Autism Symptoms in Young Children*" – ActiveBeat.com)

Jake also exhibited additional behavior signals, many noted in the referenced article by Emily Lockhart for ActiveBeat.com.

Disconnection with others. Jake seemed distant, never quite connected to those around him as a child. His facial expressions didn't change much, whether happy or sad. "It's important to keep in mind that autistic children are not disconnected emotionally themselves; they simply don't understand or pick up on social cues as efficiently or quickly as other children."

Emotional outbursts. Jake did not like surprises or unfamiliar circumstances and often reacted to show his displeasure with occasional outbursts, no matter where or who might be around. But thankfully, his underlying nature kept these to a minimum and never took on an aggressive manner. As Jake matured, his amazing smile in the face of such a bleak future endeared people worldwide to him.

Delayed Language Development. "By three years of age, most infants start to babble or mimic the language of those they interact with, pronouncing a single word when they point to an object or try to get their parent's attention. However, infants with autism may not start to babble or speak until much later. Some won't display significant language skills until they start working with a speech therapist."

"Jake didn't say a word until he was about four," Jake's mom remembered. "We then put him into a preschool with a speech therapist, and within a year, he was saying two 3-word sentences."

Difficulty Understanding Figurative Expressions. They may not also detect communication cues delivered through tone of voice; for example, they can't distinguish a happy tone of voice from a sad or angry one, and unlike children following standard development paths, they don't develop the ability to identify sarcasm or understand body language.

A related symptom is that autistic children tend to have more trouble distinguishing between what's real and what is make-believe. While most (if not all) children have active imaginations and can't differentiate between fact and fiction the way older children and adults can, for autistic children, there often seems to be no line at all between what's real and what's imagined.

Repetitive Behaviors. Individuals with autism are somewhat prone to repetitive behaviors. For instance, they may arrange and rearrange the same group of objects, rock back and forth for extended periods, flutter their hands, or repeat the same word or phrase in what appears to be an obsessive manner. This is one of the most easily identifiable symptoms of autism, and it's one most parents will be on the lookout for early in the child's development.

Sensitivity to External Stimuli. Sensitivity to external stimuli is another early warning sign of autism. For example, autistic individuals may become stressed or agitated when exposed to specific noises, bright lights, smells, tastes, or textures. They may also become hypersensitive to certain stimuli; in other words, they will insist on wearing certain items of clothing or colors, prefer rooms with bright lights or loud sounds, and enjoy touching or playing with specific body parts. Many autistic children also display emotional stress when deprived of their preferred stimuli.

Obsessive Behaviors. Children with autism will often show signs of inflexibility. This includes obsessive and repetitive behaviors. They will find one or a few activities they enjoy; sometimes, these activities are very unusual, and they will want to do them repeatedly throughout the day.

Helpguide.org provides detailed examples of what these obsessive behaviors might include, especially as they age. For example, their need for a rigid routine might include taking the same route to school every day, an inability to adapt to changes in schedule or environment, an unusual attachment to toys or strange objects, or becoming obsessed with a narrow topic of interest, usually something that involves numbers or symbols. They will enjoy repeating the same actions over and over again, spending long periods staring at moving objects like a ceiling fan, or instead of playing with a toy, they'll only focus on one aspect of it, like spinning the wheels on a toy car.

Lack of Communication. Healthychildren.org says that children with autism will also struggle with communication in a much more general sense. Not only will they be unable to speak or significantly delayed in their language development, but they might also seem utterly uninterested in communicating at all. As a result, they will not show any interest in sparking conversation or be able to participate in even a simple conversation. They will not respond to facial expressions, use them, notice when their name is being called, or even point at things when they need something. When they do start speaking, their language is often underdeveloped. For example, they might confuse their pronouns and use "you" when they should be saying "I" and vice versa - or repeat sentences they hear without understanding the meaning behind them. Healthychildren.org says this is called "parroting" or "echoing."

Seemingly Unresponsive. According to Autism Canada, signs of autism can begin as early as 12 to 24 months. While it is often hard to get a diagnosis before the age of 24 months, one of the best indicators of autism is the absence of expected behaviors. Many other signs on this list can't be recognized until the child is older, but a child's responsiveness can be tested while young.

Don't Like Being Touched or Cuddled. This behavior was evident in Jake. He did not like to be touched by anyone but his mother. However, I made it my goal to coax him into my arms every time I saw him, and eventually, those "long hugs" between grandfather and grandson became something Jake looked forward to, thus allowing me into the ring of hug-honor.

It can be devastating for a parent to learn something is wrong with their child, but luckily, with autism, an early diagnosis (ideally by 18 months) can make a huge difference. Once a baby is past its infancy stage, parents might begin to notice their child does not like to be touched or cuddled as a typically developing child would.

Autism Canada also notes that children with autism will also not like to be touched, making it hard to console them during emotional outbursts or tantrums, especially when young. It can affect their ability to bond with parents and siblings or even make friends with other children.

Autism is commonly characterized as a mental condition that affects communication and behavior, which is present from an early age. Several medical theories exist about autism, some more backed by science than others. For example, some celebrities caused a false buzz by stating the condition is caused by vaccines.

Although Jake's autism was less severe than the highly impacted, he still carried many of the symptoms noted above. These symptoms would only exacerbate once he started formal education. Jake's behavior problems soon became a challenge for his parents and teachers. One by one, they threw up their hands and requested Jake be sent on to one program after another until there were no more. At the age of eight, Mighty Jake left the school system to be home-schooled by his mother.

Around the age of nine, Jake started having bowel elimination problems, resulting in extended hospital stays of one or two-week periods to clean out his colon and feed him nutrients. The Doctors poked and prodded and conducted test after test without diagnosing the root of the problem, only to send Jake home feeling better until he returned a few weeks later with the same problem.

Jakes's mom would not leave his bedside, quizzing every Doctor or nurse who attended Jake to learn as much as she could about his care. She soon realized these medical professionals had no clue what was wrong with her son. They gathered facts and test results for months without a clear consensus about Jake's condition. Through a miracle and tender mercy from God, Jake's condition was noticed by a family and church friend, who happened to be a medical Doctor. "Have Jake's Doctor run tests for Mitochondria Disease," he suggested.

The "powerhouses of the cell;" that's how many people know mitochondria. The parts of cells that turn sugars, fats, and proteins that we eat into forms of chemical energy that the body can use to carry on living.

Every living thing is made of cells–tiny compartments contained by a membrane. Cells are the smallest things that can reproduce themselves. When we look inside cells, we see that they have smaller sub-compartments, known as "Organelles," which perform different functions essential for the cell to live.

Mitochondria are organelles found in the cells of every complex organism. They produce about 90% of the chemical energy that cells need to survive. No energy, no life! Jacob was officially diagnosed with Mitochondrial Disease in 2013 when he was just eleven.

How do you explain to a young boy who had faced rejection from so many in his adolescent years that he would likely never experience adulthood? That he would probably die a slow and painful death, one day at a time. While most of us experience bouts of near-death periods in our life cycle, we generally recover some or most of what we lost physically during those dark periods. For those with diseased mitochondria, Paradise Lost would never be regained.

Jake, however, would gain something far "greater" than physical strength; he would develop the ability to encourage others. He would become–Mighty Jake!

The road to "mightiness" is never straight or level but instead filled with twists and turns–and occasional potholes. How one reacts to the winding road of life is what this book is all about–it is how heroes are born. Jake's diagnosis did not level or straighten the road ahead, nor did life get easier. In fact, the treatment of Jake's symptoms would become almost unbearable because of the little-known medical history of how to treat this incurable disease.

Each time Jake's bowels would back up and need medical treatment, whoever was on call at the hospital would go through a learning curve at Jake's expense, requiring test after test during each lengthy stay. Eventually, feed ports were added to Jake's body to bypass the need for solid foods, an attempt at reducing the pain of digesting and eliminating such foods. This procedure was only intended as a short-term fix while other options were explored, but there were no other options, and Jake remained hooked up to these feeding ports for several years, creating a recurring nightmare of emergency hospital visits caused by infection from the entry port into Jake's body.

When Jake was about to turn thirteen years old and become a teenager, his mother asked him what he wanted for his birthday. Expecting to hear a wish list of toys and electronic games, Jake replied: "I would like birthday cards!" He was spending so much time in hospital rooms that his best friends were the nurses and aides assigned to his care. He longed for friends outside the confines of the multi-story hospital(s) where he spent such a big part of his life, and he enjoyed reading the comments, stories, and well-wishes of the few cards he did occasionally receive.

"How many cards would you like? His mother asked.

"400!" was Jakes's reply. "I would like 400 birthday cards!" Just saying those words caused Jake to form the smile that would become his trademark.

Jake's mom put on social media Jake's wish for birthday cards. She didn't expect the local news channels to pick up on it, gaining more than just friends and family attention. However, a local news reporter called to see if he could do a story on Jake and to raise awareness about autism. What the reporter came away with was far more exclusive and revealing than he ever expected. This was a story about a young boy, robbed of a normal childhood and exposed to daily, weekly, and monthly treatments for his *other* disease, which would ultimately take his life. And the kid couldn't stop smiling!

That picture of a young boy smiling in the face of certain death went viral, and soon, hundreds of birthday cards addressed to Jacob Priestley, the boy who just wanted birthday cards, began arriving. The local post office called and asked what was going on. They had received more mail for one individual than the entire morning's delivery for the town.

Jake received over 2,000 birthday cards that year–mostly from locals, first responders, and schools. It was amazing! Jake's mom and dad were overwhelmed with the love and support from the community and brought over post office crates full of letters to open and read. It was one of the most spiritual experiences of my life as I read story after story of others who shared Jake's trial and added words of encouragement and stories of their own. We lasted one night until after 2 am, completely exhausted from the emotional outpouring for our grandson.

Jake took stacks of birthday cards with him to the next hospital visit and the next–sharing them with Doctors and nurses alike. It kept him preoccupied with something other than the increased emergency visits to the ER and more extended stays at the hospital due to a spike in temperature or other infection symptoms. Early in the diagnosis of the disease, we almost lost Jake due to an infection that could not be controlled. It almost took his life because we had waited too long before bringing him in for antibiotics and other fluids. So, every time after that, even the slightest fever was a reason to bring him in.

Diseased Mitochondria disarms the body's normal function to fight invading organisms, so another part of Jakes's life was spent avoiding the public. Jake had no real friends his age other than online or in written form. His world revolved around health professionals and his immediate family. The birthday cards added a welcomed new dimension to Jake's life.

Like every trial, conditions either get better and the sun shines again, or they take another turn, delivering another punch or two. In Jake's case, it would be the latter. It was near Christmas 2016, and we were all worried that Jake would have to spend Christmas in the hospital fighting another bout of infections, which would not go away for him to be released. Periods between home and hospital stays were becoming shorter, forcing Jake's caregivers to arrive at a grim decision–they had to remove Jake's feeding tubes and let nature take its course.

A second bit of news trumped the decision to remove Jakes's only means of receiving life-sustaining nourishment–Jake had a large blood clot in his chest. Because of Jake's fragile condition, no Doctor would operate. They were sending our Jacob home to die.

In writing this book, it has been my sincere effort to help prepare you for the next trial in your life. Left to our own responses, most will react instinctively–in anger mode, striking out, without purpose, control, or plan. Our minds shut down, focused only on the bitter pill of disappointment and pain, leaving the trial's outcome to chance–and more often to failure. But remember the five P's discussed earlier in the book? Proper Preparation Prevents Poor Performance. This acronym encourages us to condition ourselves for opposition and trial *before* it comes. The first activity of preparation is to understand the purpose of trial as a schoolmaster and not as a taskmaster handing out punishment. Understanding that trial has purpose and conditioning ourselves to look for the purpose with a tender and humble heart is significant in winning *thru* trial.

I still remember sitting in Jake's hospital room, the only sound being the heart monitor hooked up to Jake–the air in the room being sucked out with the sobering news that Jake was coming home for Christmas, but it may be his last. A family prayer was offered, asking the Lord for a miracle, or at the least a tender mercy.

The hoped-for miracle came the next day, after a sleepless night–a surgeon had come forward and said he would operate on Jake to remove the blood clot in his chest. Our prayer was answered, at least in this one instance. It would not be the blood clot that claimed victory over Jake.

That afternoon, Jake's family gathered around his hospital bed, filling the room with nervous laughter, as we Malone's are wont to do when the beating of our hearts exposes our soft shell–the attending physician's words still resonated in our memory. "He may not survive the surgery!" But Jake earned his place in the ring of bravery with his own declaration after the Doctor had finished with his sober explanation of the seriousness of the operation, when he said to everyone's surprise, "Do I get to ride in an ambulance?"

The wait for Jake's ambulance ride was the most agonizing clock-watching time I had ever spent, the silence broken only occasionally to share and laugh at something found on one of our devices–our hearts (and eyes) riveted upon the partially closed door to Jake's room, and then to the clock, as minutes turned into hours, with no arrival of the ambulance.

I did not want to be the one to show my lack of faith, but I heard a voice whisper anyway. *"Somethings wrong!"* My shaky declaration would prove prophetic, as the doorway filled with two figures clad in white–both attending Doctors, followed by a third, Jake's nurse for the morning. The words "strength in numbers" came to my mind. *How many doctors and nurses does it take to announce the arrival of an ambulance?* I asked myself. The answer to my attempt at self-humor came instantly from the older doctor. "The surgeon who had agreed to perform the surgery this morning backed out. He says the chances are too high that Jake would not survive the surgery. He is sorry."

It was as if a bomb had been detonated in the room, as the implications of the Doctor's words hung in the air before exploding. "What now?" Jake's mom breathed out, already knowing the answer. "Take him home, Mrs. Priestley. Feed him. Make him comfortable. Enjoy your time with him…" (*because it won't take long for him to die* – I filled in the rest of the unspoken message, myself).

"How will he eat with the feeding tubes removed," I asked, searching for further confirmation of Jake's death sentence. He had not tasted solid foods for years, choosing to stay home when family gatherings filled the air with foreign smells that brought back memories and unfulfilled pangs of hunger, unable to be satisfied. Was he now to 'start eating' as if merely breaking an extended fast?

When the men in white looked at one another as if to gauge which one would break the news, I already had my answer and saved them the unpleasant task of answering my question. "He won't," I said softly to my daughter, who had begun to sob, tears hidden for days, weeks, months, now flowing freely over their banks, no longer able to contain them.

"There is no physical reason why Jake cannot eat enough to sustain himself," one of the white coats broke in. "Let him eat what he wants, a little at a time." And they all disappeared down the hallway to attend to other patients, their job done here.

Frankly, there was nothing to do but go home and wait. And for the first time in this exhaustive journey, we began planning a funeral, thoughts of a blood clot time bomb playing out in everyone's mind.

At least Jake and his family got to come home for Christmas, a gift from God for sure. And a beautiful Christmas it was–every thought turned more to Christ than ever... and to Jake. It was during this bleak period that Jake's Bishop suggested Jake arrange for a patriarchal blessing, a spiritual blessing administered by a humble man called by revelation and priesthood authority, to serve as a Patriarch within the boundaries of the stake (geographical area of The Church of Jesus Christ of Latter-day Saints) in which he resides, serving those individuals and families who lived therein.

Patriarchal blessings are usually scheduled during a person's middle-to-later teenage years, but Jake's Bishop felt inspired to arrange for one now, not knowing if Jake would live to experience adulthood. His recommendation would be a tremendous blessing of peace to the family and further confirmation that Jake was securely bound to a loving Heavenly Father who knew of his condition very well.

"A patriarchal blessing is a revelation to the recipient, even a white line down the middle of the road, to protect, inspire, and motivate activity and righteousness. A patriarchal blessing literally contains chapters from your book of eternal possibilities. I say eternal, for just as life is eternal, so is a patriarchal blessing. What may not come to fulfillment in this life may occur in the next. We do not govern God's timetable. *For my thoughts are not your thoughts, neither are your ways my ways,* saith the Lord. ("Your Patriarchal Blessing," by President Thomas S. Monson, Second Counselor in the First Presidency, Ensign Magazine, November 1986)

Unlike a Priesthood blessing to heal the sick, a patriarchal blessing is intended as a glimpse into the eternal realm of possibilities, not as a fixed prophecy, but as insight into your lineage and revelation into what may come to pass... upon your "faithfulness" and obedience to continued revelation from God.

Do you remember the story of the Old Testament Israelites during their trek across the wilderness to reach the Promised Land and how God intended to prepare them to become His covenant people? But they did not heed the revelation and instruction from God and chose instead to worship idols, complaining that God took too long to provide for their needs. They chose to overlook the mighty miracles God performed on their behalf, and therefore their generation forfeited the blessings intended for them. Such are the promised blessings received through a patriarchal blessing, conditioned upon one's choices in life and responsiveness to God's spiritual promptings.

Jake's patriarchal blessing revealed much about his spiritual life before receiving a body of flesh and bone as part of his earthly experience. He was indeed an extraordinary young man, personally acquainted with many noble and great ones who came to earth as prophets, seers, and revelators. Jake had come to earth not to become great, in terms of his station in life or church callings he may hold–but he would indeed become "mighty!"

That special Christmas, a miracle would happen in the form of Mighty Jake—he did not die! One can only imagine the terror Jake's mother felt every morning after realizing she had fallen asleep without checking almost every hour on her oldest son to be sure he was comfortable and still breathing—and then forcing herself to peer into his bedroom, preparing for the worst, only to find his body rising, ever so slowly, with every precious breath.

Imagine the joy felt every morning as my wife or I called to check in on Jake, preparing for the worst but quickly forming a smile in reaction to his mom's words: "He is still with us!"

Jake lost forty pounds over the next month, settling into a body weight of around seventy-five pounds, adjusting to his new norm of life without food. We kept asking ourselves, "How? How can this fragile boy continue to survive with only a few bites of whatever he asked for?" Then, a paragraph in Jakes's patriarchal blessing came ringing clear. His mission on earth had been accomplished—a physical body had been obtained. He was now under his Heavenly Father's care. The timing of Jakes's return to his heavenly home would be between Jake and his Heavenly Father. This comforting revelation eased the stress around the Priestley household and the MaloneZone of grandparents, aunts, uncles, and cousins. We all breathed a little easier knowing God was in charge now. Our role would be to enjoy Jake for as long as possible.

Instead of planning his funeral, the family started planning Jakes's fourteenth birthday. Once again, Jakes's request was only for birthday cards, so his mom went to her friends on social media asking for help planning Jakes's birthday–a milestone she never expected to celebrate with her son. The response was immediate.

The letter was marked with the insignia of a police shield, with letters forming Brooklyn North, NYPD. The letter said they had seen the article on the news about Jacob, the boy who just wanted birthday cards, and realized just how special this young man facing death was... and they wanted to do something special for him, so they sent out an email to the whole NYPD asking those who saw Jakes story and wanted to send in a card to send them to Brooklyn North so they could fill a box full of cards to send to Jake. But they were astonished over how many cards and letters came in and decided to do something a little more.

Jake and his family had been invited to New York City at the request and expense of the fine men and women in blue of the Brooklyn North Police Department. Someone with the NYPD had been following Jakes's story since the previous year and had suggested the idea of Jake's invitation, which was met with enthusiastic approval. An itinerary for the week in NYPD was sent, full of sightseeing and public appearances. The more the word got out about Jake's story, the more requests for him to visit hospitals, schools, and dedications–the list grew so long that Jake's hosts had to begin turning down requests.

Jakes's parents were stunned as they tried to find a "catch" to the invitation. Plane tickets and hotel accommodations would be provided, as well as a tour of NYC by Jake's entourage of both plain-clothed and uniformed officers. Their suspicions satisfied–replaced by excitement and joy for their son, the Priestleys had no idea of what lay ahead of them in response to birthday cards for their son. The NYPD experience was only the tip of the iceberg of surprises.

"Mom, it's Fox News," came the excited announcement from Jacob's younger brother, Tyler. "They want to do a story about Jake!"

The reporter from Fox News arrived shortly after the phone call asking for an interview with Jake and his family–which meant protector Grandad Malone would be on hand to ensure the reporter's intent was indeed about Jake's request for birthday cards and not something else. Thankfully, it turned into a wonderful experience for all. Jake flashed his famous smile and responded to questions like any fourteen-year-old kid with autism would do–capturing the hearts of viewers and affiliates alike.

Soon, the Phoenix Suns and Mercury professional men's and women's basketball teams were behind Jake's wish, sending their respective mascots to the Priestley home with fun antics accompanied by autographed basketballs, hats, shirts, and other fun gifts for Jake. It was sad to see them go, walking down the street like a parade at Disneyland for all the neighbors to see.

That year, social media's "Adventures with Mighty Jake" was born. Cards and letters came pouring in so fast that the post office dedicated a bin just for the kid who only wished for birthday cards–and more than once had to call Jake's mom to ask her to please come pick up the hundreds of cards, letters, and packages, addressed to Mighty Jake.

Jake's trip to New York City was nothing but first class all the way. After a long flight from Phoenix, a bite or two of New York Pizza was enough for Jake, followed by an early morning call to visit an inner-city school assembly, at which Jake was treated like a rock star. Jake was introduced to the Mayor of Brooklyn North, who proclaimed Mighty Jake Day, followed by a "modified" tour of the Empire State Building (who wouldn't want to be carried, wheelchair and all, by Brooklyn's finest), a close and personal view of Lady Liberty, the 9/11 Museum, Time Square, and even a Broadway Show, with dinner afterward.

Jake's adventure, although a once-in-a-lifetime event for anyone, would prove exhausting–a reminder of the progressive terminal illness that lay beneath the winning smile. While New York wanted more of Mighty Jake, they only had a taste of the fighting spirit this young man possessed. But the officers assigned to Jake's detail got to see firsthand what this boy–a mere child in terms of age–endured every day of his life, and their respect and admiration turned into a fast friendship long after the visit had ended, continuing even to present day 2023.

Although Jake's body would give out after a few hours of activity each day, he still gave his all to those who had been so gracious, caring, and kind in providing this opportunity for Jake to see and experience New York. From appearing live on a morning radio talk show to being the center of attention in a school assembly that same afternoon–while Jacob's dad gave an encouraging talk to the youth, as he does weekly back home, where he is known as "Coach Tom" to young boys on his baseball team–Jake gave all he could.

Back home in Arizona, Jake's mail bin was overflowing with literally thousands of birthday wishes for this brave young man who had inspired so many with his infectious smile despite his circumstances. Needless to say, Jake's wish for hundreds of birthday cards had exceeded his wildest dreams, as he spent most of his birthday waking hours in bed, surrounded by hundreds of yet unopened cards, interrupted by occasional texts to Jake from his many New York fans.

I cannot mention in this writing the many–and I do mean many, kindnesses of complete strangers to Jake and his family for fear of missing someone. People went out of their way to reach out to this boy with no hope of experiencing a normal childhood and blessed his life with their words, deeds, and gifts. It was truly a miracle, resulting in happy distractions from the daily reminder of a debilitating and progressively fatal disease.

After such a marvelous birthday experience, one might think the end of Jake's journey would surely come to pass. Not so in Jake's case. Even though he could not physically show his uplift from the birthday events and attention, he showed it in other, less noticeable ways. He did not succumb. He did not become depressed. He did not cry because he couldn't eat the birthday cake or play outside and experience what it was like to ride a skateboard. He smiled. He slept. He chatted with his new police friends in New York on social media. He played video games. And yes, he continued the best he could with his online studies–his parents trying to provide as much normality to Jake's life as possible. But Jake's life was anything but ordinary. I mean, who gets invited to a SWAT demonstration in a private facility filled with the latest and greatest crime-fighting equipment? Who gets to watch man-against-beast training? And operate a remote-controlled surveillance device used to check out hostile environments? Mighty Jake, that's who. Many thanks to the Phoenix, AZ SWAT Team for this experience that even "Granddad" was invited to attend.

Who has the Phoenix Suns Gorilla bouncing an autographed basketball down the street to Jake's house for a personal visit? When was the last time you saw a group of Motorcyclists cruising a neighborhood on their way to deliver signed birthday cards to a hero of theirs? And the list goes on as Jake's *mightiness* gained notoriety and captured the heart of America, ports abroad from Australia to Canada and beyond. It soon became apparent that this was to be Jacob Priestley's mission in life–to bring encouragement and blessings of hope to the afflicted and downtrodden, the well and the sick, the rich and the poor. If Jake can go through life with a smile, knowing his would likely end sooner than expected, then what about me? What excuse do I have for not becoming all that I can be with what I have to work with?

Jake's story did not end his fourteenth year, nor his fifteenth, again defying medical science. His fifteenth birthday was celebrated as Grand Marshall of "NYPD Walk and Run, a 5k and 10k Run to draw awareness to unique diseases, such as Autism, Mitochondria, and other rare diseases, held in Brooklyn, New York, USA, called upon to assist a Catholic Priest in pronouncing a blessing at the start of the race, and shook hands with the Mayor of Brooklyn, New York as he took his place at the front of the parade of which he would lead as Grand Marshal.

Jake accepted invitations to visit schools–In one, he would participate in art day, beaming with the others surrounding him at his colorful creations. In another, he just sat in his wheelchair, listening to musical chorales. But on this second visit to New York, his friends noticed something different about their hero: he often tired and took longer to recover. The disease was taking its toll on the body of this mighty warrior, and there was nothing he could do but endure.

Jake loves Disneyland, so his parents purchased a season pass so his mom could drive him over to LA every few months to give Jake a pause from his reality and enjoy a bit of fantasy. But one need only look at his social media photos to see the change in Jake; subtle but unmistakable, nonetheless. His big smile is slower to peak, and his endurance is limited to maybe an hour or two at the most at Disneyland before he is found asleep in his wheelchair, covered with a blanket from head to toe, his mom left to herself, fearing the worst for her son as this terrible disease continued to advance.

As Jake approached his sixteenth birthday, a date his family never imagined he would see–the change in Jake was dramatic. He had grown up... to be over six feet, one inch tall. Yet, he was still only seventy-five pounds or so. He would sleep much of each day, waking to check social media or spend an hour in his online class at his mother's insistence, and then back to sleep, having eaten maybe a morsel or two before succumbing. His mannerisms were much subdued, but his eyes still reflected the presence of an inner soul–a mighty warrior sent to earth for a brief time to inhabit a temporary body of flesh and bones, to experience joy... and pain.

Jake developed a fever at one point, signaling his body's inability to fight off infection. But with prayers, a blessing, and a little time, Jake was able to avoid an ER visit and return to his new routine–except for a few days prior when his younger brother went in to wake him one morning and couldn't. With a shrill in his voice, like a child in distress, young Tyler yelled for his mom. Even the loud scream did not rouse his sleeping brother until several minutes later. After multiple attempts at gently shaking and whispering in his ear, he responded, confused and disoriented. We believed this was a precursor of things to come and most likely how this valiant warrior would be received into the next life, shedding the mortal diseased body for a clothe of glory and heralded by those whose lives he had touched while on earth and those who awaited his return. But until that day, we continue to celebrate each day he is with us, coming to realize more fully the impact one eternal soul of humanity can have upon even strangers who only know him from a distance as *Mighty Jake,* the boy with a terminal disease who only wants birthday cards for his birthday.

A few years later, we celebrated yet another milestone we never believed we would see–Jake turned eighteen. He was an adult now, by the world's standard, anyway. And He continued to grow, sprouting to six foot, four inches, and a skeletal weight of one hundred pounds, leaving us wondering if he might one day become taller than his dad at six foot, five inches; but that thought has now been erased with another curve ball thrown, bringing back the reality that this disease may have been working slowly during Jake's teenage years, but it is not through testing the resolve of Mighty Jake to endure.

As Jake grew taller, we noticed one leg seemed to be getting a little shorter than the other, causing Jake to slump to one side. Over the past two years, it became apparent that Jake had developed another problem–his spine was deteriorating, caused by a disease known as "neuromuscular scoliosis."

Jake had entered his Twentieth year with a 70-degree curve at the bottom of his spine, causing further debilitation in his desire to walk on his own accord and grow taller than his dad; his curved spine, no longer centered, now began to impact Jake's stomach organs by shifting them out of their natural location, causing internal feeding issues, pain, and additional weight loss. Jake's growth spurt was now receding as he leaned more to the side, following the continued deterioration of his spine. Yet, no matter the prognosis of medical science to offer "last-rites" to Jake's earthly presence, this young man continued the fight, day after day.

Living in a world completely changed as a result of the spread of the deadly COVID-19 virus in 2020 brought new fears and precautions into the lives of most inhabitants of planet Earth but for those like Jake, whose body has a compromised immune system, the impact of coming in contact with this virus would be unthinkable. So Jake, like many others, stayed confined, hoping for a vaccine to kill this monster and allow them to resume a somewhat "normal" life outside of their confinement.

Jake's parents have lived with his changing special needs since his birth, earning them, and others like them, a place at the table with the mighty… but nothing could have prepared them for this virus. The loudly proclaimed news updates of the millions of deaths reminded Jake's parents and brother of another challenge to Jake's earthly stay. Yet, they continued to embrace their faith in God that Jake was here for a reason, and when that reason had been accomplished, he would return home... and not until. I believe that also makes them mighty.

My worry, as a grandparent, is not for Jake–his future is solid, his endurance of earthly trial almost complete, his *mightiness* assuring a legacy for loved ones and admirers alike to look back upon whenever their personal trial leans in just a little too hard, and they need encouragement not just to endure, but to win! My worry is personal. How will I run my course after Jake is safely in the arms of his Father in Heaven? How will I face my next trial knowing I can't text Mighty Jake with a silly joke and expect one back in return?

The pain felt by losing a loved one cannot be measured in earthly terms, yet our reaction can. We can choose to use the legacy of the one who has passed as a constant reminder of our purposes in life–never to give in, never give up the fight to become better, to become all we can be–to become *Mighty!*

"Some will magnify their purpose for being on earth and choose to rise above worldly expectations. These are the mighty!" -Author

I have chosen to spend this entire chapter on becoming mighty because there is such a negative front out there trying to convince us that we are not... led by the same enemy to God who violated his oath, as Isaiah the prophet referred to him in the book of Isaiah, Chapter 14, verse 12... "How art thou fallen from heaven, O Lucifer, son of the morning," to deceive a third of the spirit children of God into believing they had no purpose or reason to grow into someone mighty.

Winning Way #7— Choose to Become Mighty, is centered

on two significantly important principles of truth: (#1) Choice! We retained our "agency" from the great "war" in heaven. We do have the power to choose to become mighty. And (#2) We can "become" all that we were sent here to be. We "can" become mighty!

If you are struggling with this final Winning Way because you can't relate or because you can't visualize how to become Mighty, then perhaps these "words" of mightiness will help:

Courage — "Be strong and of great courage." (Deuteronomy 31:6)

Steadfast — "She was steadfastly minded to go..." (Ruth 1:18)

"Be steadfast and immovable, always abounding in good works" (Mosiah 5:15).

Valiant — "be ye valiant," 2 Sam. 2:7 (13:28).

Willingness to change — To have the Spirit of the Lord cause a mighty change in a person's heart so that he has no more desire to do evil but rather desires to seek the things of God. *LDS Guide to the Scriptures* (Ezekiel 11:19,18:31, 36:26)

Emerson's quote — "That which we persist in doing becomes easier for us to do—not that the nature of the thing has changed, but that our power to do has increased."

One becomes mighty through persistence.

From this mixture of biblical and motivational literature, you can see that "becoming mighty" does not necessarily conform to what the world's definition would lead us to believe:

Free Dictionary definition — 1. Having or showing great power, skill, strength, or force: a mighty orator; a mighty blow. 2. Imposing or awesome in size, degree, or extent: a mighty stone fortress.

Other dictionary definitions include Boss, powerhouse, muscular, lusty, indomitable, stalwart, stout, strength, strong, vigorous, etc.

Quite a difference between the two lists, isn't there? Do you see how "becoming" mighty has little to do with physical strength, title, or skill, at least in the context of "becoming" more like God, developing Christ-like behaviors, and gaining power over the natural man within us?

Mighty Jake cannot fly, or scoop down from the sky to save the fair maiden, nor can he show great power to knock down buildings or bench press five hundred pounds. He is neither a great orator, persuading thousands to write a happy birthday greeting on a card and invest another $.45 to deliver the greeting. Although Jake continues to grow – up... his weight is just a little over one hundred pounds. During a recent "haboob" windstorm in the Arizona desert, Jake was almost blown off his feet while moving from his parent's car to the house. He is certainly no stone fortress.

But he is mighty!

You see, mightiness is a sum of parts, not a stand-alone victory. Achieving mightiness is not a 100-yard dash but rather a marathon. And the award for "being" mighty may not be achieved until you and I have crossed the finish line into the next life. Until that time, we will be in a state of "becoming."

It will be our legacy that will define our mightiness–our reaction to trial, how we dealt with adversity, and conversely, how we handled success.

But "why be *mighty?*" You ask. "Why the pressure to be something I'm not?

My answer to your question is: "But you are/were! You stood, with two-thirds of Heavenly Father's spirit children before the world was, against the powerful persuasions of the Son of the Morning, Lucifer himself (Book of Genesis). You chose agency (the right to choose) over guaranteed success offered by Lucifer despite the certainty that you would experience some measure of physical and mental pain while living on earth. Is that not "mighty?"

There would be many unanswered questions stemming from the trials we would face as human beings, but most of us will move on in life anyway, perhaps unprepared for the next trial but facing it regardless. Is this not a continuation of the mightiness within us when we faced Lucifer in the pre-existence?

Are not each of us the spiritual offspring of the Creator of Heaven and Earth? How could such a spiritual intelligence clothed with an Earthly body, a son or daughter of a King, become anything less than mighty with such heritage and equipped with the Light of Christ coursing through his or her soul?

We came to earth as mighty warriors but stripped naked of any such remembrance so that we would develop faith sufficient to make correct choices. I absolutely love this poem written by the immortal William Wadsworth (1770 – 1850), titled: *Intimations of Immortality from Recollections of Early Childhood.*

"Our birth is but a sleep and a forgetting: The soul that rises with us, our life's Star, Hath had elsewhere its setting, and cometh from afar: not in entire forgetfulness, and not in utter nakedness, but trailing clouds of glory do we come from God, who is our home."

Trial was intended to fall upon all men and women in varying degrees. Agency would rule the universe. Lucifer, disguised as Satan, the Father of lies, would tempt us, try us, even rule us through addictions if we would give in to such habits. His presence on earth, along with the other one-third of God the Father's fallen children, would be to possess our bodies if we would but let them–by giving up when trial strikes hard.

There is always a willing tenant to occupy a vacant soul who gave up on becoming.

The goal of Winning Way #7–*Choose to become mighty,* is to build within each of us faith, belief, and action, which will strengthen our resolve never to give up trying to be the best we can be and to encourage the use of each of the Winning Ways listed in this book as a means of not just enduring trial, but "Winning!"

This chapter is dedicated to Mighty Jake but also to those who have mightiness within them yet to be discovered. This chapter is dedicated to those who fall yet get back up, perhaps to fall again. It takes mightiness to conquer a poor self-image. To fight off the pains of addictive behavior while focusing on a goal of healthy living. After years of doing what is wrong, it takes mightiness to do what is right.

My years serving in the Arizona State Department of Corrections prison system as a religious volunteer provided me a front-row seat to the atonement of Jesus Christ. During these many trips to the state prison in Florence, Arizona, I gained my perspective about "mightiness." I witnessed firsthand how one could fall further from God as humanly possible and yet make his way back into the loving arms of his eternal Father in Heaven to taste forgiveness and eternal joy.

The journey back was inconceivable given the state of mind that existed at the time Frank (not his real name) stood before the camera at the processing counter shortly after being led from the orange bus with a small caravan of cuffed and shackled men destined to spend a good portion of their lives behind bars, having been convicted of various crimes against another.

The collateral damage to Frank's family led to their undoing, and Frank found himself lost and alone–forgotten as the man once loved by a beautiful woman, adored by two children, and respected by neighbors, work associates, and practically anyone who knew him. Frank was even tapped for a promotion at work before he allowed himself into the world of pornography. The door had been opened, and Satan–the father of all lies, was more than willing to convince Frank to step through it.

Pornography led to lies to cover up his growing addictive habit, followed by over-use of prescribed medicines to numb the pain of feeling like a traitor to his family, followed by illegal painkillers, which led to making selfish decisions, then covering up for such choices, affecting Franks judgment even more.

As Frank got bolder and bolder with his need to escape reality and responsibility, he eventually sought after and found individuals like himself who gladly accepted him into their world of sex and drugs.

Their fabricated escape vehicle from the realities of life soon carried Frank deeper into a life with no self-control. He ultimately exhibited no discipline in his life to counteract these inner man lusts and cravings—only living to satisfy and indulge until the fantasy wore off and he was left with nothing but the reality of how far he had fallen, only to be temporarily erased with another round of drugs and fake love from his new friends.

During this free-fall, Frank's family did everything they knew how to do to save Frank from himself, but it soon became painfully apparent to them that Frank was no longer the happy husband, provider, or responsible person those who knew him could attest. Frank was on a free-fall, with Satan as his parachute partner, only to bail on him in his hour of need, leaving Frank alone and afraid, now dressed in orange coveralls for having severely broken laws of the land for which there is little tolerance in the courts. Frank would serve twenty years without the likelihood of parole for good behavior. He was a convicted felon and would be treated like one.

Frank first attended one of our religious services at the invitation of his cellmate. When I first laid eyes on Frank, he looked ten or more years than his birth certificate would confirm—his almost all grayish hair was long and frizzy. His blue-gray eyes void of any sparkle. It was clear that Frank had given up and would welcome death over his current conditions. There was no life to return home to—no children to visit, no wife to love. Frank was truly alone.

It is always an amazing sight to behold, and I never tired of it—watching this line of orange-clad men walk across the prison yard, often to catcalls from others, all with scriptures in hand–all except Frank. The prison culture will not tolerate weakness, and it was often looked upon by the few who ruled the yard that those who attended church and other religious services were made soft by their teachings of turning the other cheek. My journal is full of such stories of our Christian brothers being persecuted and those of other faiths. Satan has a deep hold in the prisons of America, and it takes mightiness to break out of that grasp.

I remember as if it were yesterday–teaching the topic of Christ's atonement was always my favorite, and this particular Sunday would become memorable as the men filed into the dining hall where services would be held. The day was hot outside, which meant humid inside the hall, but no one complained. It was indeed a blessing–a privilege offered incarcerated human beings by the state institution to assemble outside their "house" and enjoy the spirit of fellowship. How they embraced one another in the spirit of friendship caught me by surprise the first time or two I visited the prison. I soon came to realize it was genuine love.

I reflected upon my own services at my home church, especially when the men and women met separately in men's priesthood and women's relief society breakouts. I admit to feeling a little embarrassed as I observed how these men welcomed the newcomers to our service. I had been a Sunday visitor in another town only weeks before and had literally no one welcome me, a stranger in their midst. It must have been the sign around my neck, "Don't welcome me; I'm a visitor and will be gone tomorrow." (Sarcasm, sorry!)

Here I was, within the walls of a prison, in a dining hall filled with round, stainless steel tables and six small cylinders for seats per table. The air was moved by a circulating swamp cooler, offering little comfort when the summer sun beat down on the arid desert of Arizona, and yet those attending welcomed all who came in after them, new attendee or regular–all were welcomed with seemingly happy hearts to see one another in a setting without an officer's presence bearing down on them.

There were no comfortable pews, no folding chairs with soft cushions attached. There wasn't even a metal folding chair with a back on it, which is relegated to latecomers and those of us with noisy children or just not wanting to be noticed by the ward leadership in case they were scanning the congregation for someone to give next week's Sacrament talk–or teach in the nursery. Yes, one would choose a hard seat over a soft seat for many reasons. Choice!

Frank chose to sit at a table as far from the front and those presiding at the service as possible. His head was down for most of the service. Even when his bunkie introduced him at the beginning of the service, Frank would not look up. He was clearly uncomfortable in these surroundings.

I had seen others come at the invitation of a fellow inmate and suddenly leave after the opening prayer. The spirit in these prison services was unexpected, even to those of us who were prepared spiritually. To someone with no clue–it can be a bit overwhelming. But Frank did not run. Nor did he lift his head until one part of the lesson when I bore testimony of the truth of the atonement of Jesus Christ being a gift to all who would accept it.

I explained that Jesus Christ was sent to earth to provide a way for "each of us" to return to the heavenly home from which we came, no matter our earthly choices–no matter our crime, "if we would but repent," and seek to change from the ways and choices which led us here. Frank's head jolted upright with these words, but apparently embarrassed, lowered his head once again but kept his eyes directly upon me.

The spirit spoke to me in a way I almost looked to see who had spoken. *Forgiveness!* Came the impression loud and clear. *These men need to have hope of forgiveness,* came the impression again–more clearly this time.

"Brethren, there is hope of forgiveness for each of us in accepting Jesus Christ as our Savior and Redeemer," I taught, my eyes now watering from the emotion of the personal relationship I had built over the years of my own change–and forgiveness. "I am a living witness that sin can be forgiven, burdens can be lifted, and a rebirth of the inner man can take place so that any sin, fully repented of can be expunged from your soul as if it had never happened" (See Isaiah 43:25). "Behold, he who has repented of his sins, the same is forgiven, and I, the Lord, remember them no more" (Doctrine and Covenants 58:42).

Frank did not move–his head slightly bowed, but his eyes remained affixed upon me, now blinking wildly. *The spirit has touched this man,* I remember thinking to myself just before my heart stopped.

There was this commotion in orange in front of me so fast I could only stare, watching as Frank jumped off his round, stainless steel seat, orange hoody drawn up over his head, and marched out the door–his roomie right behind him.

Believe it or not, this occurrence is relatively common in the prison environment, albeit not as dramatic. These men had long since snuffed out the Light of Christ in their lives, contributing greatly to their choices and actions. When the spirit manifests itself as strongly as it did on that Sunday to Frank–the shock to their system can be rather dramatic, causing them to lose control. It disrupts their steel persona, making them feel vulnerable. This is not a positive when your health and safety depend upon your awareness and ability to remain unnoticed.

I am reminded of an instance at the Pinal County Juvenile Detention Center ("Juve") in Florence, AZ, where I also taught occasionally. These youth were placed in this facility for many reasons–the most repetitive being border violations. But one common thread did exist among them: "anger!" They were mad at being caught, and angry at family, police, the institution holding them, and life in general. But when it was announced that "religious instruction was available in ten minutes," I was always amazed at how many "angry" youths showed up–voluntarily.

A stay at Juve was only temporary before its occupants were either sent back to their own country or moved to another facility, so we rarely saw the same kids more than a half-dozen times. But in their brief stay, it was our goal as "religious volunteer instructors" to provide a spiritual experience that would hopefully re-ignite the Light of Christ within them that all inhabitants of planet Earth were once equipped with at birth. It was through "choices" that this precious seed of conscience was covered up–once a North Star for right choices and an alarm device for wrong, the spirit of God likely never burned within them any longer sufficient to influence their choices.

I watched intently as these boys and girls dressed in orange shirts and pants filed in, escorted by two officers, their hands not cuffed but clasped behind their back at the waist. I would take the English-speaking kids, and my teaching companion would take the Spanish speakers into separate areas of the large recreation room, where we would teach principles of life directly from the Bible–with a male or female officer present.

I usually had a particular topic I wanted to teach when I visited this group, but this night, I was winging it (aka, let the spirit dictate the topic). I was impressed to ask if anyone had ever seen someone die? Several hands raised, along with a few smart remarks. One young girl, about 15 years old, said her grandpa was asleep in his chair and died without anyone knowing it–of course that brought another round of laughter. I admit that I had a hard time not adding to the laughter thinking about some of my fellow high priests after about twenty minutes into that Sunday's lesson.

I described that I had watched my mother pass away. I felt her spirit leave her body as she breathed out her final breath of life, as it had entered in the same way at her birth. I then asked: "Is there life after death?" Before anyone could answer, I shot out another question directed at the young teen whose grandfather had passed away in his chair. "What if I told you that your grandfather watches over you, loves you, and is even with you tonight? And before I could utter another word, a warm blast of air passed through the room, causing all thirteen detainees to react—all emotionally, some more than others, but it was so evident that some spiritual phenomenon had just occurred—even my teaching partner out of our direct sight with his group stopped teaching and beckoned his group of Spanish speakers to join us.

My point in using this example is to share that most of these kids wept when this spiritual experience happened. They had a look of confusion on their faces, their eyes wide and fearful. **They did not recognize the spirit of God** trying to pierce their heart. It was not a feeling they welcomed—so they rejected it. But not the granddaughter!

I witnessed a change in this cocky teen who made light of her grandfather's passing. With tears streaming down her face and head bowed, she whispered so only those next to her—and me, could hear: "I felt him!"

My tears began to fall as I tried to verbalize what had just happened, but the scene must have unnerved the two officers present because they, too looked confused and vulnerable. The one with the Spanish speakers called out to the other officer that time was up, and all stood as if part of a drill and put their scriptures back on the desk as they each filed out—except the granddaughter. She hesitated a moment, looked at me with tears still fresh in her eyes, and asked if she could keep the Bible to read in her room tonight.

Becoming mighty is a process, not an event; a marathon, not a one-hundred-yard dash—yet there must be a beginning. I believe in both cases mentioned above, the granddaughter *and* the inmate Frank, the seed for change was sown by an unfamiliar presence of the Holy

Spirit trying to penetrate the hard shell that had grown thick around the heart. Somehow, the spirit was able to testify sufficient to cause uncomfortableness. The granddaughter perhaps was more open to letting the spirit in initially than Frank, who bolted out of the service, but in time, Frank returned to become a weekly regular, embracing the gospel of Christ as solid as I had ever seen someone do before. But true change in nature takes time; given Frank's history and low self-image, his change came gradually. To Frank's credit, however, he used his time in prison to become converted through the scriptures, reading everything he could get his hands on.

Boyd K. Packer, a former President of the Quorum of the Twelve Apostles of the Church of Jesus Christ of Latter-day Saints, was known to teach the principle, "True doctrine, understood, changes attitudes and behavior. The study of the gospel doctrines will improve behavior quicker than a study of behavior will improve behavior." Frank's legacy would support this principle. Frank developed a love of Christ, which replaced his desire to sin. His weakness toward the urges of the natural man soon came under control and was replaced with a burning desire to follow Christ and perfect himself–even living within Satan's lair.

I remember when the prison policy against us in the Branch Presidency giving individual "hands-on" blessings was changed to allow the inmates to receive a blessing, at their request, at certain times each month, and only a limited number. Frank was among the first group to request a blessing.

That Sunday in the Arizona desert, the humidity was almost unbearable as we made our way to a location within the prison confines where we would have a little privacy to give those who requested a blessing. The flies were unusually unmerciful as we placed hands on heads, unable to swat them from our mouths or eyes, and waited for the Lord's spirit to direct our blessing. The electricity I felt once I laid my hands upon Frank's head was instant as if God Himself was anxious to bestow his love to Frank.

The words that left my mouth came rapidly, without thought or pretense, giving comfort and assurance to Frank that should he repent of his crimes, with a broken heart and contrite spirit, and attempt restitution where possible–God would also apply restitution and remember his sins no more. I could feel Frank's body tremble as the Lord's words, not mine, poured into his soul as manna from heaven, giving this wretched soul hope that he could indeed be forgiven of his sins as promised by God in written scripture (See Hebrews 8:12; Isaiah 43:25; Doctrine and Covenants 53:42; and Jeremiah 31:34).

This blessing given to Frank was the catalyst for more change. Frank did indeed confess his sins to the proper authority called and set apart to receive such confessions, and deep within the confines of prison walls, Frank began his long road back. I was fortunate to see, during my five years of service, Frank's nature change from the fallen and forgotten man he was at the processing point at the prison entry to a man with many friends who chose to serve rather than take, and who walked the grounds of prison confinement to encourage and bless the lives of others. Frank was indeed a blessing to those who came to know him.

Mark Twain was credited for saying, "The two most important dates in your life are the day you were born, and the day you find out why."

Becoming Mighty is discovering "why" you were born during this time in history. Think about it before dismissing this idea because you feel you haven't done anything to warrant such a declaration as "This is why I was born!" Frank, in the prison story, realized his worth by deciding to become an encourager to those who had given up on themselves. Becoming an encourager doesn't require talent or expertise to become one. It takes desire to make a difference. It takes practicing unselfishness by overlooking your own hurts and disappointments to help another.

I am reminded of a church member friend of mine who responded to the Bishop's plea to those members attending church to clean up around the area they were sitting during sacrament service so that the next ward congregation meeting in the chapel would have a clean place to sit. My friend waited for most of the people to leave the chapel before he started picking up debris left behind. Doing so gave him a sense of "mightiness" for doing something for others who would never know who had prepared the chapel for their use.

My church friend didn't pursue a cleaning profession and find his life's purpose in franchising, but this little act of service gave my friend the right touch of self-worth to gain a positive feeling about himself, affecting his marriage and relationship with his kids. He was a happier person because he found a simple act of service that was needed, which he could fulfill.

This example seems to set a pattern for us all–dream to find our passion for something that makes us happy. Finding our purpose requires that we get out there and follow our dreams. If we fail, then we must reevaluate and keep failing forward.

"Becoming Mighty" and finding our purpose in life has less to do with personal status, worldly acclaim, or winning Super Bowls than slaying our own personal Goliaths. One becomes mighty by experiencing failure in the battlefield as when they win a battle, because it takes just as much, or more, character, determination, and discipline to rise again after failure than it does actually to win.

I remember as if it were yesterday–but it was likely BC (Before COVID). I asked my Heavenly Father in prayer, *"Am I becoming all I can be? Am I doing what I was sent here to do? Am I learning all I am to learn to better serve You in this life and in the next?"* Becoming mighty is an outfall from asking such questions and then listening for the answer–and then having the guts to follow that inner voice. Well, maybe having faith sufficient to follow the promptings of the inner voice is a bit less heroic but more definitive. When you can walk into the night with nothing more than a desire to become and allow those promptings to guide you even through the darkest times–that is faith. That is becoming mighty.

For me, and my quest to become, the answers have never been scripted in a vision or from a knock on the door with someone on the other side with a sign hanging from his neck that said: "I have the solution!" For me, the answers were never clearly imprinted in my mind. I think had they been–I would not be writing my fifth book from a treadmill at the gym. I would not have felt the *sweetness* of the atonement from my trial because I never would have humbled myself sufficiently to rely totally upon God if I had seen the answers. I had to learn to trust that inner voice no matter the outcome and learn to trust whatever the outcome... it was for my good, for my development, and for my "becoming."

A former head coach of the Arizona Cardinals professional football team in the NFL was often quoted as saying: "No risk it, no biscuit!" Bruce Arians internalized the words of this quote into his personal motto, clearly creating passion for his choices on the football field each week, leading the Arizona Cardinals to many successes as one of the elite football teams in the NFL (Prejudice showing here, sorry).

Coach Arians' passionate declaration led to failures and successes when measured in terms of the final score, week after week. But the score only tells part of the story. Each loss would open the door for opportunity to grow as individuals and as a team "if" the coach and his players and assistant coaches approached the loss as an opportunity to refine and become better.

Losses and setbacks can expose a team's weaknesses and vulnerabilities, often providing a clearer picture of the team's shortcoming to be addressed and corrected. Super Bowl champions in the NFL are rarely untested in their climb to the top, and they are stronger for it. But you might argue that my example of using football as an example to follow is out of character, with football being just a game. I would agree that football is a game, but each team is also a business, returning large profits or in some cases suffering huge deficits. The decisions made before, during, and after each game are critical to the success and health of each franchise.

In our quest to become all we can be (aka to win), we, too, must develop a passion within us to find our purpose. This may sound easy, like picking out a fine steak from the local meat market, but how many of us have come to understand our purpose in life before the last sands of time run out? I mean think about it for a minute–we come to earth, accept a body, learn to walk and talk, make decisions, have experiences, grow old, and die. Along the way, we may finish college, find a job, marry, have children, maybe grandchildren, and perhaps follow the American dream and even retire someday, playing golf and traveling the country. Sounds rather good right now, doesn't it? But what if you found your passion along the way? How would your legacy read then?

Yes, you are still going to die at some point–but what if you altered your thinking just a bit to include finding a passion that would drive you to become better, live life fuller, pack more into it, and get more joy from it?

Why would I want to do that, you ask?

Because the journey of life does not carry a round-trip ticket. You have one shot–why in the world would you waste even one minute just "waiting" for something to happen?

The greatest legacy you could leave is not how much money you made or how many college degrees you obtained, but rather how you "lived life." Imagine finding your passion and becoming so excited to rise each day just to see what new experiences await you. Imagine discovering your purpose early enough in life so you can spend the rest of it "becoming all you can be!"

Just think of the possibilities that could open up for you if you only looked at life a little differently. Give your current status of happiness a little appraisal. Are you happy? How often? At what level? How do you spend your free time? Is it spent doing something you love? Is it fulfilling, or just filling time?

Is it time to risk it? (Please do not get a second mortgage on your home to start a flea breeding business). Maybe it's committing to a relationship? You are afraid that because your parent's relationship failed, yours will also, and you don't want to risk a broken heart. Maybe it's risking the ending of an abusive relationship, and you are afraid to go it alone.

I once took a risk. As mentioned earlier within the pages of this book, I once joined a Toastmasters group sponsored by the City of Mesa for their employees. I was the only non-employee, if you remember me saying, but they met at 7 am each Wednesday morning, which fit into my always-busy schedule as a local home builder/Realtor. I felt like a fish out of water that first day as I entered the conference room where the group met in the City building in downtown Mesa, all ten heads turning to the doorway to see who had just entered. I didn't know a soul, but I willed my shaky legs into the room and took the closest chair between two ladies, who each extended a hand of greeting.

The moderator had everyone at the large conference table stand and introduce themselves, and add a 60-second bio, as a box was being passed around the table–each attendee reaching in and drawing a card. When the box came to me and I picked one of the three remaining cards, I quickly glanced at the writing on the card as I stood to introduce myself and gulped!

With my eyes still on the words of the card I uttered, "Hello, mmy n-ame is, and then I froze... my brain trying to decide if I should introduce myself as Chuck, or Charles.

"And you are?" prompted the moderator, bringing a hint of humor to his question, not unnoticed by the group.

"My name is Chuck Malone!" I finally blurted out. "But if one of you is my mother, you may call me Charles." The group roared with laughter. I had just hit my first home run. Telling about myself was easy, something I loved to do when given a chance.

"I am a native Arizonan, with roots in Northern Arizona–Holbrook, to be exact. My father was the local Fire Chief of the Holbrook volunteer fire dept; my mother worked for the state department of transportation, and my older sister was Miss Perfect!" Second base hit noted, as the group responded with smiles and light laughter.

"I am a graduate of Arizona State University and a music scholarship recipient to Northern Arizona University, where I majored in music for two years. I served as a missionary in Eastern Canada for two years and returned to meet and marry my eternal companion, Linda Faye Malone!"

"You married your sister?" a voice from the group interrupted, drawing more laughter than any of *my* attempts. I then realized I had used my wife's married name of, Malone instead of her maiden name of Johnson. I quickly backtracked and corrected the mistake. Strike one!

The moderator then thanked me for introducing myself with the use of humor but indicated my time was up and deferred to the next person. I had not followed the intent of the opportunity to introduce myself. Learning about me was secondary to staying within the 60-second template. I had strayed outside the lines, and I knew it.

Finding your passion may not be any harder than identifying what leaves you wanting more. I believe this to be a significant component in being mighty because it is continual, not absolute or final. Your passion is realized in the journey. Satisfaction may be realized in the accomplishment of the dream, but if that achievement is not replaced with another goal or dream you may find yourself once again struggling to become all you could be.

My twelve months in Toastmasters provided great experience in adding structure to my presentations, and I gained much confidence in myself as a speaker by adding sufficient structure to get my intended message across, but also allow my humorous side to improvise and take a different road, if so impressed. This freedom I allowed myself to pursue fed the passion within me to drive my points home and finish with a planned closing to leave the listeners wanting more. But it was I who wanted more, as well. I had discovered a passion.

Discovering passion(s) within you become stepping stones to finding purpose in life.

There are rarely free passes to success in life. Anything worth pursuing should come with a cost if you expect to gain more than just experience. Identifying passions and perhaps discovering your purpose in life is a marathon effort, not a one-hundred-yard dash or a weekend motivational seminar with your favorite speaker/author. I wanted more than just to learn to handle myself in front of a small Toastmasters group.

I wanted to learn how to direct this energy I felt within me for bigger things. I wanted to become a motivational speaker and travel the world, healing hearts and spreading words of encouragement to all who would listen–bringing value, laced with humor.

In your quest to find purpose, you may find your life out of balance for a time. To use a couple of over-used statements of purpose–you must "keep your eye on the ball," (Tom Robbins [not Tony] and others) and "keep the main thing the main thing" (Pat Riley, Stephen Covey, etc.) or you may find yourself enjoying worldly success without feeling the true joy of happiness. But to discover one's purpose, it is not uncommon to commit intense focus for a given length of time–just don't forget "the main thing" in your life as you pursue your passions. In the end, when time on this earth has run out, rare is the person who wished they had worked harder. More in line with our earthly purpose, the dying have reached out to family, friends, and loved ones.

Too much of one thing, no matter the righteous intent, tends to askew our perspective in life with little regard for those who may disagree. Keep evaluating your passions to reflect a righteous intent, and you shall not stray.

What have we learned about Becoming Mighty? You don't have to be Mighty Mouse, Superman, or Wonder Woman to become mighty, but you do need to "want" to rise above worldly expectations and be more than just a placeholder in life. You must want to count for something–be something–make a difference in someone's life.

Rise tomorrow with a burn to succeed! Dwell in possibilities. Your passions could lead you in many different directions to find fulfillment. Explore your life and unearth all the things that bring you joy. Pursue that which brings you joy and develop your passions into purpose.

It has not been my successes that have brought the most change toward becoming.

Well, I cannot believe our time together is ending, at least [and hopefully] until you reach into your bookshelf and pull me out once again to share my heart, my failures, and my successes with you in an attempt to encourage you to discover your own mightiness.

My purpose in closing out this book with Winning Way #7 – "Choose to Become Mighty," is to instill in those who may be struggling in any way with who you are or who you may become–a sense of hope, a clearer self-image, and perhaps a desire to find your passion in life.

I hoped to build within you a sense of direction that will cause you to always look up. There is purpose in this life, and we each have varying timelines to discover ours–so why wait? Start today! Start now! Become Mighty!

Here is to *becoming!*

Chapter Eight

CONCLUSION

"Parting Is Such Sweet Sorrow!"

This famous line from William Shakespeare in *Romeo and Juliet* seems to reflect the void I have begun to feel, knowing our time together is coming to an end. We have become friends, you and I–brothers and sisters from the same Heavenly Parents, united by an earthly purpose to become all we can be and not just endure.

I have visualized you throughout the creative process of writing this book, and I have cried with you as I felt your loss, even stiffened as I felt your negative self-talk mirroring the history of my own. I prayed to God for a blessing upon you as I, too, have felt the pain of struggle, trying to regain a stable footing in an unstable world.

In the many pleadings I lifted upward to Heaven on your behalf, I also prayed that I might be raised above my worldly failings to express to you the Heaven–inspired words of hope and encouragement to carry you over the bar of trial, not only to place or show (endure) but to "Win!" And Become Mighty!

As an author and brother-in-spirit, it has been my pleasure to share a significant piece of my life with you in hopes of helping you prepare for the next trial and fortify you against unexpected opposition. My experiences of tasting a "sweetness" while in the depth of despair opened portals of opportunity to change, seven of which were shared as "Winning Ways" within the pages of this book.

Let's take a stroll down memory lane, you and I... and try to remember a few of the highlights of each Chapter.

I shared with you in **Chapter One**, when trial struck a blow, how long it took before my "first" call was to God. I hope Winning Way #1–to "Call upon God" as "your" first call when trial strikes, has made a lasting impression on you. If you internalize only this one principle of truth taught in this book, my sacrifice of many hours of precious time to "get it right" will have been worth the effort I put into this book–for it sets the foundation of every truth principle taught herein.

Another setpoint in the ring of life was taught in **Chapter Two**, introduced as the Five P's. "Proper Preparation Prevents Poor Performance" is a reminder that unlike attaining success in life, "trial" will likely hit when you *least* expect it, so internalize the Boy Scout® motto to "Be Prepared."

Remember to determine your anchor in life... and then "secure it" as part of your preparation before the next trial hits.

Another essential truth principle in your preparation for trial and/or success in life is the condition of your "attitude." Remember the chapter title, "Attitude Begets Behavior?" **Chapter Three** is dedicated to teaching you how to feed your brain on foods of success instead of grazing at the smorgasbord table on empty content. You will want to spend more time in Chapter Three studying how to program your brain with "positive" responses to opposition.

What I love about the study of attitude is that we have a "choice" of which flavor of attitude we will possess. We also are in control of our mindset. Will we train our brain to see the glass half full or half empty? In this case, we are each the author of our own play. You can write the script for your legacy of how you want to be remembered. Chapter Three will help you learn how.

I have mentioned "choice" a few times in my closing comments... but **Chapter Four** was "all" about choice!

To make correct choices "consistently" takes discipline. It also takes commitment. And this is where "choosing your anchor" proves to be a valuable decision. You really need to give some serious thought to what kind of person you "want" to be, then choose how you want to anchor yourself... and to whom. This is like fixing your eyes on the North Star for direction and stability.

Remember my anchor? I chose God and Jesus Christ as my co-pilot(s) and have never been sorry for that decision.

Winning Way #4 taught us how to keep an open mind when trial and opposition strikes. Where is the opportunity in trial? Good question! Do you remember the definition of opportunity I used in Chapter Four, as found in the dictionary? *A set of circumstances that makes it possible to do something!*

Don't you just love that definition? Ok, I admit, I had to search a bit to find it, but there it was, in Mr. Webster's dictionary. This entire book, "Winning Thru Trial," aligns with that definition. It teaches from page one that trial is necessary to create circumstances powerful enough to open the door to your mind and heart to change, otherwise, we are usually just too consumed with "being" (status quo) and not at all looking for opportunity to "become."

Each of us will experience "hinge-points" throughout our life, and it has been my perfect hindsight 20-20 vision that trial has been most often one of the hinges.

Would you happen to remember me telling you how **Chapter Five** came to be? Oh, I didn't want to listen! But I ended up acting upon those impressions anyway and created a chapter just for "Spiritual Gifts, Hidden Talents, and Miracles," which are often born during periods of trial and opposition.

Chapter Five was so exciting to write and ponder over every truth principle taught. There is so much room for personal interpretation of Chapter Five... I just love it! Each gift, talent, and miracle is *personal!* They belong to "you!" And there is no measurement or grading by the curve to tell you which attribute is a gift... *or* a talent. And each miracle? I see miracles quite often in my business, spiritual, and family life... but they never make the "Church News!"

A gift is just that, a gift! But it is to be shared for it to grow. You might inherit a family trait or talent from ancestral genes, but if you keep it under a bushel, "it won't grow!" In fact, it will likely die!

I hope so much that you followed the training in Chapter Five to help you discover your gifts and talents and that you feel so blessed to be "you!" I promise, there is no one like you!

And yes, there are some miracles worthy of making the Church

News, but that isn't the purpose of miracles, mostly. They are miracles only if you see them as such with your spiritual eyes and humble heart.

I am a commission-only real estate agent; I have been for fifty-three years and counting. I can tell you without a shadow of hesitation that God is in the details of our lives and will show His hand so often. Like the time during COVID-19 when I just "happened" to send an email to a former client of mine, asking how things were and if I could help in any way? This circumstantial email led to a family referral wanting to move closer to their daughter, and with the shortage of homes available, the wife was inspired to call a builder in a retirement section of a local community, which led to me getting involved, which helped secure an inventory home that had just fallen through. And yes, this was a miracle! The buyer initially wasn't even interested in looking at a retirement community.

Winning Way #5 taught us to "Trust in God." If you can't think of one gift or talent or miracle in your life… then ask God for one! I promise, He is in the details of your life and has made it clear throughout the ages that He wants to bless you to grow and become successful in all your righteous endeavors. You can trust Him.

Chapter Six prepared us to better understand the nature and purpose of trial in our lives. We learned the importance of trusting in the Lord… and now we are going to learn to look at trial very differently than the neighbor down the street who just lost his job and acts out feelings of despair and anger, just like the movies portray a person should act when such trial hits… he puts on his pouty-face, defeated, still in his PJ's at noon, unshaven, empty root beer cans strewn all over the kitchen, accompanied by stacks of half-empty pizza boxes, and just stares at the blank TV screen, forgetting to even turn it on. Maybe he attaches a skull and crossbones picture to his home office door and won't come out! Try seeing *opportunity* with all that goin' for ya!

"Without Battle, there is no Win," (Sub-title of Chapter Six) is a battle cry of sorts, or call to arms, that "change is a-comin." And it is to be our "choice" as to what that change will be.

Winning Way #6 taught us that failure is necessary for discovering who we really are. And that inserting the *Failing Forward* mindset is a *choice,* a higher plane of understanding that "God didn't make no junk," and He certainly didn't make us to "stay down" once we were dealt a right hook in the ring of life!

Chapter Seven turns very personal and is dedicated to my grandson, Mighty Jake–an invitation to us all to "Be Mighty!"

We learned that being mighty leads to winning, and winning is a state of becoming. So, do you remember how one *becomes* mighty? Ah, the quiz! There has to be a quiz (LOL).

If you accept the world's interpretation of the word *mighty,* then "showing great power, skill, or strength in battle" would probably be your first choice of definition. Maybe imposing size, in the form of a Goliath? Or a seemingly unreachable station in life? Colorful stripes on your uniform? How do you think you are doing on the quiz?

But in our time together, you learned a few "new" definitions of *mighty* that did not include one having an advantage over another or the feeling of fear. It didn't include "any" of the world's characteristics of one we might think of as mighty.

My grandson Jacob would certainly qualify as one who is mighty. He was born autistic, shunned at school, not welcomed in quiet surroundings, underwent never-ending hospital stays, and lives with an everyday uncertainty of whether today may be his last, from a blood clot in his chest to a diagnosis of the fatal disease, Mitochondria.

I could fill up another book listing conditions that would qualify someone as being mighty, but I think, for the purpose of our conclusion to this book, if you have arrived on planet Earth as spirit offspring of Heavenly Parents, to possess a body of flesh and bone, to gain experience to more fully achieve a full measure of your creation in preparation for your future eternal life throughout the eternities, then, my dear brother and sister, you already have the "seeds of greatness" within you to *become* mighty.

Our Exemplar, Jesus Christ, was sent to earth by the Father to "show us the way" to become mighty. His people, the Jewish community, misinterpreted his mission as one of mighty strength to rescue them from bondage to Roman law by "force and power," but His message then and now is still the same, "Come unto me, all ye that labor and are heavy laden, and I will give you rest. Take my yoke upon you and learn of me; for I am [meek] and [lowly in heart:] and ye shall find rest unto your souls. For my yoke is easy, and my burden is light." (Mathew 11:28-30, emphasis added)

Jesus came to free us from personal bondage in the form of burdens carried as a result of trial, poor choices, unforeseen circumstances, and spiritual and physical weariness–that we may become *mighty* through His word and in deed (service to others), by "yoking ourselves" to Him through His atonement; that our burdens may be made light (lifted from us).

I think the Apostle Paul would understand what this book is about when he boldly instructed his longtime friend, Timothy, to "fight the good fight of the faith."

In Paul's own words, he has left for each of us no better vision of having completed our own personal journey toward becoming than is stated so beautifully in 2 Timothy 4:7: "I have fought a good fight, I have finished my course, I have kept the faith."

It is my humble prayer that in our time together within the pages of this book, you have better understood who you are and who you can become!

You have the seeds of greatness within you, to be nourished and fed, sometimes broken and bruised, then healed to become stronger, and live to achieve the *full* measure of your creation as a son and daughter of God. You are nobility! You are special! You are mighty! You were born to *Win*!

In the spirit of my Irish ancestry, may I leave upon you a little Irish blessing... that you may have:

A world of wishes at your command.
God and His angels close at hand.
Friends and family their love impart,
And Irish blessings in your heart.
-Anonymous

Until we meet again,
-Chuck Malone

About the Author

Charles P. Malone

Charles Patrick ("Chuck") Malone knows trial personally – considering he wrote this book mainly using his own experiences to guide the reader into the "sweetness" described herein. His unique writing style of approaching a subject with clarity and expression, sprinkled with humor and just a touch of mischievousness, has earned him published copywriting success with such titles as "Decluttering! An Eternal Perspective" and "Dutch Oven Cooking and the Plan of Happiness."

Awarded "Prison Volunteer of the Year" by the Arizona Department of Corrections, Chuck uses his experiences from a front-row seat to the atonement - from serving in prison ministry and as a Sealer in the Gilbert, AZ Temple, and Stake Patriarch - to skillfully guiding the reader into the eye of trial to taste the "Sweetness" of the Savior's embrace and to do more than endure trial, but to *Win*.

An active Arizona real estate broker for over 53 years, Chuck continues to serve his new and longtime clients, placing him among the top producers of the company's licensees, and still finds time to cheer on his seventeen perfect grandchildren from five incredible adult children – and stay married to the love of his life, Linda, for over fifty-six years... and counting.

The author has written his many published articles and three full-length books on his iPad (fourth in process) at the local fitness gym while on the treadmill/elliptical/stationary bike, with only one slightly-embarrassing fall. He loves public speaking, probably a result of the "fall," and was a paid motivational speaker in the field of business development and entrepreneurship.

You can find Chuck on YouTube – Facebook – Instagram – and Twitter... and on the WWW at Facebook.com/ijustwriteit, and Amazon.com/books (search for Charles P. Malone), and gilbertazhomestoday.com. He loves to speak at private gatherings, church, and special events and promises not to fall off the podium.

You can also "hear" Chuck on Spotify.com reading his first published book, "The Sweetness of Trial," at https:://podcasters.spotify.com/pod/show/charles-p-malone

Chuck loves to hear from his readers and listeners at cmijustwriteit@gmail.com or Facebook at facebook.com/ijustwriteit/ or his personal Facebook page at facebook.com/chuck.malone

www.ingramcontent.com/pod-product-compliance
Lightning Source LLC
Chambersburg PA
CBHW070551100426
42744CB00006B/255